HUMANIZING CHILD DEVELOPMENTAL THEORY

HUMANIZING CHILD DEVELOPMENTAL THEORY

A Holistic Approach

EUGENE M. DEROBERTIS

Assistant Professor of Psychology, Brookdale College

iUniverse, Inc.
Bloomington

HUMANIZING CHILD DEVELOPMENTAL THEORY
A Holistic Approach

Copyright © 2008 by Eugene M. DeRobertis

All rights reserved. No part of this book may be used or reproduced by any means, graphic, electronic, or mechanical, including photocopying, recording, taping or by any information storage retrieval system without the written permission of the publisher except in the case of brief quotations embodied in critical articles and reviews.

iUniverse books may be ordered through booksellers or by contacting:

iUniverse
1663 Liberty Drive
Bloomington, IN 47403
www.iuniverse.com
1-800-Authors (1-800-288-4677)

Because of the dynamic nature of the Internet, any web addresses or links contained in this book may have changed since publication and may no longer be valid. The views expressed in this work are solely those of the author and do not necessarily reflect the views of the publisher, and the publisher hereby disclaims any responsibility for them.

Any people depicted in stock imagery provided by Thinkstock are models, and such images are being used for illustrative purposes only.

Certain stock imagery © Thinkstock.

ISBN: 978-0-595-44924-8 (pbk)
ISBN: 978-0-595-69098-5 (cloth)

Printed in the United States of America

iUniverse rev. date: 03/08/2011

CONTENTS

PREFACE xv

ACKNOWLEDGMENTS xvii

CHAPTER 1 HUMANISM, EXISTENTIAL-PHENOMENOLOGY, AND CHILD DEVELOPMENT 1

Humanism and Child Developmental Theory *1*

Two Humanistic Currents in the Study of Child Development *4*

The Theoretical Perspective of This Book *5*

    The meaning of humanism. *5*

    The meaning of phenomenology. *6*

Fundaments of Existential-Humanistic-Developmental Thought ... *8*

The Structure and Goals of This Text *12*

CHAPTER 2 A HUMANISTIC THEORY OF SELF-DEVELOPMENT: ROGERS AND HORNEY 14

Carl Rogers: Development of the Congruous Self (or Self-Actualization) vs. the Incongruous Self *15*

Karen Horney: Development of the Real Self (or Self-Realization) vs. the Idealized Self *20*

Rogers and Horney in Mutual Encounter: Synthesizing a Humanistic Theory of Child Development *27*

    The nature and nurture of self development. *28*

    Healthy parental influence. *28*

    The nature of healthy self development: the self-actualizing child. *28*

    Unhealthy parental influence. *29*

    The course of unhealthy self development: self-alienation. *29*

Concluding Remarks *31*

    Comments on the synthesis of Rogers's and Horney's ideas. *31*

Critical remarks on the theory presented here. *33*
Strengths of the current approach. *34*

CHAPTER 3   AN OBJECT-RELATIONS THEORY OF SELF-DEVELOPMENT: WINNICOTT & KOHUT **37**

D. W. Winnicott *38*
    The good-enough mother. *39*
    The True Self. *43*
    The not-good-enough mother. *45*
    The False Self. *46*
Heinz Kohut *47*
    The optimal mother. *47*
    The nuclear self. *50*
    The unempathic mother and the unhealthy self. *52*
    Final remarks on Kohut's self theory. *53*
Winnicott and Kohut in Mutual Encounter: Synthesizing an Object-Relations Theory of Child Development *55*
    Healthy parental influence. *55*
    The nature of healthy self development. *57*
    The course of unhealthy self development: self-depletion and self-fragmentation. *58*
Concluding Remarks *59*
    Comments on the synthesis of Winnicott's and Kohut's ideas. *59*
    Critical remarks on the theory presented here. *61*
    Strengths of the current approach. *61*

CHAPTER 4   AN EXISTENTIAL-HUMANISTIC THEORY OF SELF-DEVELOPMENT: CHARLOTTE BÜHLER **64**

Global Characterization of Charlotte Bühler's Existential-Humanism *65*
    Bühler and Freudian theory. *65*
    Bühler and behavioral theory. *66*
    Bühler on the context of development. *67*

Bühler and the self..67
Bühler and ego psychology..68
Bühler's self and healthy development....................................70
The Four Basic Tendencies of Human Life Span Development 71
Charlotte Bühler's Four Phases of Child Development...............................73
    Infancy (birth to two years old)..73
    Early childhood (two to eight years old)...............................75
    Late childhood/early adolescence (eight to twelve years old). 76
    Adolescence/early adulthood (twelve to twenty-five years old)...............78
Overview: Charlotte Bühler's Stage Theory of Self-Development..................80
Strengths of Bühler's Approach and Critical Remarks 82

CHAPTER 5   AN EXISTENTIAL-ANALYTIC THEORY OF SELF-DEVELOPMENT: RICHARD KNOWLES.. 89

Erikson's Stages of Psychosocial Development..89
Knowles's Reinterpretation of Erikson in the Light of Heidegger 92
Phenomenology of Embodied Facticity as a Developmental Progression 95
Ego Development Outside of Analytic Strictures...97
Phenomenology of Self-Development 100
Deviations from Healthy Development...104
In Summary: Strengths of Knowles's Approach and Critical Remarks.........107

CHAPTER 6   DANIEL STERN'S ANALYTIC-DEVELOPMENTAL SELF THEORY 112

Stern's Theory and Existential-Humanism...112
Four Senses of Self..113
    A sense of emergent self...113
    A sense of core self. 114
    A sense of subjective self..115
    Emergence of the verbal self...116
In Summary: Strengths of Stern's Approach and Critical Remarks.............117

CHAPTER 7 EARLY CONTRIBUTIONS TO THE PHENOMENOLOGY OF CHILDHOOD EXPERIENCE: KURT KOFFKA AND ERNEST G. SCHACHTEL 125

Kurt Koffka *126*
Ernest Schachtel *130*
    Autocentric and allocentric perception. *130*
    Emotional development: embeddedness and activity affect. *134*
Criticisms of Koffka and Schachtel *137*
An Introduction to the Phenomenology of Childhood Perception *138*

CHAPTER 8 TIME AND SPACE AS LIVED IN CHILDHOOD 145

Lived-Time *146*
    Time in childhood: temporal rhythm. *147*
    Time in childhood: the focus on the present. *147*
    Moving beyond the present. *149*
    The development of public time. *149*
    Time-in-space. *150*
Lived-Space *151*
    Lived-space and embodied perspective. *151*
    Lived-space and affect. *153*
    Lived-space: things and others. *154*
    Personal meaning and self-discovery in lived-space. *154*
An Illustration: Lived-Space-Time in the Preschool Classroom *156*

CHAPTER 9 FINDINGS FROM A PHENOMENOLOGICAL STUDY OF PSYCHOLOGICAL MALTREATMENT: THE CHILD'S RELATIONS TO THE MATERNAL FIGURE 161

Phenomenology as a Methodological Option *163*
The Present Study *165*
Method *166*

  Participants. *166*
  Procedure. *169*
 Results..*173*
  Inadequate maternal nurturing and affection. *173*
  The impact of being cast aside. *174*
  Verbal abuse and resultant self-blame. *175*
  Resignation and the internalization of abusive messages. ...*175*
  Negative comparisons. *176*
  Communication deficits. *176*
  Self-destructive behaviors. *177*
  Avoidant behaviors..*177*
  Misplaced aggression and the need for control. *178*
  Embattled self-awareness and self-definition. *179*
 Discussion of the Research Results..*179*
 The Research Results Inverted *181*
  Pedagogical considerations. *181*
  Developmental inferences...*182*

CHAPTER 10 EXISTENTIAL-HUMANISTIC SELF DEVELOPMENT THEORY (EHSDT) 185

What Is the Self?..*185*
What Are the Fundamental Characteristics of Optimal, Healthy Self Development? *192*
Does Self Development Occur in Stages?...................................*199*
When Does Self Development Begin? *200*
Is Self Development a Matter of Nature or Nurture?.................*201*
 General position...*201*
 Research-specific position. *202*
What Kind of Parenting Is Conducive to Self Development?......*202*
 1. Bringing an Ordered World to the Child. *202*
 2. Affectionate Holding and Handling. *203*
 3. Genuine Care and Involvement. *203*

  4. Constancy and Reliability of Loving Care............................204
  5. Empathic Bonding..204
  6. Nurturing Felt and Symbolically Represented Experience......204
  7. Receptive Mirroring..205
  8. Sensitivity to Changing Needs...205
  9. Tempering the Severity of Discipline without
   Overgratifying the Child..205
  10. Displaying Prosocial Models of Behavior...........................206
 Are Children Active or Passive Participants in Their Development?..........206
 Is Self Development Continuous or Discontinuous?.................................207
 What Kind of Parenting Threatens Self Development?.............................207
 What Does Unhealthy Self Development Look Like?...............................208
  Mild imaginative-integrational impairment....................................209
  Moderate imaginative-integrational impairment............................210
  Severe imaginative-integrational impairment.................................211
 Concluding Remarks...212

REFERENCES..**221**
INDEX..**235**

LIST OF ILLUSTRATIONS

Figure 4.1   Schematic Representation of the Self and Its Four Basic Tendencies 72

Figure 4.2   The Primary Integrative Tendencies of Bühler's Stages of Development 84

Figure 5.1   Representation of the Self According to Knowles 102

Figure 5.2   Schematic of Knowles's Existential-Analytic Developmental Theory 107

Figure 7.1   Construction Paper Lion Made by a Child of Four 141

Figure 7.2   Pig Drawing Made by a Child of Four 142

Figure 7.3   Pig Drawing Made by a Child of Five 143

Figure 10.1   An Evolving Process of Personal Integration Beginning in Infancy 188

Figure 10.2   Disrupted Self Development along a Continuum of Severity 212

LIST OF TABLES

Table 2.1	Characteristics of a Healthy, Congruent, Actualizing Self According to Carl Rogers	18
Table 2.2	Characteristics of the Self-Realizing Person or Real Self According to Karen Horney	23
Table 2.3	Examples of Parental Behavior Adverse to Self-Development Given by Karen Horney	24
Table 4.1	Infancy (birth to two years): The Primary Motivational Tendency Is Need Satisfaction	74
Table 4.2	Early Childhood (two to eight years): The Primary Motivational Tendency Is Self-Limiting Adaptation	77
Table 4.3	Late Childhood/Early Adolescence (eight to twelve years): The Primary Motivational Tendencies Are Self-Limiting Adaptation and Creative Expansion	78
Table 4.4	Adolescence/Early Adulthood (twelve to twenty-five years): The Motivational Tendency of Creative Expansion Facilitates the Overriding Drive Toward Self-Fulfillment	80
Table 5.1	Two Psychoanalytic Theories of Child Development	93
Table 5.2	Knowles's Ego Issues for Each Stage and Additional Ego Manifestations	100
Table 5.3	Pathological Deviations from Healthy Self Development According to Knowles	105
Table 9.1	Contrast of Quantitative Research and Phenomenological Research	165
Table 9.2	Brief Characterization of the Participants	168
Table 9.3	A Portion of an Edited Synthesis (Bob)	170
Table 9.4	A Portion of One Participant's Meaning Unit Analysis (Bob)	171
Table 9.5	Flowchart of the Research Method	172
Table 10.1	Self-Enriching and Self-Transcending Motives According to EHSDT	190

Table 10.2   *Contrasting Characteristics of Healthy and
              Unhealthy Self Development*.. 208

PREFACE

In their respective texts on child development, William Crain and Guy Lefrancois asserted that the study of child development is intrinsically harmonious with the basic principles of humanistic psychology. As Crain (2005) put it, "There is one place where the developmentalists' concerns are seriously expressed. This is in humanistic psychology" (xvi). Moreover, both Crain and Lefrancois admonished that child development ought to be viewed as a truly human process. In Lefrancois' (2001) words, "Self-actualization is simply the process of development" (562). The current text is in accordance with these views in that it explores how humanistic perspectives in psychology can be applied to the study of child development. It is an attempt to make humanistic ideas relating to child development more accessible to college or graduate instructors and their students. I wrote the book out of my own needs as an instructor. I struggled with the issues in the text for years and slowly accumulated what is now the work in its entirety. It has been used successfully in the honors sections of my child psychology classes at Brookdale College.

Humanistic theoretical perspectives are represented in a great many courses at the university level, including general psychology, health psychology, educational psychology, abnormal psychology, counseling techniques, theories of personality, and so on. However, despite the importance that humans place on the welfare of their offspring, humanism has not found a way into the field of developmental psychology, certainly not at the college level. Introductory child psychology texts typically open with an account of how Westerners appear to be placing an increasingly high value on the welfare of their children. However, there has not been a proper analogue to this cultural metamorphosis in psychological theorizing about child development. Theory in the area of child psychology has tended to conceptualize child development in mechanistic, reductionistic terms (e.g., the id, stimulus-response, information processing, etc.). In short, attempts to see the truly human elements of development remain atypical. This text hopes to make a significant contribution to remedying the disparity between the above noted cultural transformation and the current state of developmental theorizing.

The text presents two closely related humanistic currents in the area of child development: humanistic self-development theory and phenomenological child psychology. The first chapter discusses the need for the text, its theoretical orientation, and the structure of the book. In the next three chapters, theories of self-development are derived from the works of Carl Rogers, Karen Horney, D. W.

Winnicott, Heinz Kohut, and Charlotte Bühler. Chapters Five and Six introduce the reader to existing self-development theories created by Richard Knowles and Daniel Stern. Chapters Seven, Eight, and Nine explore major aspects of childhood experience (i.e., perception, affect, time, space, and maternal relations) from a phenomenological perspective. The concluding chapter is the culmination of the text, which consists of a comprehensive theory of self-development from an existential-humanistic perspective.

In terms of the pedagogy of the text, summative observations are included at the end of each chapter. The summation usually appears in the form of critical remarks and/or comments. In addition, there are illustrations peppered through the book and some empirical findings. Finally, I have listed key terms and concepts at the conclusion of each chapter.

In my eleven years teaching in the developmental area, I have noticed that it is difficult for students to attain a holistic grasp of development by the end of each semester. This relates directly to the controversial issue over whether to use a chronological book as opposed to a topical book. Unfortunately, the two different book designs have not ameliorated this problem. Whether the material is presented in a few major time "chunks," as it were, or in fifteen individual chapters, students tend to leave the course without having developed a synoptic grasp of the metamorphosis from childhood through adolescence. It is my sense that theoretical continuity is the key to a synoptic understanding of development.

Chapter Ten provides an overarching theoretical viewpoint that can be used to put developmental issues into perspective. The perspective offered there is holistic and open to dialogue between various schools of thought, such as American humanism, postmodern psychology, existential-phenomenology, psychoanalysis, Gestalt psychology, neo-analytic and psychodynamic theories, Vygotskian theory, and ecological psychology.

ACKNOWLEDGMENTS

This text would not have been possible without the help of Miss Heather, who allowed me to observe her preschool class. I am indebted to her for her help, encouragement, and expertise. She is the most innately talented teacher I have ever known. I am further indebted to the *Journal of Emotional Abuse*, the *Journal of Humanistic Psychology*, and *The Humanistic Psychologist* for publishing articles that have become chapters in this text. Finally, I owe special thanks to Heather Lionetti for creating the art for this text.

CHAPTER 1

HUMANISM, EXISTENTIAL-PHENOMENOLOGY, AND CHILD DEVELOPMENT

Humanism and Child Developmental Theory

As a college instructor, I have been teaching child psychology nearly every semester since 1997. The topics of the course never cease to stir my enthusiasm, and teaching child psychology remains a positive experience for me. At the same time, updating the course each new academic year brings with it a somewhat frustrating experience. Having an existential-humanistic theoretical orientation, I struggle with the problem of how to go about introducing students to humanistic-developmental frameworks and methodologies.

Child psychology textbooks rarely include material on humanism that can be used as a guide for students. Freudian and Eriksonian psychoanalysis, behaviorism and social learning theory, genetic perspectives, the cognitive approaches of Piaget and Vygotsky, and ecological theories all regularly appear in child psychology textbooks. While there are humanistic currents in Eriksonian psychoanalysis, Vygotsky's theory, and ecological approaches due to their holism (e.g., their emphases on the child's social context and enculturation), these approaches are not specifically dedicated to a systematic and rigorous humanization of psychology per se. Hence, they are generally not referred to as humanistic theories, nor are they presented in textbooks as belonging to the tradition of humanistic psychology. To date, I have found only one introductory child development text that has included a section specifically dedicated to a presentation of humanistic theory. Namely, Lefrancois (2001) cited Abraham Maslow's hierarchy of needs as a humanistic theory of development. This is somewhat unfortunate, however, as Maslow's hierarchy of needs is not a theory of child development. The needs that comprise the hierarchy are not tied to chronological time frames, and Maslow never schematized the steps along the path to self-actualization in such a way as to imply that they were phases of lifespan development (e.g., a "biological-needs phase" preceding a "safety-needs phase," and so on). This is not to imply that a developmental theory must be a stage theory. Rather, the important point is that Lefrancois presented Maslow's ideas as if they were developmental in nature without discussing how Maslow's works might be reinterpreted in order to shed light on child development (86).

The dearth of humanistic theory in developmental textbooks is indicative of humanism's relative lack of popularity in developmental psychology on the whole. Compelling reasons for this state of affairs can be found in the history of psychology and the history of humanism. In the early 1900s, Sigmund Freud was articulating the view that newborns are the manifestation of our truest animal nature, "in the raw," so to speak. For Freud, children were first and foremost pleasure seekers. Freudian psychology envisioned the course of child development as a process of taming our animalistic drives, the eventual appearance of an ego and a superego. While early movements like psychophysics, structuralism, functionalism, and Gestalt psychology all made their contributions to the burgeoning field of psychology, it was psychoanalysis that would eventually become the first major contributor to child developmental theory. By grounding his psychology and approach to therapy in a theory of development, Freud influenced developmental psychology as well. Due to the influence of psychoanalysis, many psychologists came to view children as hedonistic beings relentlessly driven by "instincts" for attaining pleasure and being aggressive.

Eventually, John Watson was inspired to create a psychology without reference to intrapsychic dynamisms. In America, behaviorism became the dominant force in psychology for many years. Behavioral theory, or learning theory as it is often called, conceptualized human behavior as the cumulative result of the environmental forces which shape and mold it. Behavior was held to be the consequence of environmental contingencies or conditioning (e.g., the distribution of punishments and reinforcements). While development was no longer viewed from the perspective of animal instincts, applying behaviorism to child development was perhaps even more physicalistic, reductionistic, and deterministic. Children were considered to undertake courses of action that brought them rewards in the past and avoid behaviors that elicited punishments in the past. To understand the behavior of children is to understand their history of reinforcement.

To be sure, it is the positivistic-empirical current in Freudianism and behaviorism (and all forms of psychology that attempt to pattern themselves after the natural sciences) that promotes the creation of a reductionistic, deterministic developmental perspective. As Allport (1955, 10–11) put it:

> One final presupposition marks Lockean empiricism, namely, the assumption that what is earlier is more fundamental than what is late in

development. The early impress upon the wax of the mind is important. First impressions, to be sure, may later be compounded and criss-crossed, but the original simple ideas are still the elements of later mental life. This type of geneticism has taken a firm hold upon American psychology. In keeping with the doctrine of tabula rasa, American geneticism holds that what is important is childhood learning, childhood fixations, childhood conditioning.

Viewing prior influences as universally more fundamental and important to later experiences in the life of an individual comes as a consequence of a causally determined view of the universe, which psychologists influenced by positivistic natural science applied to the issue of human development. Development became a linear procession, with the past, present, and future being thought of similar to the way billiard balls collide into one another. In other words, the past causes the present, and the future is predictable even though it has not come simply by looking at the causal chain of events that precede it. The dominance of this model of development has created some resistance to the study of development as such within humanistic psychology. Many humanists have been put off by the idea of a concerted effort to explore the significance of child development, as they associate that kind of research with the causal, deterministic view of human existence that dominates natural science psychology (e.g., Yalom 1980, 10–11).

This is not to imply, however, that all humanists were uninterested in developmental psychology. For instance, Charlotte Bühler was intensely interested in issues pertaining to child development. However, her interests were not typical within humanistic circles. Humanists and existential-phenomenologists have traditionally been enamored with adult existence. This is not only due to misgivings about developmental psychology, but also the influence of existential philosophy on humanistic and existential psychologists. Needless to say, philosophers such as Søren Kierkegaard, Max Scheler, Martin Heidegger, Martin Buber, and Paul Tillich were not interested in developmental science. Thus, on the whole, the third force in psychology (i.e., humanism) has simply not been very interested in "developmental reform," as it were.

Nonetheless, as an existential-humanist, my overriding interest in child psychology can be summed up with the following question: To what degree is it possible for psychologists to see child development as a truly human process? Rather than maintaining the status quo of developmental science, I want to be able to look at child development and see distinctly human elements. I would like to be able to consider how child development can play a part in the unfolding of a human existence. To be sure, there are some works pertaining to child development that allow one to view child development in a more humanistic fashion. I have found these works within two related humanistic currents in developmental psychology: humanistic-developmental self-theory and phenomenological child psychology. However, these works have not been brought together into an organized form that would allow them to attract more attention in child psychology on the whole. To this end, this book explores humanistic-developmental self-theory and phenomenological child psychology as options for instructors who wish to expose students of child psychology to humanism at the college or graduate level.

Two Humanistic Currents in the Study of Child Development

There are several options to consider when introducing students of developmental psychology to humanism via self-theory. D. W. Winnicott, Karen Horney, and Heinz Kohut, for example, have all been referred to as "humanists," specifically due to their respective emphases on selfhood (e.g., Hall & Lindsey 1978, 166; Mitchell & Black 1995, 141; van den Berg 1972, 138), and each theorist has made significant contributions to an understanding of child development within psychoanalysis. Apart from the psychoanalytic tradition, Carl Rogers (1951, 1959) and Charlotte Bühler (e.g., 1968c) articulated approaches to child development that stressed the development of selfhood as well.

Among existential-phenomenological developmental psychologists, Knowles's (1986) work stands out as more accessible than average. His interpretation of Erik Erikson's stage theory in the context of Heideggerian philosophical-anthropology steers the psychoanalytic study of development extending from Freud (1962) to Erikson (1963) in an existential direction. Knowles effectively humanized the Eriksonian framework by compensating for what he called the psychoanalytic "omission of the self" (1986, 3–4). In his words:

> Erikson's work has enabled us to be constantly mindful that the human being cannot be considered solely in bodily terms but must also be seen as an ego and as a social being. The traditional psychoanalytic insights concerning the person as bodily being are integrated into a larger view which does, to some degree, alter them. In the same way, Erikson's approach must be broadened since he, like most psychologists, seems to overlook or to minimize what is most characteristic of human beings and that is not their bodies, their rationality, or even their relationships with others.

Knowles goes on to note that what is most essential to the person is "his or her authentic, though always limited, selfhood" (7).

All of these developmental theorists demonstrated that the concept of selfhood can be used to efficiently and effectively bring a more humanistic approach to students of child psychology. This is promising since some child psychology texts are beginning to include self-styled psychoanalytic authors into their chapters on developmental theory. For example, Seifert and Hoffnung provided a short summation of Daniel Stern's (1985) and Heinz Kohut's (1977) ideas concerning self-development (2000, 39–40). However, these synopses were quite brief (i.e., limited to one to two paragraphs) and were not given focal attention in the chapter. Nonetheless, the inclusion of self-styled developmental theory in child psychology texts is a legitimate and promising way to advocate a more humanistic approach to child development. Thus, the first chapters in this text are dedicated to an explication of self-development, utilizing contributions to this area that have been made by humanistically oriented psychologists.

Various phenomenological authors have also made valuable contributions to developmental psychology by focusing on the nature of childhood experience (e.g., Benswanger 1979; Briod 1989; Lippitz 1983; Schachtel 1959). Phenomenological research has yet to make a significant impact on developmental psychology in the United States. Nonetheless, the insights gained from phenomenological research into the lived world of childhood existence are invaluable to an understanding of child development, so chapters dedicated to the phenomenological approach are also included in this text.

The Theoretical Perspective of This Book

As I mentioned earlier, my theoretical background is primarily humanistic in nature. In particular, I have a preference for existential-phenomenological thought. It is for this reason that I use the combined term, existential-humanism. When I analyze and construct self-theories in this book, it will be from this theoretical vantage point. However, since the words *humanistic* and *phenomenological* are subject to much confusion in psychological literature, they are in need of immediate clarification.

The meaning of humanism.

The word *humanism* is used in three different ways in psychological literature, though the three uses are rarely explicated. One meaning of humanism is the use of psychological knowledge toward humane ends. This is the broadest definition of humanism. In this sense of the word, any school of thought can be considered humanistic (Fischer 1985, 346; van Kaam 1966, 357). This is not primarily what

I mean when I use the word *humanism* in this text, though it is related to my use of the term.

More often than not, humanism is identified with the work of certain American psychologists, especially Carl Rogers and Abraham Maslow. This is the most narrow and specific use of the term. Rogers, Maslow, and others like them (e.g., James Bugental) attempted to free American psychology from the strictures of psychoanalytic and behavioral thought using concepts such as self-esteem, self-acceptance, self-actualization, or self-realization. While some existential-phenomenological psychologists such as Rollo May were a part of this effort, the humanistic movement is more commonly identified with the work of individuals like Rogers and Maslow who were not explicitly phenomenological or existential in orientation. For me, being a humanist does not refer to the specifically American humanistic movement that was popular through the 1960s either.

By referring to myself as humanistic I mean being a humanist in a more moderate sense of the term. I mean something more specific than simply having humane intentions and something broader than American humanistic psychology. As a humanist, I strive to contribute to psychology's knowledge base in hopes that my contributions can be used toward humane ends. However, I find it confusing to refer to Freud, Skinner, Rogers, and Bühler, for example, as humanists when they have such obvious differences between their metapsychological principles and the implications of their ideas. Humanism in psychology is concerned with the truly human qualities of existence, such as "the role of values in culture and history, acknowledging the power of a person's experience and will, and taking a holistic, growth-oriented stance" (Fischer 1985, 345). Looking at the history of psychology, it is obvious that certain thinkers and schools of thought have clearly been more preoccupied with such aims than others. American humanism can certainly be considered a movement that sought to address the aforementioned concerns. However, many individuals who did not belong to the tradition of American humanism sought to address these concerns as well. Thus, phenomenologists, existentialists, Gestaltists, American humanists, and a wide array of post-Freudian psychoanalysts can all be considered humanistic according to my usage of the term. However, behaviorists, for example, would not be referred to as humanistic in the context in spite of whatever humane intensions they might have due to their reductionistic perspective.

The meaning of phenomenology.

There are many usages of the term phenomenology that are different from the phenomenology of the current work. Phenomenology, as discussed in this text, refers to a distinctly European tradition that originated in philosophy. To delve into the manifold meanings of phenomenology in psychological literature goes beyond the scope of this book. However, to avoid misunderstanding, I will quickly mention the two most common uses of the term *phenomenology* that deviate from the current usage before introducing my conceptualization of it.

First, phenomenology is a term that is often used to describe the focus of American humanistic psychologies, such as those of Carl Rogers and Abraham Maslow (e.g., Rathus & Nevid 1999, 54). While Rogers and Maslow certainly espoused theories with a phenomenological thrust, they were not formally trained in phenomenology as originally developed by Edmund Husserl (1859–1938) and other European philosophers. This first popular usage of the term defines phenomenology as "having to do with subjective experience" (Rathus & Nevid 54). While phenomenology as originally developed does focus on perceptual phenomena, the European phenomenological tradition has taken great pains to eliminate the artificial distinction between pure subjectivity on the one hand and the supposed realm of pure objectivity on the other. American humanistic psychologists tend to use the terms "subjectivity" and "objectivity" without explicitly noting that subjectivity and objectivity are but two interdependent poles of experience. Thus, phenomenology as a description of American humanistic psychology is a rather informal and imprecise use of the term.

The second popular use of *phenomenology* comes from the American Psychiatric Association's Diagnostic and Statistics Manual (DSM) classification system for mental illness. Phenomenology, as the term is used in the DSM, deals solely with the so-called "objective" manifestations of the patient's subjective world. Phenomenology refers to objective evidence in the form of signs or symptoms of a disorder. It does not penetrate into the meaning of the patient's symptoms or how they may have evolved. Moreover, the psychiatric usage of *phenomenology* maintains the traditional subject-object dichotomy that European phenomenology sought to overcome. In this sense, it is the exact opposite of *phenomenology* as it appears in the current text.

The phenomenology discussed in this text is existential-phenomenology. Phenomenology and existentialism are two different currents of thought in philosophy that are nonetheless related. Phenomenology is typically considered a methodology, while existentialism is considered an overarching mood or attitude that characterizes phenomenological description.

Phenomenology can be defined as the description of human experience as it is lived. It is not, therefore, a theory of what human experience is like, nor a theory of the conscious mind. Phenomenologists aim to characterize human experience in as unprejudiced a manner as possible, resisting the temptation to constantly rely on theoretical frameworks for interpreting psychological phenomena. Therefore, phenomenologists do not search for simple cause and effect relationships when it comes to human experience and behavior. Their primary aim is to describe the nature of an experience—what a phenomenon means to a person—rather than asking what caused the phenomenon to occur. In essence, phenomenologists seek to understand the qualitative significance of human behavior and "mental processes" above all.

Existentialism is a philosophical movement that stresses the fact that human beings are not solely or even primarily thinkers, but rather that they are first and foremost caring, desiring, choosing, and acting beings. To existentialists, a human being is not a detached observer of the world, but rather "in-the-world," always already caught up in a situation and living out the possibilities inherent to their concrete predicament before they are reflectively aware of this involvement. Thus, the existential-phenomenological approach focuses on explicating the highly significant meanings embedded within personal experience from the viewpoint of the feeling, valuing, behaving individual who is ever "caught up" in-the-world.

Fundaments of Existential-Humanistic-Developmental Thought

Having noted the general purpose of the current work and delineated its global theoretical thrust, an outline of how existential-humanism relates specifically to the study of child development is in order. In brief, there are six basic elements to an existential-humanistic-developmental perspective, whether self-styled or phenomenological. These elements are presented as bulleted items below and then subsequently discussed in a more detailed fashion:

- An existential-humanistic-developmental perspective is holistic;
- An existential-humanistic-developmental perspective recognizes individual uniqueness;
- An existential-humanistic-developmental perspective views child development as inherently worldly and contextual;
- An existential-humanistic-developmental perspective views development as historical without being a historical determinism;
- An existential-humanistic-developmental perspective views development as a project of becoming oneself rather than a purely passive process
- An existential-humanistic-developmental perspective values an understanding of healthy development

An existential-humanistic view of child development is a holistic perspective. Emphasis is not given to subdivisions of the child's personality, nor is the child considered a mere sum of interacting parts, whether physical or mental. Some humanistic authors use the notion of selfhood to guide their observations and discussions of the child as a whole, while others rely on primarily phenomenological descriptions of the child's lived world (i.e., the total action-perception Gestalt that constitutes the experiential world of the child).

Whether humanists focus their efforts on exploring the nature of self-development or arriving at phenomenological descriptions of childhood experience, their holistic understanding of the child assumes that each child is a unique individual. To study self-development is to explore the significant issues, themes, challenges, and other core structural elements that frame each child's efforts at personality integration as he or she grows to develop a unique style of being-in-the-world (Heidegger 1962, 153). Phenomenology acknowledges the inherently individualized nature of perception, action, and development by admonishing that phenomenological descriptions of childhood experience always remain fundamentally open-ended. In other words, the living, breathing, developing human child cannot be explained away or totally comprehended in terms of philosophical or scientific systems of thought about development. A humanistic-developmental psychology strives to illuminate being-a-child-in-the-world to the utmost degree while being cognizant of the fact that the child's lived-openness to the world can never be encapsulated within a totalizing system of thought or explanation.

As an individualized process, development occurs in a particular context. A truly existential-humanism refrains from describing any course of development as if it were occurring independently of the child's embodiment, social relations, language, culture, and history. An existential perspective on development entails viewing development as an inherently worldly process of personal growth and evolution. Thus, the self, as it is understood from an existential-humanistic standpoint, does not refer to a "little person inside the big person" or even the singular individual in the sense of an organism demarcated from the world and others by the boundary of the epidermis. The self is not a cogito, a homunculus, or any other solipsistic construct. Rather, selfhood implies a fundamental relatedness to the world in which the child is always already involved before conscious, reflective awareness intervenes to conceptualize this relatedness. As the phenomenologist Wilfried Lippitz (2002, 7) noted, "Even the self is only understandable in difference to the other and the stranger."

Of the various aspects of worldly childhood existence, history is of particular importance to developmental psychology. One of the assumptions of child developmental theory is that an individual's life-history plays a significant role in his or her becoming. Thus, Murray (1986), referring to the phenomenology of perception, observed that "Perception ... is historical, having a decided, pronounced relationship with one's history" (42). Put more strongly, Lippitz (2002, 8) noted, "To have been a child is ... a fact which affects the present."

The past (i.e., life-history) is an important part of an existential view of human becoming because time is central to existential-phenomenological philosophical-anthropology. Martin Heidegger (1962, 42), for example, described human existence as fundamentally comprehensible in terms of time. For Heidegger, to articulate how a person lives time is to illuminate the particular way an individual lives out his or her life (i.e., how does one interpret and narrate the story of his or her past so that it becomes a personal hi*story*? How is one "present" or not present to the world around him or her? How does one "look forward" or not look forward to the future?). One's past, in the sense of a lived-past, a life-history, is essential to our existence. As Heidegger put it, "Historicality is a determining characteristic for [human existence] in the very basis of ... Being." Heidegger also maintained, however, that past, present, and future were equiprimordial. In other words, there is no overriding primacy given to past events such that they would be seen as determining present and future realities. It is in and through one's present frame of reference, looking ahead toward a future, that one interprets and remembers a past. The past of authentic life-history is not a fixed set of occurrences, a collection of objects within a causal chain of events that is the same for everyone who was a part of those occurrences. If two people have different memories of the same event, this does not mean that one or both of their memories are simply subjectively biased. To have a memory of the past is to re-member. It is to put past experiences back together again in an act of interpretation on the part of the person. Just as past, present, and future are interrelated, subjectivity and objectivity are bound together, and the scope of meaning that one can appropriate from one's past is inexhaustible.

Having a past, a life-history, is an absolute requirement for a person to be a person. To erase one's memories is to erase one's very identity as an individual. Having a past full of learning experiences and meaningful relations with others provides a context for future growth. This context (i.e., the past) is an overabundance of "raw material," so to speak, which comes in the form events that would tend to cultivate strengths and opportunities as well events that tend to bring about limitations on one's ability to mature and grow. At the same time, the past is not set in stone. Past experience is not a segment from a purely objective linear order. Again, how the person imaginatively projects himself or herself toward the future provides a frame of reference for interpreting the nature and significance of the past. One's past and one's future have a reciprocal relationship. The past one is gathering up and the future one is projecting from one's present predicament co-contextualize and thereby co-constitute one another. In van den Berg's (1972) words:

> The conditions of a decision are given by the past; the act itself originates from the future, from the expectance, the wish, the fear, the desire. This is true for one's entire life. The past provides the condition for what is going to happen in life, but the acts of life are rooted in the future. (86)

Later, he continued:

> The past appears in what is coming to meet us; if it does not appear, it is absent. So that, indeed, the past is that which lies there behind us, but only because a future permits it to lie there. And the future is indeed yonder, before us, but only because it is fed by a past. (91)

Thus, an existential-phenomenological view of historical development is not a historical determinism. Rather, to understand human perception and action in an evolutionary context is to see history as one of many important influences in the life and growth of an individual. As an existential-humanist, I am not inclined to see life-history as "the" determining force of human experience and behavior. At the same time, I am not willing to marginalize its significance on the grounds that there are so many other forces at play in the life of an individual, including freewill and decision making. Like Murray (1986, 43), I find the middle, more moderate position to be the most accurate description of human becoming: "Perception is signifying in the way and to the extent that one is historically prepared for the perception and that means in the way and to the extent that we have put it together for ourselves."

From an existential-humanistic viewpoint, child development is understood to be a significant (though not exclusive) formative factor in a human being's general project of becoming a person. That the process of becoming is a project implies that existence is not ready-made or predetermined by internal or external variables (e.g., genetics, bio-chemistry, familial or social environment). Becoming, in other words, is not a purely passive process. Growing, developing, maturing, and becoming a healthy self-with-others-alongside-things is a personal accomplishment that is carried out in and through meaningful worldly relations throughout the lifespan. From this broad perspective, the challenge of human development is to make life meaningful and fulfilling in a world that is not completely our own doing and which harbors threats to our being. This is evident across the lifespan, from the awareness of vulnerability felt in infancy to the articulated fears of death that manifest in old age.

Unfortunately, however, psychology has tended to focus more on the issues and problems that are integral to human development rather than the process of growth itself. Nowhere is this more striking that in Freud's work, where he offers no notion of human health as such, only conceptualizations of the different subtle levels of developmental aberration (e.g., Freud 1960). This one-sidedness has created a need for an explication of healthy developmental progress. Self-developmental and phenomenological theories address this need. An existential-humanist understands that child development cannot be adequately described by focusing on human sickness. Rather, unhealthy development is best understood as a deviation from healthy developmental progress. As Levinas (1969, 115) put it: "Life is affectivity and sentiment; to live is to enjoy life. To despair of life makes sense only because originally life is happiness. Suffering is a failing of happiness; it is not correct to say that happiness is an absence of suffering."

The Structure and Goals of This Text

To reiterate, the general purpose of this book is to provide educators with options for introducing humanism to students of child psychology. Humanistic-developmental self-theories and phenomenological descriptions of childhood experience will be used in pursuit of this goal. In addition, I hope to accomplish a further aim: the construction of a unified humanistic-developmental self-theory that is rooted in existential-phenomenological psychology. The existential-phenomenological roots of the theory will come from my own interpretive viewpoint and the fact that some phenomenological psychology runs through the self-theories covered in this book.

Self-theories are covered first in the pages that follow. In order to more firmly establish the phenomenological underpinnings of the unified theoretical framework, phenomenological descriptions of childhood experience will be subsequently examined, especially for their potential to contribute to the construction of the humanistic-developmental self-theory proposed at the conclusion of this volume.[1]

---

1   It is important for the reader to note that phenomenology is first and foremost a methodology and maintains its power as an illuminative force in psychology by resisting theoretical systemization. Thus, self-theory and phenomenology will always remain distinct contributors to child psychology.

KEY TERMS AND CONCEPTS

Active becoming
Existential-phenomenology
First force psychology
Healthy development
Historical determinism
Holistic perspective
Humanism
Humanistic-developmental self-theory
Individual uniqueness
Natural science psychology
Phenomenological child psychology
Second force psychology
Third force psychology
Worldly development

CHAPTER 2

A HUMANISTIC THEORY OF SELF-DEVELOPMENT: ROGERS AND HORNEY*

Two theorists' ideas provided the foundation for the humanistic-developmental scheme presented in this chapter: Carl R. Rogers (1902–1987) and Karen Horney (1885–1952). Carl Rogers (1951, 1959) generated some basic humanistic understandings of child development to ground his person-centered model of therapy. Karen Horney, although she is considered a neo-psychoanalyst, has been referred to as both humanistic (Paris 2002) and phenomenological (Knowles 1986, 3; van den Berg 1972, 138). In very much the same way as Rogers, Horney (1937, 1939, 1945, 1950, etc.) used developmental ideas to conceptualize human growth and psychological illness, which provided a basis for her ideas regarding psychotherapy.

Both Rogers and Horney used the same method of observation to gather their ideas concerning development: a retrospective, case-based style of data collection, meaning that they each disclosed themes of child development via the reconstruction of their patients' childhoods. Briod (1989, 116) referred to this method of data collection as one of the richest sources of data regarding the life-world of children. Although Briod added the caveat that retrospective research with patients has a tendency to yield results that support therapists' particular theoretical biases (116), it is interesting to note that Rogers's and Horney's findings overlapped considerably despite the fact that they came from different traditions of thought. Thus, Rogers (1951, 489) cited Horney's ideas concerning the self-realization process as being similar to his understanding of the self-actualizing tendency in human development. Conversely, Paris (1996a, 140) noted that Horney's later theory was most similar to the works of third force psychologists such as Carl Rogers. This inherent harmony added credence to the possibility that an encounter between the two theories appeared viable and promised to be productive.

---

* This chapter is based on an article titled "Deriving a Humanistic Theory of Child Development from the Works of Carl R. Rogers and Karen Horney." *The Humanistic Psychologist*, Volume 34, No. 2, 177–199 ([Mahwah, New Jersey]: Lawrence Erlbaum Associates, 2006).

Rogers and Horney were also chosen for this chapter because they are well-known theorists. Both thinkers regularly appear in various textbooks and a variety of courses because of the influence of their personality theories and their ideas regarding therapy. Therefore, using theorists whom students are more likely to be familiar with promises to provide a very efficient, effective means for introducing college students to humanistic ideas about child development.

What follows is an explication of Rogers's and Horney's thoughts on child psychology. Their theories are introduced separately. Should the reader prefer one of the theories as originally formulated, each is available in a manageable outline form. Next, highly significant structural themes from Rogers's and Horney's works are integrated into a single humanistic perspective on child development. Finally, the potential strengths and vulnerabilities of the humanistic-developmental framework are discussed.

Carl Rogers: Development of the Congruous Self (or Self-Actualization) vs. the Incongruous Self

Carl Rogers examined the development of the personality in a holistic fashion. Rather than making psychological constructs such as the id or ego the focus of his observations, Rogers sought an empirically verifiable theory of the whole person. Rogers tended to use the terms *organism* and *person* interchangeably. However, *organism* was preferred when he referred specifically to "sensory and visceral equipment" (Rogers 1951, 500). The term *person* was favored when Rogers referred to one's mental capacities, one's phenomenal field of experience, one's self-concept, and one's self-ideal, that is, the more psychological dimension of existence (Hall & Lindzey 1978, 292). This is not to imply that the person exists in isolation from the world with others. In Rogers's words, "There is ... no possibility of a sharp limit between organism and the environment" (1951, 497).

According to Rogers, the developing organism has a single sovereign motivational predisposition: the "actualizing tendency" (1959, 196). The actualizing tendency is the innate tendency of the organism to develop all of its biological and psychological capacities in ways that serve to maintain or enhance itself. The ultimate aim of the actualizing tendency is that of increasing autonomy for the organism and a correlative lessening of control by external forces (1959, 196). The actualizing tendency is present at birth and observable in infancy.

As infancy progresses and children begin to experience more and more of a sense of autonomy and control over their surroundings, they start to develop what Rogers called "a dawning awareness of 'I experience'" (1951, 499). At this time, a particularly significant dimension of the organism becomes manifest, which

Rogers referred to as the "self." As Rogers (1986, 128) put it, "One aspect of this basic tendency is the capacity of the individual, in a growth-promoting environment, to move toward self-understanding and self-direction."

Rogers's self is not a homunculus. The self is but "one expression of the general tendency of the organism to behave in those ways which maintain and enhance itself" (1959, 196). However, the self is not the total organism either, but is rather "the awareness of being, of functioning" (498). The self and the self-concept tend to be interchangeable terms for Rogers (286; Murray 2001, 46). In his words, the self is "an organized, fluid, but consistent conceptual pattern of perceptions of characteristics and relationships of the 'I' or the 'me,' together with values attached to these concepts" (1951, 498). This is not to say that the self always remains within focal consciousness. For Rogers, the self is more precisely "available to awareness, though not necessarily in awareness. It is a fluid and changing gestalt, a process" (1959, 200). Elsewhere, along similar lines, he noted, "It is, then, the organized picture, existing in awareness either as figure or ground, of the self and the self-in-relationship, together with the positive or negative values which are associated with those qualities and relationships" (1951, 501). In stronger terms, Barton (1974, 197) noted that the "real self" in Rogers's works is "not primarily a thinking self." In Barton's view, Rogers's notion of the self-implies both "perceptual-life" and "feeling-life" (200).

As the self-concept evolves, infants arrive at more sophisticated understandings of themselves in relation to others and their environment. This process is value laden, meaning that children begin to see certain kinds of worldly and interpersonal relations as good, neutral, or bad. Under healthy circumstances, children positively value experiences that they perceive as enhancing themselves and negatively value experiences that appear to threaten their development (1951, 498–499). The self is said to be congruent with the organism. As a result, a complementary self-actualizing tendency begins to develop in consort with the global actualizing tendency.

When the actualizing tendency of the organism is adopted by the self, the self-actualizing tendency orients the person's development in the direction of "socialization, broadly defined" (e.g., Rogers 1951, 488). Thus, Tobin (1991, 16) noted that Rogers's theory is a field theoretical view of self-development. The self both develops in an interpersonal context and desires good interpersonal relations during the growth process. The person is also oriented toward future development, in the direction of who he or she would ultimately like to become (i.e., his or her ideal state of selfhood or "ideal self"). In Rogers's words, "Ideal self ... is the term used to denote the self-concept which the individual would most like to possess, upon which he places the highest value for himself" (1959, 200).

Whether or not children develop a healthy self-actualizing tendency in the direction of a genuine ideal self has to do with the nature of their upbringing, especially their interactions with their primary caretakers. When children are old enough to comprehend parental judgments such as "good boy" or "bad girl" accompanying their behavior, these social experiences are related to the evaluative dimension of the self-structure (1951, 499). Healthy developmental conditions are those in which children experience unconditional parental care and affection The result of these conditions is that children will most likely view themselves as good, as worthy of love (1951, 499). In Rogers's words:

> The parent who is able (1) genuinely to accept ... feelings of satisfaction experienced by the child, and (2) to fully accept the child who experiences them, and (3) at the same time to accept his or her own feeling that such behavior is unacceptable in the family, creates a situation for the child very different from the usual one. The child in this relationship experiences no threat to his concept of himself as a loved person. He can experience fully and accept ... himself. (1951, 502)

Children who are not threatened by the loss of love are open to the full range of their organismic experiences (1951, 503). As Rogers put it, "The behavior which would result [from unconditional positive regard] would be the adaptive behavior of a separate, unique, self-governing individual [whose self structure] would be realistic, based upon an accurate symbolization of all the evidence given by the child's sensory and visceral equipment" (1951, 502). Thus, the self-structure of healthy developing individuals is, in Rogers's words, "integrated, whole, genuine" (1959, 206). This experientially open, "congruent self" actualizes in consort with the more global actualizing tendency in the direction of a particular self-ideal. As Rogers (1961, 27) noted, these individuals can let the flow of their experience carry them in a forward-moving direction toward tentative goals and ideals. Rogers observed that the actualizing self has numerous qualities. The qualities of healthy, congruent self development according to Rogers are compiled and listed in Table 2.1.

Table 2.1
Characteristics of a Healthy, Congruent, Actualizing Self According to Carl Rogers

- Down-to-earth, perceptions and judgments are grounded in facts, realistic
- Open to experience without feeling threatened or being defensive
- Mature and responsible, owns one's own feelings
- Accepts others as unique individuals different from himself
- Accepts and prizes oneself unconditionally
- Accepts and prizes others for who they are
- Has an internal locus of evaluation when judging oneself
- Willingness to be "in process," tolerance of change and ambiguity
- Appreciation of the uniqueness of each moment of one's life
- Experience of oneself as "fully functioning," general sense of richness of one's life experience
- Spontaneity, displays unpredictable creativity
- Trusts oneself, confidence in one's skills, perceptions, and evaluations
- Displays a life-affirming nurturance of all living things
- Open, expressive, flexible, and willing to take risks in relationships
- Independent, autonomous, self-motivated to seek fulfillment
- Seeks enhancement over the maintenance of one's organism overall

Note. Adapted from Rogers (1959, 1961, 1980).

When children are not given unconditional positive regard, however, healthy self-development is jeopardized. For instance, should children experience their parents as disapproving of certain behaviors that they enjoy or would otherwise value positively, they may perceive their parents as saying, "You are bad, the behavior is bad, and you are not loved or loveable when you behave this way" (1951, 500). This threatens their self-worth, their feelings of fundamental lovability as a person. There is, in Rogers's view, no greater threat to development. For this reason, the children undertake measures to survive this threatening situation: the denial or distortion of organismic experience. In Rogers's words:

> Certain results then follow in the development of the ordinary child. One result is a denial in awareness of the satisfactions that were experienced. The other is to distort the symbolization of the experience of the parents. The accurate symbolization would be: "I perceive my parents as experiencing this behavior as unsatisfying to them." The distorted symbolization, distorted to preserve the threatened concept of self, is: "I perceive this behavior as unsatisfying." (1951, 500)

Thus, in order to guard against losing the sense of being loved, children find themselves compelled to refashion their phenomenal field of experience to fit what they perceive their parents as wanting in exchange for their love. Rogers expressed this situation in the following terms: "I want to be acceptable to my parents and hence must experience myself as being the sort of person they think I am" (1951, 526). Consequently, the values that are attached to children's experiences and made part of the self-structure are in some instances genuinely experienced, but in other instances they are "introjected" or taken over from caregivers. Moreover, these values are perceived in a distorted fashion, as if they were indeed one's own experiences (1951, 498–500). Children introject the parental value system in an effort to uphold the specific "conditions of worth" imposed upon them by their parents. As Rogers put it, "self-structure is characterized by a condition of worth when a self-experience or set of related self-experiences is either avoided or sought solely because the individual discriminates it as being less or more worthy of self-regard" (1959, 209).

As the process of denying and distorting one's own experience in favor of introjected values proceeds, the self-concept becomes increasingly alienated from the organism (1951, 505). Accurate representations of experience are not allowed to be made conscious. Experiences other than those that meet children's conditions of worth cause children anxiety because such experience threaten their feeling of value and lovability (1951, 500). Instead of developing healthy, maturing, congruent selves, children with conditions of worth manifest incongruent selves that are at variance with their organismic experience. A rift occurs between the actualizing tendency and the self-actualizing tendency. Self-actualization is no longer genuine, but rather false as it is disconnected from the child's real feelings and desires. Children's distorted self-concepts inspire a self-actualizing tendency that is disingenuous and prevents optimal functioning (Ford 1991). Rogers noted that this rift can imply either good or derogatory evaluations. That is, individuals may deny that they have a good or bad trait in order to preserve a distorted self-image (1951, 506).

Incongruence creates inner tension (1959, 203). The self becomes defensive, rigid, and confused with regard to its own motives, feelings, and behaviors (1951, 505). In Rogers's words, "Behavior is regarded as enhancing this self when no such value is apprehended through sensory or visceral reactions; behavior is regarded as opposed to the maintenance or enhancement of the self when there is no negative sensory or visceral reaction" (1951, 501). Moreover, the self-concept as regards to one's relations to other people and one's environment must not be threatened by the conscious awareness of incongruity. Through the denial and distortion of experience, then, the developing child displays little or no "real understanding of the other as a separate person, since he [or she] is perceived mostly in terms of threat or nonthreat to the self" (1951, 521). Again, Rogers:

> The defensive person tends to see experience in absolute and unconditional terms, to overgeneralize, to be dominated by concept or belief, to fail to anchor his reactions in space and time, to confuse fact and evaluation, to rely upon abstractions rather than upon reality-testing. This term covers the frequently used concept of rigidity. (1959, 205)

Karen Horney: Development of the Real Self (or Self-Realization) vs. the Idealized Self

Horney's reputation as a humanistic analyst stems in no small measure from her holistic orientation, which is exemplified in her emphasis on self-development. Thus, Bühler (1968c, 19) noted, "It is to Karen Horney's great credit that she emphasized the 'self' as a 'whole' person against Freud's subdivided personality." Horney rejected the reductionistic, mechanistic view of the mind that Freud espoused (Paris, 1996b, 219). As a holistic concept, Horney's self does not refer to a psychic apparatus, nor is the self a homunculus (Paris, 1999, 164). In Westkott's (1998, 288) words:

> The concept of the real self refers to the seamlessly whole psyche where judgment, desire, and reasoning are not splintered off from each other into different functions (as in the superego, id, and ego) but are integrated into a whole discerning, feeling, and thinking person.

According to Horney, the self is "that central inner force common to all human beings and yet unique in each, which is the deep source of growth" (1950, 17). Being one's "real self" means realizing one's particular talents and living in accord with one's uniqueness within a context of interpersonal relatedness (18). For Horney, this real self is to be distinguished from the more traditional understanding of selfhood within psychoanalysis. For instance, her self is forward moving and growth oriented, whereas traditional psychoanalysis focuses on the child's past. Thus, in comparing her work to Freud's, Horney noted:

> In his concept of the "ego" he depicts the "self" of a neurotic person who is alienated from his spontaneous energies, from his authentic wishes, who does not make any decisions of his own and assume responsibility for them, who merely sees to it that he does not collide too badly with his environment. If this neurotic self is mistaken for its healthy alive counterpart, the whole complex problem of the real self as seen by Kierkegaard or William James cannot arise. (376–377)

Nascent within this passage are some clues as to the nature of the self that are central to Horney's clinical observations and theoretical formulations. The real self has the potential to be spontaneous, to be in touch with one's own wishes and desires, to be responsible, to exist in some way other than in the mode of conflict resolution and adaptation, and to feel alive.

According to Horney, children's relationships with their primary caretakers powerfully influence whether the real self emerges during human development. Children's families are the most important aspect of their developmental milieu (Paris 1999, 159). This does not mean that early childhood development is the exclusive determining force in human development. As Paris (1999, 158) noted, Horney considered development to be rooted in a set of intrinsic potentialities. Horney, like Rogers, appeared to have much confidence in the genetic endowment of every individual. She did not consider the evolution of selfhood to be a learned process (1950, 17). In her view, human beings are born with an innate drive toward self-realization, a concept which further illuminates Horney's understanding of selfhood. Moreover, though development prior to the adolescent transition into adulthood is potent and highly influential, it does not preclude, for example, the development of free choice except under highly adverse circumstances (Horney 1945, 45; Maiello 1996, 187).

Horney held that adequate parenting allows self-realization to occur unimpeded. A health-conducive parental relationship is one that provides children with proper parental love (1945, 18). Her belief concerning child development is that the real self naturally emerges as an inherent part of human nature if children are allowed to grow and mature in an uncorrupted manner. In particular, Horney held that children must be "permitted to grow according to [their] individual needs and possibilities" (18). Parents need to empathize with and understand their children as the particular individuals they are (18). Empathy must be communicated to children via "genuine warmth and interest" (87). The result of this loving warmth is that children develop a deep and validating sense of belonging, or what Horney called "we-ness" (18–19). This sense of belonging, in turn, brings out what Horney called a "basic confidence" in children (86). Children are emboldened by their nurturant social milieu, given a fundamental sense of adequacy and self-worth (87). These feelings of self-assuredness stimulate the development of various positive, growth-facilitating qualities that Horney identifies as hallmarks of self-realization (17).

According to Horney, there are five characteristics of healthy self-development that are especially significant indicators of the self-realization process (1945, 38). Children developing a strong sense of self are spontaneous rather than calculative or detached. The real self is first and foremost a felt self (Paris 1999, 157). They are able to act upon and enjoy their wishes and desires in an inspired fashion. Actualizing their imagination in creative effort comes naturally to them and is experienced as invigorating. Self-realizing children recognize their limitations. Though they are inclined to engage in creative pursuits and strive to adapt to their surroundings, these activities are done in a realistic fashion. Such children have a functional sense of their finite skills and abilities. Self-realizing children are in touch with their growth and their increasing physical, mental, and social skills. They can feel themselves maturing and developing as individuals, which Horney referred to as a feeling of evolution. The evolution of a strong, stable, consistent sense of values and goals throughout development contributes to an ever-strengthening sense of identity in children. They will come to know who they are as individuals and be able to be themselves. Thus, Horney noted that self-actualizing children display the quality of really "being." Finally, self-actualizing children see themselves, others, and their relationships with others in an accurate manner. They are able to assess their worldly relations on an emotional and intellectual level in a nonprejudiced way. These children are open to experience without defensiveness and thus live, Horney noted, in truth (1945, 38). All of these qualities empower children to develop fulfilling interpersonal relationships to the utmost of their ability (1950, 308). Table 2.2 lists the qualities of the real self (i.e., the self-realizing person) according to Horney.

Table 2.2
Characteristics of the Self-Realizing Person or Real Self According to Karen Horney

- Being in touch with one's own wishes and desires;
- Responsibility for one's thoughts, feelings, and actions;
- A sense of vitality or "feeling alive;"
- Accepting and embracing one's uniqueness;
- A sense of belonging or "we-ness;"
- "Basic confidence" in one's adequacy and value as a person;
- Clarity and understanding with regard to one's feelings, thoughts, wishes, and interests;
- The ability to tap resources and exercise will power;
- The ability to actualize one's special capacities or gifts;
- The ability to relate to others;
- The ability to find one's set of values and aims in life;
- Spontaneity of feeling and expression with others;
- The ability to recognize one's limitations;
- The ability to live in truth with oneself and others;
- The ability to be oneself when alone and when with others;
- Experiencing a feeling of evolution in one's personal development.

Note. Adapted from Horney (1950).

Just as proper parental love facilitates the self-realization process, inadequate parenting increases the potential for poor self-development. According to Horney, primary caretakers may truncate their children's self-development if they are unable or unwilling to somehow communicate loving affection and thereby emotionally bond with their offspring. The styles of behavior that constitute inadequate parenting are manifold for Horney. She believed that there were countless ways for parents to create an unsupportive, unhealthy childrearing environment. References to the varieties of behavior that would threaten a child's self-development are strewn throughout Horney's works (i.e., 1937, 1939, 1945, 1950). These examples are cataloged on Table 2.3.

Table 2.3
Examples of Parental Behavior Adverse to Self-Development Given by Karen Horney

- Unpredictable changes between overindulgence and scornful rejection;
- Making unfulfilled promises;
- Impairing a child's self-sufficiency, self-reliance, or initiative (e.g., ridiculing independent thinking or behavior, disturbing or impeding the child's friendships);
- Parenting that elicits the feeling from the child that he has no rights of his own;
- Parents who transfer their own ambitions to the child, thereby developing in the child the feeling that he is loved for imaginary qualities;
- Indifference or a lack of reliable warmth or guidance;
- Erratic, unstable, anxiety provoking behavior;
- Lack of respect for the child's individual needs;
- Direct blows to the child's self-esteem (e.g., derogatory, disparaging attitudes);
- Too much admiration or the absence of it;
- Forcing the child to take sides in parental disagreements;
- Too much or too little responsibility;
- Over-protection;
- Creating an intimidating atmosphere (e.g., irritability, over exacting behavior);
- Partiality to other siblings (e.g., emotional neglect, unjust reproaches).

Adapted from Horney (1937, 1939, 1945, 1950).

For Horney, however, a particular parental behavior in and of itself may not necessarily constitute inadequate parenting (1950, 18). Rather, the more essential issue is the spirit in which parents care for their children and, correlatively, the way children perceive their parents' attitudes toward them. In other words, the total affective atmosphere or emotional tone of the parent-child relationship ultimately determines the adequacy of parenting. Horney associated the kinds of behavior in Table 2.3 with inadequate parenting because the more parents rely on them, the more they would tend to block children from attaining the fundamental warmth and security that they seek in their parental relations. The danger, Horney felt, was that children would perceive a "lurking hypocrisy in the environment," meaning that children see their parents' love as nothing more than pretense (1945, 41). In Horney's words:

> The basic evil is invariably a lack of genuine warmth and affection. A child can stand a great deal of what is regarded as traumatic—such as sudden weaning, occasional beating, sex experiences—as long as inwardly he feels wanted and loved. Needless to say, a child feels keenly whether love is genuine, and cannot be fooled by any faked demonstrations. (1937, 80)

When children do not feel adequately loved, the immediate result is that they feel "helpless and defenseless and … conceive the world as potentially menacing" (1939, 9–10). They feel alone in a hostile environment (1950, 18–19). This experience of isolation and vulnerability creates a desperate situation for children, a basic lack of self-confidence (1950, 86). Horney called this fundamental lack of confidence "basic anxiety" and noted that in order to manage it, children find themselves forced to discontinue the development of their real selves (18–19). The lack of genuine warmth and interest gives children "the feeling of being unloved and unworthy—or at any rate of not being worth anything unless [they are] something [they are] not" (1950, 87). In other words, if being themselves arouses basic anxiety, then the only viable alternative to quell their fears of abandonment is to avoid the real self (376–377). As Horney (1939) put it:

> All these influences, varied as they are, make the child feel that in order to be liked or accepted he must be as others expect him to be. The parents have so thoroughly superimposed themselves on the mind of the child that he complies through fear, thus gradually losing what James calls the "real me." His own will, his own wishes, his own feels, his own likes and dislikes, his own grievances, become paralyzed. Therefore he gradually loses the capacity to measure his own values. He becomes dependent on the opinion of others. (91–92)

Thus, a parental relationship that arouses basic anxiety derails children's self-realization process. Instead, a process of self-alienation ensues. As Westkott (1998, 291) observed:

> The child is forced, then, to repress her true feelings. Out of fear of ... further loss of "love," the child represses legitimate anger: The feared and resented parent becomes admired and the child turns her hostility back on herself ... the child loses touch with and, indeed, comes to fear and hate her real self.

Once the real self has been abandoned in this way, Horney observed that various coping strategies are adopted in an attempt to overcome the fundamental sense of insecurity (1945, 42). In Horney's view, any particular attempt to manage basic anxiety can be classified as either a "moving toward," "moving against," or "moving away" strategy (1950, 18–19). Children will develop a passive and dependent interpersonal style (i.e., moving toward), an aggressive and dominant interpersonal style (i.e., moving against), or a withdrawn and isolative interpersonal style (i.e., moving away). Each mode of comportment promises to help children manage their deep-seated fears of abandonment and rejection. To be sure, these strategies are not adopted consciously and with full intension (18–19). They are a desperate reaction to an unbearably painful and difficult relationship to their primary caretakers. The coping strategies are thus defensively and tenaciously guarded:

> He is no longer, so to speak, the driver, but is driven.... The individual alienated from himself needs ... something that will give him a hold, a feeling of identity. This could make him meaningful to himself and, despite all the weakness in his structure, give him a feeling of power and significance. (1950, 21)

Since the three basic coping strategies are mutually exclusive in style, Horney also noted that one style must be chosen as the predominant trend as a substitute for genuine personality integration (1950, 19). Thus, children begin to display a reliance on one of the three styles more than the others. Moreover, these children find that they can strengthen their defenses against their feelings of helplessness and insecurity by creating an idealized image of themselves in their moving toward, against, or away from others. Consequently, they will "lift themselves above others" by forming an aggrandized mental representation of their particular mode of flight from their "painful feeling of nothingness" (1950, 20–22, 92). In her words:

> Self-idealization entails a general self-glorification and thereby gives the individual a much-needed feeling of significance and superiority over

others ... a feeling of ... unity. He idealizes, to begin with, his particular "solution" of his basic conflict: compliance becomes goodness; love, saintliness; aggressiveness becomes strength, leadership, heroism, omnipotence; aloofness becomes wisdom, self-sufficiency, independence. (1950, 22)

Upholding a glorified image of oneself is, for Horney, a way for children to prevent themselves from being crippled by the feeling of being "thoroughly bad" (1950, 77). Rigorously identifying themselves with a glorified, idealized self-image, promises to compensate for the inadequacy of the real self (13, 368). Horney referred to the drive to actualize the perfectionistic goals of the idealized self-image as a "search for glory," which exists in contradistinction to the genuine strivings of self-realization (1950, 37–38). Rather than developing the characteristics of the real self (see Table 2.2), Horney noted that individuals searching for glory are compulsively preoccupied with appearing perfectly aligned with their particular "solution" to basic anxiety (38). The fantasy of perfection creates egocentrism and a sense of entitlement (48–50). That this perfection is merely self-deception is evidenced by the prevalence of self-hate and hypersensitivity among these same individuals (1950, 81). Their defensiveness is indicative of the fundamental conflicts of their psychological lives: (a) the contradictory attitudes toward others and (b) the rift between the idealized self and the hated real self, which is tied to basic anxiety and feelings of worthlessness (1950, 368).

Rogers and Horney in Mutual Encounter: Synthesizing a Humanistic Theory of Child Development

What follows is an outline of a developmental perspective synthesized from the works of Carl Rogers and Karen Horney. Rogers and Horney are not named in connection to specific ideas throughout the narrative. Nonetheless, the theory is an amalgam of their developmental views. As a humanistic-developmental perspective, this theory emphasizes the development of the whole child rather than subdivisions of the personality (e.g., the id, the intellect, and so on). The current approach focuses on the development of the self embedded within the social world. The self is not a homunculus. That is, the self is neither a psychic apparatus nor any faculty existing on the inside of the child's body. Rather, selfhood is an expression of the inherent desire to grow and thrive within every human child, which is primarily lived, felt, deeply personal, and interpersonal rather than intellectual. A child's "self" refers to the manner in which he or she integrates and organizes his or her experiences into a fluid, dynamic pattern of perceptions, feelings, and personal meanings within a context of interpersonal relatedness. In each case, the child's integrative efforts are unique. According to this view, the sovereign motivational force in development is the striving toward a strong sense of self-with-others called self-actualization.

The nature and nurture of self-development.

Children are born with an innate drive toward mature selfhood that, when nurtured, brings about psychological health. Self-development is not something that must be taught to children by way of formal instruction. Moreover, the development of the self is not something that is the result of training. Self-development naturally occurs in the care of parents who do not stand in the way of its development. In other words, although the development of the self is innate, parents nonetheless facilitate or impede self-development. In this sense, self-development is a matter of both nature and nurture.

Healthy parental influence.

The optimal environment for self-development is one in which parents display heartfelt warmth to their child. The parents take a genuine interest in their child's growth and communicate through affectionate words and actions that their love is without conditions. In this kind of familial environment, the child develops an unwavering sense that his or her parents value and care for him or her, even when the parents disapprove of certain behaviors. Moreover, optimal parenting for self-development is empathetic parenting. Specifically, understanding parents permit their child to grow according to his or her individual emotional and psychosocial needs, allowing him or her the freedom to pursue the courses of action that promise to bring happiness and fulfillment in life.

The nature of healthy self-development: the self-actualizing child.

The results of this kind of parenting are that the child develops a foundational sense of safety. That is, the child feels secure rather than fearful or anxious in a potentially hostile world. The child also comes to develop a sense of self-acceptance and self-esteem. He or she feels valued as a person in his or her interpersonal milieu. Together, the child's sense of safety and self-worth constitute a fundamental sense of self-confidence that provides him or her with the emotional stability and resilience needed to avoid perceiving the world as threatening or otherwise rejecting. Thus, this emotional stability is the basis upon which he or she is open to the world. Openness in this context refers not only to the ability to perceive without distorting or falsifying experiences, but also to the ability to openly relate to others. In short, the safety and self-esteem that the child develops provides the basis for integrating and organizing his or her experiences in the direction of future growth within the social world (i.e., self-actualization). Tables 2.1 and 2.2 outline the various characteristics of the self-actualizing tendency. Looking at these tables one will notice the stress on realistic perception, responsibility for one's feelings, self-acceptance, and feelings of vitality, spontaneity of expression, self-confidence, and relating to others.

A healthy self-actualizing child is oriented toward the future in the direction of a genuine self-ideal. The self-ideal represents who the child would like to become at any given time during development. The values, moral principles, and personal goals that the child comes to adopt over the course of development are essential components of the integrative movement toward the child's self-ideal. Furthermore, the genuine, healthy self-ideal is not individualist in nature. A healthy child develops his or her unique skills and talents in and through fulfilling social interactions. As a healthy self develops and becomes increasingly independent, the child never relinquishes his or her desire for empathic, intimate relations with valued others. Actualizing people accept and prize others in their difference. The healthy self is first and foremost an interpersonal relatedness-in-the-world and fundamentally pro-social in the widest sense. Through proper parental love and nurturance, the self develops a deep and validating sense of belonging that he or she will seek to develop and explore throughout the lifespan.

Unhealthy parental influence.

In stark contrast to the optimal parenting noted above, parents who impede self-development do not unconditionally accept and love their child. In one way or another, the child comes to feel that his or her parents' love is conditional, tenuous at best, or altogether disingenuous. Many different forms of parental behavior can give a child the impression that his or her parents' love is lacking or absent. Table 2.3 provides examples of these forms of behavior. However, the essence of the child-parent relationship that is inadequate for self-development is a relationship that is lacking in love, attention, affection, genuine interest, and empathy. In other words, the child becomes the victim of emotional deprivation via conditional or disingenuous love.

The course of unhealthy self-development: self-alienation.

The primary result of conditional or disingenuous parental love is that there is no foundation for the development of the basic self-confidence, emotional stability, and openness to experience noted above. The child cannot develop an unconditional acceptance and love himself or herself. Thus, the child's ability to integrate and organize his or her perceptions, emotions, and personal meanings in sustained relations with valued others is compromised.

Children who feel that their primary caretakers do not sincerely love them without conditions do not feel free to comport themselves in accordance with their genuine perceptions, feelings, and desires. To act spontaneously and unreservedly would mean being the person that one's parents have deemed undeserving of love, care, and empathy. These children feel threatened and anxious at the possibility of being themselves. Consequently, these children behave in ways that are at variance with their real motives and defend this behavior rigidly for their own emotional survival. They defend against actualizing their real needs and desires as well as the consciousness of their growing alienation from their true feelings and experiences. In short, children's self-understandings and perceptions in general are distorted and denied. Thus, through their anxiety and defensiveness, they become increasingly conflicted, disintegrated, and self-alienated. At the same time, they become increasingly alienated from others due to their preoccupation with egocentric projects designed to manage anxiety and conflict.

As was noted above, emotional deprivation can take the form of conditional love or absent love. Moreover, the severity of conditional love exists on a sliding scale, so to speak, depending on both the parents' behavior and the child's perception of that behavior. In instances of mild emotional deprivation, the child perceives the conditions to be relatively clear and in some instances attainable. Thus, the child experiences instances of gratifying parental love, though the presence of conditional love constitutes an emotionally unfulfilling parental relationship overall. At the severe end of the conditional love spectrum, the child perceives the conditions to be vague, elusive, and typically unattainable. Thus, the child rarely experiences gratifying parental love. However, the most severe and damaging instance of inadequate parenting is complete emotional deprivation, where the child perceives his or her parental love to be utterly disingenuous and thus altogether absent.

A victim of mild to moderate emotional deprivation is more likely than a child who has not been emotionally deprived to pursue acceptance and affection in ways that sacrifice his or her genuine self-actualization. He or she experiences an unfulfilled need for the unconditional positive regard that promotes positive self-regard, self-acceptance, and self-esteem. The child will maintain a distorted self-concept in hopes of attaining acceptance from his or her parents. The child will rigidly comport himself or herself in a manner that promises to win his or her parents' loving care and affection. In other words, a child given conditional love will value behaviors that confirm their distorted self-concepts and either negatively value or not value behavior that is at variance with this self-concept. The motivation for this is to feel acceptable as per the conditions of worth imposed upon him or her from the parents. Hence, the behavior and experience of the developing child in these circumstances are increasingly regulated by what they believe will please their parents. In effect, the parents have "superimposed themselves" on the mind of the child, so the child complies, but eventually loses touch with his or her own authentic self-actualization in the process.

In instances where the child's emotional deprivation is moderate to extreme, meaning that unconditional love and acceptance was rarely if ever experienced, his or her self-development is put at a greater risk. The child responds to this situation with feelings of threat, vulnerability, insecurity, and anxiety. Primordial fears of rejection and abandonment give rise to even more extreme attempts at managing the emotional deprivation. This becomes evident in the child's behavioral dynamics, especially his or her behavior toward others. The child's behavior begins to include increasingly stereotyped behavior and mental processes. As Yalom (1985, 254) states, "The grosser the pathology, the greater the predictive accuracy." In particular, the child tries to manage basic anxiety and helplessness through moving toward (i.e., dependency), moving away (i.e., withdrawal), or moving against others (i.e., aggression and domination). Here, genuine self-actualization is further truncated due to the child identifying himself or herself with an "idealized" self rather than a genuine self-ideal. Through this identification, the child seeks a glorified substitute for genuine love and affection. Even a child "moving toward" others does not seek genuine love and an authentically fulfilling relationship. Rather, he or she is self-effacing and morbidly dependent in his or her attempts to actualize the ideal of a perfectly merged self-with-other.

Concluding Remarks

Comments on the synthesis of Rogers's and Horney's ideas.

Two primary differences between Rogers's and Horney's understandings of self-development had to be worked through in order to arrive at the theoretical framework presented above. First, Rogers and Horney differed in their manner of conceptualizing the self. Rogers provided a clearer conceptual definition of the self than Horney. Horney defined the self as "that central inner force common to all human beings and yet unique in each, which is the deep source of growth" (1950, 17). While this definition did not run contrary to Rogerian thinking on the subject, Horney has nonetheless been criticized for her lack of clarity regarding her conceptualization of the self (e.g., Elkind, H. 1958–1959; Munroe, 1955). Paris

(1999) has recently noted that Horney's concept of self will appears vague, mystical, and elusive to individuals who have not experienced the later phases of analysis (157). Rogers, on the other hand, was detailed in his characterization of the self or self-concept as opposed to the whole organism. Rogers's conceptualization of selfhood brought clarity and specificity to an understanding of the self, which is wanting in Horney's works.

An example of how Rogers's notion of the self (as distinguished from the whole person or whole organism) provided a sounder theoretical foundation for the above theory can be found in their respective notions of pathological development. Horney's theory had a more dualistic quality about it than Rogers's approach. Horney spoke of the idealized self of pathological development as hateful of the real self (e.g., 1950, 368). This assumes that there is a repressed real self, which has nonetheless retained some measure of personality integration and exists "beneath" the idealized self that dominates the personality (1939, 229; 1950, 189). While other thinkers in the psychoanalytic tradition have proposed similar positions, such as Winnicott's (e.g., 1965, 150–151) notion that a False Self protects the True Self when an individual exists in a threatening environment, this type of theory is phenomenologically problematic. According to Horney, the real self is essentially abandoned in pathological development in favor of identification with the idealized self. Rather than a self-realization process guiding development, a search for glory ensues and dominates the developing person's character. At the same time, Horney maintained that the person's genuine thoughts, feelings, and judgments remain integrated enough such that they constitute another self (a "real" self) that is involved in the person's inner conflict. Simply put, Horney did not explain how the real self is able to maintain enough awareness and integration to truly be considered a self even though it is "mostly blocked out" (1950, 189). For this reason, Rogers's distinction between the self and organismic experience appeared to be a preferable, more theoretically sound corrective to Horney's theory of an essentially repressed, unconscious self.

Rogers and Horney also differed in their accounts of how children who develop in an unhealthy manner respond to their inadequate parental relationships. Rogers held that children respond to conditional positive regard by rigidly comporting themselves in a manner that they believe will win their parents' loving care and affection. The motivation for this, to reiterate Rogers, is "I want to be acceptable to my parents and hence must experience myself as being the sort of person they think I am" (1951, 526). Horney agreed that when parents "superimpose themselves" on the minds of children that they comply and eventually lose their real selves (1939, 91–92). However, she found that children then respond to the situation of anxiety and loss of self by striving for a search for glory through moving toward, moving away, or moving against others. What dictates development in unhealthy circumstances for Horney are the rules (the "shoulds," as she calls them) associated with these styles once one style becomes preferred, glorified, and molded into an idealized image (1950, 64–65).

Considering this difference between Rogers's and Horney's theories, it appears reasonable to assert that Horney wrote about individuals suffering from more severe instances of emotional depravation than Rogers. Horney, in other words, focused on the development of individuals who suffered from a more fundamental and potentially destructive unfulfilled need than Rogers: the need for safety, security, or in Eriksonian terms, "basic trust" (Erikson 1963, 247). In Horney's words, "A neurotic development … arises ultimately from feelings of alienation, hostility, fear, and diminished self-confidence … they are the soil out of which a neurosis may grow, since it is their combination which creates a basic feeling of helplessness" (1939, 172–173). Thus, Horney regularly spoke of neurotic development, whereas Rogers did not use terms such as *neurosis* and was disdainful of diagnostic categories in general. A similar conclusion was reached by Kahn (1985) in comparing Rogers with another psychoanalytic thinker, Heinz Kohut (1977). For these reasons, the course of pathological development was viewed as relative to the nature and severity of the emotional deprivation experienced by the individual child.

Critical remarks on the theory presented here.

I hope to have demonstrated through the preceding discussion that there is a viable humanistic framework for viewing child development within the works of Carl Rogers and Karen Horney. As a theory of self-development, this perspective is supported by the work of other self-styled developmentalists such as Bühler (1968c), Knowles (1986), Kohut (1977), and Stern (1985). All of these thinkers created theories of development that stress the overriding importance of the self as the integrative, consolidating tendency in development that is the source of growth and health within the child. Knowles and Kohut drew primarily from observations of adults to build their theories, while Bühler and Stern grounded their theories in direct observations of children. Moreover, there is phenomenological research in the area of psychological maltreatment that supports the notion that children who have been victims of moderate to severe emotional deprivation become preoccupied with pleasing their parental figures while also displaying dependency, isolation, and aggression (DeRobertis, 2004).

Perhaps the greatest weakness of the theory presented here is that it was inspired by clinical aims. That is, both Rogers and Horney developed their notions of child development for the purpose of grounding their theories of psychotherapy in a developmental model. However, neither of these thinkers were direct observers of children. Instead they drew primarily from their clinical experiences. Thus, the approach outlined here could stand to benefit from self-styled developmental research that focuses solely on the child's phenomenal field of experience in its own right, without using clinical concerns as a frame of reference. This does not mean that their ideas have no merit. A humanistic-developmental theory can benefit from multiple data sources. Descriptions of children managing developmental issues, problems, and tasks would add to the rigor and credibility of the humanistic-developmental perspective presented here. For humanistically oriented insights obtained from actual descriptions of children, the works of Bühler and Marschack (1968), Stern (1985), and Winnicott (1965) may all be of use. Additionally, there are sources of such data from phenomenological authors who have observed children (e.g., Benswanger 1979; Briod 1986; Lippitz 1983).

Strengths of the current approach.

The developmental theory presented above provides a humanistic alternative to the developmental theories of Freud (e.g., 1962), Erikson (e.g., 1963), and Piaget (e.g., 1961). However, the perspective presented here is not a stage theory. No specific phase related issues were identified or articulated. This is to be expected as both Rogers and Horney explicated social and emotional themes of childhood in a very phenomenological manner. Phenomenological research in the area of child development is not typically presented in a stage-of-life manner. While Knowles (1986) and Bühler and Marschack (1968) have shown that phenomenology is not incompatible with a stage approach, Briod (1989) argued that a phenomenological approach to development is more conducive to a theory without demarcated phases of growth.

The current theory of child development is humanistic on several grounds. First, the theory is nonmechanistic and nonreductive. The child is not held to be the mere result or by-product of material forces determining his or her development in advance of his or her active participation in the developmental process. Moreover, freedom of the will is never excluded as a possibility inherent within the developing child. Second, the current theory is holistic, both in its emphasis on the whole child (i.e., the child as a unique self) and the fact that the individual child is always a relatedness-to-others. Third, the theory presented above characterizes the child's development as a deeply meaningful, lived process. The child is not dehumanized by comparing him or her to an animal or some other organism seeking to gratify egocentric motives or drives. Further, the child's development is not viewed in the abstract or conceptualized in an impersonal, intellectualized manner. Finally, the humanistic-developmental framework presented above places importance on understanding healthy human development.

A major strength of the current approach is that it is specific about what it means to be growing and developing in a healthy manner. Rather than dwelling on the varieties of adaptive human adjustment to the environment, behavioral theorists have tended to focus on psychopathology (Hall & Lindzey 1978, 596). Freud (e.g., 1965) denied the existence of human health as such, and, with the notable exception of Erik Erikson (1963), psychoanalysis has continued to focus on sickness rather than health. While Piaget (e.g., 1961) schematized the course of intellectual growth and noted the landmark cognitive skills characteristic of mental development, the psychological health of the whole person has not been the focus of cognitive theory. One of the great contributions of humanism to psychology is its emphasis on the positive side of human existence (e.g., Maslow 1954, 340–341). Rogers and Horney have brought this valuable contribution to developmental psychology as well.

Along with Erikson's (1963) ego-psychological theory, the humanistic approach outlined here contributes to our understanding of human development by addressing what it means to develop in a healthy manner. Specifically, it articulates the nature of the growing, thriving self and the process of self-actualization. To be sure, many of the characteristics noted in Tables 2.1 and 2.2 are traits typically identified with mature individuals (e.g., taking responsibility for one's feelings). Nonetheless, a comparison of the traits of healthy development covered here and the characteristics of healthy development according to Erikson's stage theory reveal both perspectives to be complementary. For example, Erikson's basic trust (247) can also be spoken of in terms of Horney's basic confidence (e.g., 1950, 86; Paris 1996a, 139). Erikson's autonomy (1963, 251) is mirrored by Rogers's (1959, 196) stress on autonomy in the actualizing tendency. Erikson's initiative and industry (1963, 255, 258) are complemented by Rogers's assertion that healthy development is marked by spontaneity of expression and unpredictable creativity (1961, 354; 1980, 44). Finally, both Rogers and Horney continually stress what Erikson referred to as identity (1963, 261) throughout their works.

Another strength of the current perspective is that it is specific about the parental behaviors that foster resilience and growth or strain children's efforts to mature. What is regrettable is that Horney did not spend as much time spelling out the manifestations of good, positive parental relations. It is left to current humanistic theorists to explicate the variety of ways that adequate, loving parents nurture self-development.

Perhaps most importantly, however, the theory presented here offers a realistic starting point for students to begin thinking about child development in a humanistic manner. Humanistic theories also occasionally appear in life-span developmental texts (e.g., Lefrancois, 1999). However, humanistic theory is not regularly included in child psychology texts. Moreover, the humanism that tends to appear in developmentally relevant texts rarely addresses the issue of child development in any systematic manner.

KEY TERMS AND CONCEPTS

Actualizing tendency
Basic anxiety
Basic confidence
Conditions of worth
Congruence
Denial and distortion of experience
Empathy
Holistic orientation
Homunculus
Ideal self
Idealized image
Incongruence
Introjection
Moving against
Moving away
Moving toward
Organismic experience
Phenomenal field of experience
Proper parental love
Real self
Retrospective data collection
Search for glory
Self
Self-actualizing tendency
Self-realization
Self-worth
Unconditional positive regard
Whole person

CHAPTER 3

AN OBJECT-RELATIONS THEORY OF SELF-DEVELOPMENT: WINNICOTT & KOHUT

In this chapter, two psychoanalytic theorists' ideas concerning development are analyzed in order to arrive at an object-relations theory of self-development: D. W. Winnicott (1896–1971) and Heinz Kohut (1913–1981). Winnicott is considered an object-relations theorist, while Kohut is referred to as a self-psychologist. The term object-relations was chosen to represent this chapter due to the inherently interpersonal nature of Kohut's work. For example, in their detailed analysis of Kohut's works, Bacal and Newman (1990, 225) noted that Kohut's thought rests upon object-relations foundations.

Winnicott's and Kohut's developmental ideas were outlined and synthesized using an existential-humanistic frame of reference to derive a self-styled, humanistic theory of child development. Winnicott and Kohut were chosen together for several reasons. First, both thinkers are more humanistic in orientation than is typical within psychoanalytic thought. As Mitchell and Black (1995, 168) put it:

> A fundamental feature that distinguishes postclassical psychoanalysis is the shift in emphasis and basic values from rationalism and objectivism to subjectivism and personal meaning (see Mitchell 1993). Winnicott and Kohut were among the most important figures in this movement.

Second, Winnicott and Kohut both sought to describe the nature of self-development via a shared source of data collection for their theorizing: clinical data. While Winnicott also drew from his actual observations of children as a pediatrician, both he and Kohut used a retrospective, case-based style of data collection, meaning that they each disclosed themes of self-development via the reconstruction of their patients' childhoods. In Winnicott's words, "My experiences have led me to recognize that dependent or deeply regressed patients can teach the analyst more about early infancy than can be learned from direct observation of infants, and more than can be learned from contact with mothers who are involved with infants" (1960, 141).

Third and finally, a body of literature has established that Winnicott's and Kohut's theories have an intrinsic harmony between them. For example, Kohut (1977) himself has noted that his work "overlaps" with Winnicott's investigations (xix–xx). Modell (1985) regarded Kohut's contribution to psychoanalysis to be an extension of Winnicott's work (98). Bacal (1990), Mills (1997), and Tobin (1990) also view the two thinkers as bearing striking and significant similarities in their views of development, personality, and psychotherapy. Thus, the complementary nature of their ideas added credence to the notion that a mutual encounter between Winnicott's and Kohut's theories appeared viable and promised to be productive.

Like Chapter Two, Winnicott's and Kohut's thoughts on child psychology will be articulated in their original form and introduced separately. This will facilitate a clear understanding of each theorist's respective position with regard to self-development. Next, highly significant themes of the theories will be explicated and synthesized into a unified theory of child development. Finally, the potential strengths and vulnerabilities of these developmental ideas will be discussed.

D. W. Winnicott

D. W. Winnicott viewed child development in the tradition of Jean-Jacques Rousseau (1712–1778). Winnicott, like Rousseau before him, did not believe that the course of child development was rigorously dictated by the environment. This kind of radical "environmentalism" or "blank tablet" view of childhood is consonant with John Locke's (1632–1704) philosophy and the behavioral movement it inspired in psychology. Rousseau believed that children were born with innate potentials to actively make sense of their surroundings and develop in a healthy manner. Similarly, Winnicott viewed child development as guided by an inherent drive to learn, grow, and adapt to the environment. Winnicott noted that parents do not have to "make their baby" the way an artist paints a mural, for instance (1963c, 96). Rather, the child's innate potential for maturity unfolds naturally in an environment that does not impede development:

> Emotional development takes place in the individual child if good-enough conditions are provided, and the drive to development comes from within the child. The forces toward living, toward integration of the personality, toward independence are immensely strong, and with good-enough conditions the child makes progress. (1962b, 65)

As is evident from the above quotation, Winnicott held that the difference between healthy and unhealthy development was a matter of how the individuals in a child's social milieu care for the child. Winnicott systematically maintained this position, despite his insistence that parents do not single-handedly "make" the child. In particular, Winnicott spoke of the contrast between the good-enough mother and the not-good-enough mother, as well as the opposing ways that these kinds of mothers affect self-development.

The good-enough mother.

According to Winnicott, what makes a mother "good-enough" is that she provides her child with ego-coverage or, more simply, ego-support (e.g., 1959, 126). Ego-support from the good-enough mother has a variety of features, all of which revolve around adequately meeting the needs of the highly dependent infant. The most pressing need of a child in early infancy is the need for what Winnicott called continuity of being or going-on-being (1962a, 60). In essence, continuity of being refers to a sense of temporal and physical integration. A mother that "gives herself over" to her infant is genuinely dedicated and devoted to providing for her child's emotional needs. This supports "existential going-on-being," as Winnicott called it. Under these circumstances, the child does not experience impinging, disruptive periods of anxiety. The absence of unsettling feelings of impingement facilitates the gelling of a body-ego (i.e., a beginning sense of psychophysical unity) and provides the groundwork for a burgeoning sense of lived-time:

> All the processes of a live infant constitute a *going-on-being*, a kind of blueprint for existentialism. The mother who is able to give herself over, for a limited spell, to this her natural tasks, is able to protect her infant's going-on-being. Any impingement, or failure of adaptation, causes a reaction in the infant, and the reaction breaks up the going-on-being. If reacting to impingements is the pattern of an infant's life, then there is a serious interference with the natural tendency that exists in the infant to become an integrated unit, able to continue to have a self with a past, present, and future. With a relative absence of impingements to the infant's body-function gives a good basis for the building up of a body-ego. In this way the keel is laid down for future mental health. (1963b, 86)

A child-rearing environment that is free of impingement is what Winnicott (1965) referred to as a "facilitating environment." In order to create a facilitating environment, the primary caretaker must engage in holding. *Holding* is a term that Winnicott used both literally and metaphorically. It refers to actually holding the child, to protect him or her from feelings of vulnerability and from bodily harm. It also refers to the specialized sensitivity of a devoted mother tending to the particular biological and psycho-emotional needs of the individual child throughout day-to-day routines (1960a, 49). In Winnicott's words, "The main thing is the physical holding, and this is the basis of all the more complex aspects of holding, and of environmental provision in general" (54).

Holding significantly fosters the burgeoning experiences of sensorimotor unity and continuity over time in infancy (1962a, 60). The initial state of integration that occurs within an adequate holding environment has much significance for Winnicott as this constitutes the infants very first, primitive sense of identity, or "I," as he called it: "Integration is closely linked with the environmental function of holding. The achievement of integration is the unit. First comes 'I,' which includes 'everything else is not me'" (61).

It is not enough, however, that the mother engages in holding behavior. According to Winnicott, there are further requirements of the good-enough mother if her child is to develop in a healthy manner. For instance, the holding must be reliable and steady throughout the child's daily routines (1963c, 97; 1963a, 182–183). In other words, imbuing the child with a feeling of continuity must be done consistently to successfully ward off growth-stifling impingement. Moreover, the infant needs to experience the mother as genuinely devoted and loving in her caregiving role:

> There is an idea for emphasis here, for the whole procedure of infant-care has as its main characteristic a steady presentation of the world to the infant. This is something that cannot be done by thought, nor can it be managed mechanically. It can only be done by continuous management by a human being who is consistently herself. There is no question of perfection here. Perfection belongs to machines; what the infant needs is just what he usually gets, the care and attention of someone who is going on being herself. This of course applies to fathers too. (1963b, 87–88)

For Winnicott, the technical knowledge of how to parent, or merely "acting" in the role of a truly dedicated, loving parent, will not adequately assist the child in establishing the continuity of going-on-being (1963b, 88). The good-enough mother adds her own personal touch to her parenting, tending to the specific details and individualized needs of her particular parent-child relationship. In other words, in addition to holding, the good-enough mother provides a special kind of handling that benefits the developing infant (1962a, 60). The proper handling of the child facilitates the development of a "psycho-somatic partnership" that serves to personalize and individualize his or her burgeoning personality integration (62).

Winnicott noted three closely interrelated aspects of good-enough infant handling. First, proper handling of an infant entails empathy on the part of the mother (1960a, 40). In the language of modern psychology, proper child care requires affect synchrony of the mother. The infant's primary caretaker must be able to put himself or herself in the child's place in order to be in touch or "in tune" with the child's emotional needs. According to Winnicott, adequate parenting demands something more than an intellectual understanding of the child's needs. The mother-child relationship must be an empathic form of relatedness (1962b, 69). If the mother can "tune in" to the child's psycho-emotional needs, then she is in a position to protect her child from overwhelming, growth-stunting feelings of anxiety:

> Unthinkable anxiety is kept away by this vitally important function of the mother at this stage, her capacity to put herself in the baby's place and to know what the baby needs in the general management of the body, and therefore of the person. (1962a, 57–58)

The second dimension of good-enough handling, already implicit in the above quotation, is identification. In one sense, *empathy* and *identification* are essentially synonyms (e.g., 1960, 148). Take, for example, the following quotation:

> By and large mothers do in one way or another identify themselves with the baby that is growing within them, and in this way they achieve a very powerful sense of what the baby needs. This is a projective identification. This ... lasts for a certain length of time after parturition, and then gradually loses significance. (1960a, 53)

However, Winnicott also uses the term *identification* to refer to a process that goes beyond the empathic contact of mother and child. Specifically, Winnicott uses *identification* to refer to how a good-enough mother "shifts some of her sense of self on to the baby" (53). In her empathic focus on her child's needs, the devoted mother treats the child as if he or she has a self that is substantive and worthy of notice. The result is a strengthening of the child's burgeoning ego and the achievement of a fundamental sense of "I am" (1958, 33). In Winnicott's words:

> Being alone in the presence of someone can take place at a very early stage, when the *ego immaturity is naturally balanced by ego-support* from the mother. In the course of time the individual introjects the

ego-supportive mother and in this way becomes able to be alone without frequent reference to the mother or mother symbol. (32)

The third dimension of good-enough handling is mirroring. Winnicott considered mirroring to be vital to the maintenance of going-on-being (1962a, 61). By mirroring, Winnicott means that the mother reflects the child's newly developing sense of being or "I am," back to him or her in a caring, affirming way. Through her loving manner of engagement with her child, the good-enough mother validates the child's jubilant feeling of coming into being.

In addition to the proper handling of an infant, a good-enough mother also engages in object-presentation (1962a, 60). Due to the highly dependent nature of infancy, the child must rely on the mother's ability to sense his or her needs and bring the world to the child to facilitate need satisfaction. If the mother is able to achieve this sensitivity and adequately cater to her child's needs, Winnicott noted that the result is a feeling of omnipotence on the part of the child (57). This feeling of omnipotence gives the vulnerable infant a feeling of empowerment that directly contradicts his or her actual helplessness and strengthens ego boundaries (1960, 149). In Winnicott's words, "The good-enough mother meets the omnipotence of the infant and to some extent makes sense of it ... by the ... implementation of the infant's omnipotent expressions" (145).

There are two final aspects of good-enough mothering. First, as the child grows older, a good-enough mother will continue to be sensitive to the child's changing needs. She will, moreover, develop a graduated adaptation to the growing child's needs as they arise (1962b, 70–71). Second, Winnicott repeatedly admonished that the child's spontaneous, creative gesture was vital to the eventual development of an autonomous, healthy self later in life (e.g., 1960, 146; 1963a, 189). Thus, he maintained that a good-enough mother will make provisions for accommodating the child's creative impulses throughout his or her development (1962b, 70–71).

According to Winnicott, if a mother displays "good-enough" characteristics, the results will be twofold. First, the child's need-gratifications will be smoothly integrated within the whole of his or her personality. Like Erik Erikson (1963), Winnicott believed that the id and ego develop simultaneously in a parallel, yet mutually enriching relationship to each other (e.g., 1960a, 49; 1962a, 57). Unlike Freud, Winnicott emphasized the role of the ego over the id: "I think it will be generally agreed that id-impulse is significant only if it is contained in ego living. An id-impulse either disrupts a weak ego or else strengthens a strong one" (1958, 33). For Winnicott, it would be incorrect to assert that need satisfaction (e.g., feeding) or object relationships (e.g., a relation to the breast) are somehow prior to the development of ego organization in infancy (1960a, 49). Rather, these elements of development take their very significance for the child only when they can be integrated into his or her ego structure:

> There is ... no sense in making use of the word 'id' for phenomena that are not covered and catalogued and experienced and eventually interpreted by ego-functioning.... Ego-functioning needs to be taken as a concept that is inseparable from that of the existence of the infant as a person. What instinctual life there may be apart from ego-functioning can be ignored, because the infant is not yet an entity having experiences. There is no id before ego. (1962a, 56)

The second major outcome of good-enough mothering is that a True Self will eventually develop out of the child's ego formation.

The True Self.

In Winnicott's view, ego development starts at the very outset of life. In his words, "The start is when the ego starts" (1962a, 56). While Winnicott acknowledged the need for psychosexual satisfaction (i.e., the role of the id) in development, he nonetheless insisted that infancy "is essentially a period of ego development, and integration is the main feature of such development" (1960a, 40). In other words, the term *ego* is used by Winnicott to refer to the increasing unity inherent to the growing child's personality as he or she matures (1962a, 56). Again, this process of unification is a process of "personalization," meaning that the child develops a unique, harmonious sense of mind-body unification. Unification and personalization are the two dimensions of personality integration that provide the raw material necessary to help the child remain focused in the direction of healthy object-relatedness (59–60).

Selfhood is a more sophisticated, complex dimension of ego development, in Winnicott's theoretical scheme:

> It will be seen that the ego offers itself for study long before the word self has relevance. The word self arrives after the child has begun to use the intellect to look at what others see or feel or hear and what they conceive of when they meet this infant body. (56)

For Winnicott, a self with an integrated sense of past, present, and future will naturally grow out of strong ego development once the infant has distinguished itself from the surrounding world (1962a, 57; 1963b, 86; 1963d, 75). As the infant becomes aware of the mother's separate existence as a person, the child will utilize the powers of imagination to engage in the process of identifying with the mother and engage in imitative behaviors (1958, 33; 1963c, 96; 1963b, 90). The general time frame for this occurrence is approximately six months to two years old (1963b, 88). However, Winnicott noted that identification can happen as early as three months of age (90).

Selfhood is a lived sense of "I am" or "I exist" that constitutes the core of the human personality (1962a, 57). Under good-enough conditions, the self evolves from a more primitive state of vital functioning to increasingly complex object-relations. Evidence of the True Self can be found at the outset of mental organization in what Winnicott called "the summation of sensorimotor aliveness" (1960, 149). As he put it, "The True Self comes from the aliveness of the body tissues and the working of body-functions, including the heart's action and breathing … it does no more than collect together the details of the experience of aliveness" (148). In a good-enough holding environment, the relaxed, open, secure infant develops a unified sense of vitality that inspires spontaneous behavior and a process of "creatively discovering" his or her "potency as a self" (146, 148; 1963a, 189). This process of creative discovery is a dynamic, interpersonal one, always carried out in relation to others. Thus, Winnicott noted that in a state of health, a child's "personal self is not only he" (1963c, 99).

At the same time, however, Winnicott maintained that the True Self is the "still and silent spot" of the child's ego (1963a, 189). This can be seen as Winnicott's attempt to counterbalance the fundamental relatedness of the developing child with an appreciation for the uniqueness and autonomy of every individual. For Winnicott the self is permanently isolated, uncommunicative, and ultimately unknown to others (187, 190). He maintains an anthropological view of the infant that posits a self that is always unaffected by experience, existing within a theoretical "core" of the person that lies behind the boundary of the epidermis (1963c, 99). Winnicott supports his view by noting that the still, silent center of the personality is best confronted in solitude (1963a, 190). However, from an existential-phenomenological point of view, Winnicott takes this line of thought too far. He used the terms *solitude* and *isolation* interchangeably, which indicates that he was not cognizant of the phenomenological distinction between the two. As Knowles (1986, 162–163) noted, solitude is a positive, replenishing type of experience. Isolation, on the other hand, is associated with loneliness and emotional distress (van den Berg, 1972, 103–124). Thus, Winnicott's notion of an isolated self represents an element of Cartesianism in his work that ought to be rejected. In van Kaam's (1966, 209) words:

A British group of psychoanalysts, notably Melanie Klein, Farbairn, Winnicott, and Guntrip recognized the impact of culture on behavior. At the same time, their sophisticated theory of psychic internalization of the environment fell back on the isolated subject-box-theory. The Cartesian split is revived in their theory to such a degree that man is conceived to live in two worlds at the same time, inner and outer, psychic and material.

The not-good-enough mother.

The childcare situation that results from not-good-enough mothering stands in contrast to the secure holding environment associated with adequate infant care. Whereas good-enough mothering shields the child from anxiety-ridden experiences of impingement, not-good-enough mothering fragments and disrupts the infant's continuity of being. Continual interruptions in going-on-being weaken the infant's ego formation (1960a, 52). The not-good-enough mother lacks the specialized devotion of the good-enough mother. As a result, she does not give herself over to the task of making the child feel increasingly substantive, organized, and unified. Rather, the not-good-enough mother forces the child to attend to her routines, wants, and needs (1960, 145). This sort of half-heartedly committed mother thwarts the healthy development of the child (1963c, 100). No solid foundation is set in place for the child's self-development. As Winnicott put it, "If maternal care is not good enough then the infant does not really come into existence, since there is no continuity of being; instead the personality becomes built on the basis of reactions to environmental impingement" (1960a, 54).

As Winnicott saw it, delinquency and psychopathy are derivations of perceived yet actual emotional deprivation (1959, 133). For instance, Winnicott interprets the behavior of an antisocial child as an attempt to break free from the feelings of helplessness associated with unsatisfying social relations (1963c, 103). Concepts like narcissism and the death instinct were superfluous to Winnicott. He reinterpreted these phenomena as signs that an unloved, ego-weakened child is trying to compensate for environmental failure and establish real, genuine contact with others (1959, 127; 1962a, 66).

According to Winnicott, environmental failure can have a wide variety of negative consequences depending on the severity and timing of the deprivation. Environmental failure can bring about childhood schizophrenia, affect disorders, antisocial tendencies, and pathological dependence (1962b, 66). Of all of the consequences of environmental failure that Winnicott spoke of, the False Self-Disorder is arguably his most significant and original contribution to psychoanalytic theory (1960, 145).

The False Self.

For Winnicott, the fundamental feature of False Self-development is compliance. As a habitual mode of behavior, compliance compromises the child's ability to spontaneously act upon his or her genuine needs, wishes, and desires:

> Compliance brings immediate rewards and adults only too easily mistake compliance for growth. The maturational process can be bypassed by a series of identifications, so that what shows clinically is a false, acting self, a copy of someone perhaps; and what could be called a true or essential self becomes hidden, and becomes deprived of living experience. (1963c, 102)

In Winnicott's view, there is an inverse relationship between False Self-development and spontaneity. The greater the degree of False Self-development, the less the child displays the characteristic spontaneity of psychological health (1960, 147). Generally speaking, the False Self-development stands in contradistinction to healthy development (151). However, there are compliant trends in normal development as well, and False Self-development does not always indicate pathology. In the healthy individual, False Self trends are evident in the social conventions that are the result of the child's moral training, such as politeness and manners (143). When the False Self is "given pathological importance," this means that False Self-development is so powerful and thoroughgoing that a "severe handicap in emotional development" results (1959, 133–134). The child rigidly defends his or her compliant, nonspontaneous lifestyle. Thus, for Winnicott, there are many subtle levels of False Self-development. At one end of the continuum is the False Self as it exists in the healthy individual. At the other extreme the True Self is completely covered over and all that the individual presents in social relations is the False Self:

> At one extreme: the False Self sets up as real and it is this that observers tend to think is the real person. In living relationships, work relationship, and friendships, however, the False Self begins to fail. In situations in which what is expected is a whole person the False Self has some essential lacking. At this extreme the True Self is hidden. (1960, 142–143)

Irritability and disruption of biological functioning are the signs of False Self-development in early infancy (1960, 146). As the child grows, the impact of the False Self on the child's personality is more pervasive, particularly in instances where the False Self tends to dominate the personality:

Where there is a high degree of split between the True Self and the False Self which hides the True Self, there is found a poor capacity for using symbols, and a poverty of cultural living. Instead of cultural pursuits one observes in such persons extreme restlessness, an inability to concentrate, and a need to collect impingements from external reality so that the living-time of the individual can be filled by reactions to these impingements. (150)

Heinz Kohut

Heinz Kohut's view of child development is fundamentally consonant with Winnicott's theoretical model in two respects. First, both thinkers believed that children are born with a set of innate qualities that orient them in the direction of growth and healthy development. For example, Kohut (1977, 119, 121) noted that children are genetically endowed with innate confidence as well as potentials for nondestructive aggression. Second, despite this innate tendency to actualize growth-oriented strivings, Kohut and Winnicott alike believed that it is the atmosphere in which children grow up that tends to account for the conflicts of adult personalities (Winnicott, 1962a, 65; Kohut, 1977, 187). While dispositional tendencies toward pathological states are not excluded by either theorist, they are not given focal attention in either of their works. What is given quite a bit of emphasis by both Winnicott and Kohut, however, is the role of the mother in the child-rearing process. Whereas Winnicott spoke of the good-enough mother, Kohut spoke of the optimal mother.

The optimal mother.

According to Kohut, the optimal environment for the healthy development of a child is one in which there is an optimally responsive mother. An optimal mother's creative self-expression unfolds in a smooth, future-directed manner. Such a mother displays several personal qualities. Among these are self-acceptance, self-confidence, free emotionality, and especially empathy toward the next generation as they vigorously inherit the world's affairs (1977, 161, 237). Under healthy circumstances, mothers "experience joy and pride concerning the developmental progress of their ... children" (233–234). This, in turn, imbues any child with whom the mother has formed an attachment with a sense of his or her own impending personality integration and personal becoming (234).

In addition to these self-qualities, an optimal mother is able to be what Kohut called a good *selfobject* for her child. A mother is considered a selfobject when she "is experienced intrapsychically [by the child] as providing functions ... that evoke, maintain, or positively affect the [child's] sense of self" (Bacal & Newman 1990, 229). In other words, as a selfobject for her child, an optimal mother becomes a means for the child to build up his or her own mental organization. At first, according to Kohut, the child does not have a sufficient degree of personality integration to experience a strong, unified sense of self. An optimal mother, however, does not yield to this state of affairs. Rather, she assists in the formation of the child's self by relating to him or her as if the self were already firmly established:

> Under normal circumstances, maternal responses anticipate the consolidation of the baby's self—the mother imagined it to be more consolidated than it actually is; or, in different terms, the mother, by being ahead of the child's actual development, does indeed experience the joy of furthering this development by her own expectations. (Kohut 1977, 27)

Kohut spoke of the period before the integration of a clearly unified self as a time when the child only displays a nascent, virtual, or rudimentary self. This "self" represents a kind of prototype of what the child's self will ultimately be once it is firmly established:

> May we ... not speak of a self in *statu nascendi* even at a time when the infant in isolation—a psychological artifact—can be looked upon only as a biological unit? As a unit, in other words, whose behavior must be studied with the methods of the biological investigator because the immaturity of his biological equipment precludes the existence of endopsychic processes in him which we could grasp by extending our empathy to him. (1977, 100)

The nascent self is what Kohut believes to be the first evidence of primitive psychophysical unification in the child. This basic unity mobilizes the child's desire for a caring mother. As Kohut put it, "His nascent self 'expects' ... an empathic environment to be in tune with his psychological need-wishes" (1977, 85). The nascent self looks to the mother for the proper "empathic resonance." If this is not present, the child is deprived the kind of relationship with the mother that would help him or her regulate anxiety and eventually build his or her own confident, autonomous self (88–89). Again, Kohut:

> She [mother] responds—accepting, rejecting, disregarding—to a self that, in giving and offering, seeks confirmation by the mirroring self-object. The child therefore experiences the joyful, prideful parental attitude or

the parent's lack of interest, not only as the acceptance or rejection of a
drive, but also—this aspect of the interaction of parent and child is often
the decisive one—as the acceptance or rejection of his tentatively established, yet still vulnerable creative-productive-active self. (76)

While Kohut never wholeheartedly rejected the traditional Freudian notion
that need satisfaction is a vital issue during early childhood development, he nev-
ertheless insisted that need satisfaction was not the most fundamental issue of
early child development. For him, tending to the needs of the child's developing
self was the most important task of a caregiver. It is not merely the food itself that
a hungry child desires, according to Kohut, but rather an empathically modu-
lated food-giving experience (1977, 81). An optimal mother empathically senses
when the child's "psychological balance" is disturbed and will "remedy the child's
homeostatic imbalance through actions" (85). According to Kohut, a mother may
even gratify her child's every wish, but for her own purposes, and thereby ignore
his or her maturing, changing self, which cries out for confirmation, approval,
and support (79–80).

In addition to providing the empathy and security a child needs to nurture
the nascent self, an optimal mother also optimally frustrates her child. That is,
the mother slowly and gradually begins to withdraw her doting involvement
with her child so as to insist that he or she begin to become independent and
self-sustaining (1977, 188-189*n*). The child, in turn, begins to transmute and
internalize the adaptational qualities that had been previously provided by the
mother as his or her own. As Mitchell and Black (1995, 160) put it:

> Inevitable yet manageable, optimal frustrations will take place within
> a generally supportive environment. Against this secure backdrop, the
> child rises to the occasion, survives the frustration or disappointment,
> and in the process internalizes functional features of the selfobject. For
> example, he learns to soothe himself, rather than collapsing in despair;
> he comes to experience internal strength despite defeat. Kohut felt that
> this process, which he termed *transmuting internalization*, is repeated
> in countless little ways and builds internal structure, eventuating in a
> secure resilient self that retains a kernel of the excitement and vitality of
> the original immature narcissistic states. (160)

Thus, the empathy, security, and optimal frustration the optimal mother provides all contribute to a gradual process of transforming her child's nascent self
into a strong, evolving nuclear self, clearly demarcated from the mother.

The nuclear self.

Assisting in the formation of the child's nuclear self is not a project that a mother tends to do via explicit instruction. Rather, it is the caring manner in which the mother engages the child that has the formative impact on their mental organization. As Kohut put it:

> Selfobjects empathically respond to certain potentialities of the child … but not to others. This is the most important way by which the child's innate potentialities are selectively nourished or thwarted. The *nuclear self*, in particular, is not formed via conscious encouragement and praise and via conscious discouragement and rebuke, but by the deeply anchored responsiveness of the selfobjects, which, in the last analysis, is a function of the selfobjects' own nuclear selves. (1977, 100)

The nuclear self-consolidates as certain potentialities are selectively affirmed over others by the mother and consequently by the child. For Kohut, the nuclear self that forms comprises nuclear ambitions, idealized goals, and the talents and skills needed for the realization of these ambitions and ideals (1977, 243). Kohut preferred to speak of the self as a tension arc, with basic ambitions and idealized goals acting as the two poles of the self, while the child's skills and talents represent the tension gradient stretching between the child's ambitions and ideals.

In Kohut's view, the child's basic strivings or fundamental ambitiousness springs from the earliest interactions with the mother, especially those ranging from the second to the fourth years of life (1977, 179). In particular, the ambitions derive from the child's original feeling of grandiosity as he or she is lovingly and encouragingly mirrored by the mother. The idealized goals that structure and guide the child's ambitions, on the other hand, arise from later interactions as the child begins to lovingly and admiringly look to his or her caretakers for a sense of values (49). This takes place, according to Kohut, during the fourth to the sixth years of life (179). However, this developmental sequence is neither rigidly fixed nor strictly deterministic. Kohut believed that a child has multiple opportunities to derive a healthy, thriving self-structure from his or her parental relations:

> From the point of view of the child, the developmental movement (in the majority of cases) leads from the self's greatness being mirrored to the self's active merger with the ideal.… Insofar as concerns the whole nuclear self that is ultimately laid down, the strength of one constituent is often able to offset the weakness of the other. Or, expressed in developmental terms, a failure experienced at the first way station can be

remedied by a success at the second one. Briefly, we can say that if the mother had failed to establish a firmly cohesive nuclear self in the child, the father may yet succeed in doing so; if the exhibitionistic component of the nuclear self (the child's self-esteem insofar as it is related to his ambitions) cannot become consolidated, then its voyeuristic component (the child's self-esteem insofar as it is related to the child's ideal) may yet give it enduring form and structure. (186)

Moreover, the child's self-structure eventually becomes "independent of the genetic factors that determined its specific shape and content" (243).

When a child has developed a strong, healthy nuclear self, the child has set up "an independent center of initiative and perception, integrated with our most central ambitions and ideals" (1977, 177–178). As a "focus of perceptions and experiences" (94) and the origin of actions, the self provides a sense of being a "unit, cohesive in space and enduring in time" (99). Selfhood refers to the child's growing sense of being both a "central nucleus of self-acceptance and security" (161) and the vital, organizing center of skills and talents (135). Though the ego is typically considered to be the center of the personality in traditional psychoanalysis, Kohut repeatedly referred to the self as the center of the healthy personality. While the ego represents the functional, managerial, conflict resolving center of "mental apparatus psychology," Kohut held that the self is not a part of any mental apparatus (284). In order to understand a self, one must observe the behavior of a self in-the-world. As Kohut put it:

We cannot, by introspection and empathy, penetrate to the self per se; only its introspectively or empathically perceived psychological manifestations are open to us. Demands for an exact definition of the nature of the self disregard the fact that "the self" is not a concept of an abstract science, but a generalization derived from empirical data. Demands for a differentiation of "self" and "self representation" (or similarly, of "self" and a "sense of self") are, therefore, based on a misunderstanding. (311)

For Kohut, one cannot know the essence of the self as differentiated from its worldly manifestations (1977, 311). Far from being a merely functional dimension of the personality, selfhood implies that the person has a sense of being a proud, reliable initiator and performer of joyfully undertaken activities (18, 134). A healthy self is the origin of a child's creative self-expression (132–133). In Kohut's words:

The decisive issue is not whether all structures have been made functional, but whether the exercise of the rehabilitated functions now enables the patient to enjoy the experience of his effectively functioning and creative self. (134)

The unempathic mother and the unhealthy self.

Kohut contrasted the optimal mother with the "unempathic mother" (1977, 189). While the empathic, optimal mother contributes to the development of her child's nuclear self, the unempathic mother puts her child at a developmental disadvantage. Kohut saw the unempathic mother as the root of emotional disturbance rather than implicating libidinal under-satisfactions, overindulgences, overstimulations, and Oedipal conflicts as the overriding determinants of pathology:

> Behind the seeming importance of a child's sexual overstimulations and conflict with regard to his observations of parental sexual intercourse, for example, often lies the much more important absence of the parents' empathic responses to the child's need to be mirrored and to find a target for his idealization. (187)

The absence of a loving, empathic, and accepting mother blocks a child's attempts to build a strong, vital, organizing hub of experience and activity. The consequences of this state of affairs are twofold. First, the child's personality becomes fragmented and prone to an excess of negative affect. In Kohut's words:

> It is the loss of control of the self over the selfobject that leads to the fragmentation of joyful assertiveness and, in further development, to the ascendancy and entrenchment of chronic narcissistic rage. The consequence of the parental self-object's inability to be the joyful mirror to a child's healthy assertiveness may be a lifetime of abrasiveness, bitterness, and sadism that cannot be discharged. (130)

When a mother fails to empathically respond to her child's needs for security and acceptance, the child is increasingly unable to experience "the joys of self-assertion and will" (76). As a result, the child is forced to "turn to the pleasures he [or she] can derive from the fragments of his [or her] body-self" (76). For example, Kohut interpreted "anal character" as a compensatory effort to derive pleasure from life due to an empty or crumbling self-structure (76).

The second consequence of unempathic mothering is that the child is more likely to develop a disorder of the self. According to Kohut, self-disorders arise when a highly dependent child cannot derive a sense of being joined to an omnipotent selfobject that would counteract and calm his or her feelings of extreme vulnerability (1977, 87–89). As Kohut saw it, self disorders may take a variety of forms. If the mother's empathic resonance is absent or tenuous at best, the child is denied the highly important opportunity to build up a psychological organization that is vital and able to regulate anxieties. In such instances, the child is at risk for developing a "depleted self" and depressive psychopathology (89).

When an unempathic mother reacts to her child's needs for love and care with a repertoire of idiosyncratic defense mechanisms and various other pathological character traits as well, the child is put in a more precarious situation. In this kind of instance, the child must constantly work to "wall off" the noxious elements of the mother's depression, hypochondria, panic, hostility, suspiciousness, and so on (1977, 192). As a result, the child may suffer a permanent or temporary breakup, enfeeblement, or serious distortion of the self. If the self-disturbance is among the more serious (and likely permanent) varieties, the child may develop a psychotic, borderline, schizoid, or paranoid form of pathology. If the child's self-disturbance is less severe, then he or she may develop a narcissistic personality disorder, characterized by such symptoms as hypersensitivity to slights, hypochondria, or depression; or a narcissistic behavior disorder, characterized by such symptoms as perversion, delinquency, or addiction (193).

Final remarks on Kohut's self-theory.

As is evident, the structural neuroses (e.g., hysteria), which were the focus of Freud's work, were not Kohut's primary concern. Kohut was most interested in developing a greater understanding of the aforementioned forms of pathology and was especially invested in the treatment of narcissistic disorders. That Kohut was most interested in the disorders of the self rather than the structural neuroses was a consequence of his interest in the self over the "mental apparatus" (i.e., the relations between id, ego, and superego). Kohut's conceptualization of the self and the importance of its proper development is perhaps his most important and enduring contribution to both psychoanalysis and developmental psychology.

At the same time, however, Kohut's conceptualization of the self also presents one of the primary theoretical difficulties of his work (Tobin, 1991). While Kohut's emphasis on the self represents a decided movement away from classical psychoanalytic metapsychology, his use of the tension arc metaphor to conceptualize the self keeps his theoretical approach in tune with the mechanistic elements of the psychoanalytic tradition (Murray, 2001; Schafer, 1980). As Chessick (1985) noted, using the metaphor of a tension gradient to conceptualize the constituents of self unnecessarily reifies the self-structure. This contradicts Kohut's own insistence that the self is "not a concept of an abstract science, but a generalization derived from empirical data" (1977, 311). That Kohut never felt compelled to ameliorate this theoretical inconsistency can be best attributed to the fact that he found it productive. In his words:

> The definition of the bipolarity of the nuclear self and the correlated outline of its genesis is no more than a schema. Yet, although it is an abstraction—or perhaps because it is an abstraction—it permits the meaningful examination of the complexities of the empirical material the psychoanalyst observes in his clinical work. (186)

Nonetheless, from an existential-phenomenological point of view, an objectivistic, physicalistic conceptualization of the self makes understanding the nature of selfhood unnecessarily ambiguous and difficult. Kohut continually worked to distance himself from the psychology of the "mental apparatus," but his reliance on the notion of the nuclear tension-arc implicitly aligned his work with mental apparatus psychology. In this respect, Kohut's nuclear ambitions, values, and skills are liable to the same charges of Cartesianism as Freud's id, ego, and superego. Kohut's notion that ambitions, values, and skills are vital to the healthy functioning of the nuclear self can be embraced without upholding the positivistic and psychically fragmenting notion of two poles (i.e., ambitions and ideals) stretched across a nuclear tension-gradient. By abandoning the notion of the tension-arc, Kohut's ideas are made more suitable for a productive dialogue with non-Cartesian, holistic, humanistic approaches to the self.

A second, no less important place where the traditional mechanistic-psychoanalytic quality of Kohut's work creates theoretical discrepancies is in his notion of optimal frustration (Stolorow, Brandschaft, & Atwood 1987). For Kohut, the child slowly but surely develops his or her psychological organization and repertoire of skills and talents as a result of the mother's gradual failing to accommodate his or her need-satisfaction. This leaves the child in a position of having to fend for him- or herself, so to speak, in developing the strengths and abilities necessary to adapt, cope, and thrive in the world as autonomous entities. Winnicott proposed a similar idea by noting that an ordinarily dedicated mother eventually returns to the life of her own interests, forcing her child to grow and become increasingly able to care for himself or herself (Mitchell & Black 1995, 126–127). Kohut saw the process of optimal maternal failure to provide need-satisfaction as the precursor to transmuting internalization. However, while the idea of optimal frustration has its merits as a way of explaining the development of the child's self-structure, it is also true that Kohut (and to a certain degree, Winnicott as well) tended to thus downplay the more obvious role of the mother's actual responsiveness to her child as a facilitator of psychological strengths. This particular aspect of both Kohut's and Winnicott's work, the emphasis on the sequence of frustration-anxiety-adaptation, aligns them more with psychoanalytic thought than with humanism. As Tobin (1991, 20) put it:

> Bacal (1985) has pointed out that it is not what is missing, it is what was previously there between self and selfobject that makes the assumption of selfobject functions by the person possible. Bacal has coined the term "optimal responsiveness," and Stolorow (1983) has suggested the term "optimal empathy" to describe this process.

Winnicott and Kohut in Mutual Encounter: Synthesizing an Object-Relations Theory of Child Development

As was mentioned earlier, both Winnicott and Kohut saw child development as guided by an inherent drive to learn, adapt, establish interpersonal attachments, and develop in a healthy manner. Both saw child development as the result of both genetic potentials and environmental forces (especially parenting). Moreover, both thinkers upheld implicit theories of self-actualization, though they did not use the term. For Winnicott, self-actualization was implied in his notion that the child's development was guided by an innate desire to "creatively discover" his or her "potency as a self" (1960, 146, 148; 1963a, 189). Kohut came closer to the verbiage of self-actualization when he noted that the self, with its ambitions and ideals, strives toward the "realization of its own specific programme of action" (Kohut & Wolf 1978, 414). The nature of the self-actualizing process from the current perspective will be explicated in more detail during the discussion of healthy self-development. Before moving on to the issue of self-development as such, however, the kind of parental relationship that is conducive to self-development must be outlined. According to the view presented here, the mother's style of care facilitates or thwarts the child's natural inclination to growth in a healthy fashion.

Healthy parental influence.

Self-development is founded upon a strong emotional bond with a primary caretaker, especially the mother. A mother who is capable of a healthy attachment with her child is a mother who possesses the qualities of self-acceptance, self-confidence, free emotionality, self-expression, and especially empathy. In other words, the mother who is best able to facilitate self-development in her child is a mother who herself possesses a strong sense of self. As a self-accepting, self-confident person, the optimal mother is freed to care for her child in a genuinely devoted and loving manner. She is able to tend to her child's emotional needs and thus protect the child from disruptive periods of anxiety. This mother is, moreover, consistent and reliable in her care. The optimal mother protects her child, at first, by holding and handling the child in an empathic, affectionate way. As the child grows older, he or she will not require literal holding as much as he or she will rely on the mother for empathic care and understanding in order to feel safe, secure, and confident.

All in all, the optimal mother is capable of both feeling and displaying empathy. If a child's sense of self is to develop, the child must perceive the mother as possessing the proper affect synchrony or "empathic resonance," so that he or she feels truly understood and genuinely close to the mother. This closeness allows the child to identify with the mother's already well-developed sense of self. The optimal mother relates to her child as if he or she already had a firmly established self. As a result, the child is able to augment and bolster his or her primitive sense of psychological organization (i.e., the nascent self) by internalizing a model of the mother's personality integration. Thus, the mother's self becomes a means for the child to consolidate his or her own self. This process can begin as early as three months of age.

In addition to the identification process, the optimal mother for self-development engages in object-presentation, meaning that she brings the world to the relatively incapable child. Early in infancy, the child does not have the ability to explore the world as actively as he or she might wish. Until the child's sensory and motor skills advance, it is the mother who will determine how much of her child's desire to explore the world will be fulfilled. In other words, the mother is in charge of the infant's wish fulfillment. When the child wants to see or hear or hold something or someone, the optimal mother makes the world magically appear. When the child wants warmth, security, food, and so on, the mother responds to the child's gestures and satisfies the child's wishes. In this way, the child's burgeoning sense of self is repeatedly acknowledged. Over time, the instantaneous fulfillment the child's needs and wishes gives rise to a sense of omnipotence or grandiosity on the part of the child. This primitive, archaic sense of pride and confidence provides psychological resilience and a foundation for future self-development by compensating for feelings of helplessness and vulnerability. The omnipotent or grandiose self is not something to be eliminated or replaced with another self, but eventually integrated and tempered within a more mature, realistic set of understandings about how the world and others operate in relation to the child. After the child experiences continual, manageable instances of having his or her "grandeur" contradicted by experience, the seeds of the child's omnipotence are transformed into a vivacious and joyful sense of "being." This exuberant sense of existence is vital to selfhood, the core of the human personality and the truly human wellspring of the child's vitality.

In order to maintain and further strengthen her child's burgeoning self, the optimal mother engages in mirroring. That is, she regularly reflects the child's newly developing sense of self-organization back to him or her in a caring, affirming way. Throughout the course of development, the optimal mother remains sensitive to the child's changing needs and increasingly complex creative impulses. She continues to mirror the child in such a way as to convey to him or her that he or she is both safe from harm and worthy of attention.

The nature of healthy self-development.

In the presence of an optimal mother, a child is most likely to develop a strong sense of self and thus develop in a healthy manner. The development of a strong sense of self entails the formation of a psycho-emotional center of security, self-acceptance, and vital feelings of aliveness. Due to the compassion and strength of the mother, the child is able to confidently mobilize and organize his or her skills and talents in a productive, enjoyable manner. The child becomes a proud, reliable initiator and performer of joyfully undertaken activities. The child's feeling of personal significance grows. At the same time, his or her mental organization develops into a locus of experience and behavior. That is, the child experiences himself or herself as a cohesive unit, enduring in time and space, which is the origin of action.

A healthy developing self is inspired, spontaneous, creative, and pro-social. This self is not a set of functions performed by a mental apparatus. Upon a foundation of security and empathy from the mother, the healthy developing self is able to consolidate vital feelings of aliveness into an organized source of inspired, spontaneous behavior. By employing his or her creative impulses, the healthy developing child discovers his or her life-potentials as a self in relation to others. In this sense, a healthy self is the origin of a child's creative self-expression in-the-world-with-others. As the child leaves infancy and begins the phase of early childhood, his or her creative self-expression is given further impetus by the formation of ambitions that are structured and guided by idealized goals. The child's ambitiousness arises naturally (i.e., as an innate predisposition) in a mirroring, supportive environment. Idealized goals, on the other hand, are adopted over time as the child looks admiringly at his or her primary caretakers and interprets their value system. The skills and talents needed to fulfill these idealized goals are the result of both the child's genetic endowment and training. This developmental sequence is not fixed in the sense of being bound to discrete stages or phases. Nor does this theory of self-development imply a strict developmental determinism. While developmental forces such as the drives that Freud spoke of are operative in healthy development, they do not dominate the child's development. Drives enhance the strength and vitality of the self under healthy conditions, but act as a detriment to self-development under unhealthy conditions.

The course of unhealthy self-development: self-depletion and self-fragmentation.

In contrast to the optimal mother, an inadequate mother for self-development is a basically unempathic, nonmirroring mother. This kind of mother emotionally deprives her child, leading to feelings of helplessness and a lack of self-acceptance rather than security and self-confidence. While a devoted, empathic mother protects her child from anxiety and thus facilitates self-development, an inadequate mother is more likely to have a child who suffers from truncated self-development. That is, the child of the nonmirroring mother is more likely to experience unmanageable anxiety, low self-esteem, and a weakened or fragmented self-structure.

The primary characteristics of a child whose self-development is compromised are compliance or compulsion (as opposed to inspired, creative action), restlessness or disruptions of biological functioning, a preoccupation with feelings of threat and anxiety, and an excess of disruptive negative affect in general. The child is thus increasingly unable to experience joyfully undertaken action. As a result, the child is predisposed to seek out substitutes for a healthy striving toward self-actualization. As his or her personal consolidation becomes increasingly compromised, the child is more likely to turn to pleasures that can be derived from specific regions of the body (e.g., oral fixations, anal fixations, and so on). The disturbance in the child's personal consolidation will also lead to malformed interpersonal relations. These malformations are reactive attempts to compensate for the lack of empathic mirroring in early development and a subsequent inability to attain genuine happiness in the world with others. If the mother's empathic resonance is absent or tenuous at best, the child is at risk for developing a "depleted self" and depressive psychopathology. When defense mechanisms and various other pathological character traits dominate the mother's behavior, the child may suffer a permanent breakup, enfeeblement, or severe distortion of the self (e.g., permanent psychotic, borderline, schizoid, or paranoid forms of pathology). If the child's self-distortion is less severe (i.e., nonpermanent), then he or she may develop a narcissistic personality disorder.

Concluding Remarks

Comments on the synthesis of Winnicott's and Kohut's ideas.

The narrative presented above is a creative synthesis of Winnicott's and Kohut's ideas. While Winnicott focused on the period of early infancy, Kohut focused on development ranging from the second to the sixth year of life. That Winnicott and Kohut chose to focus on different developmental time frames for self-development did not make their work irreparably incompatible. Quite the contrary, it suggested that Kohut's work can be seen as a further development of Winnicott's. Moreover, since Kohut avoided making claims of a strict developmental sequence (i.e., a stage sequence), issues relating to time periods were not an obstacle to the construction of the perspective presented above.

At the same time, this is not to say that Winnicott's and Kohut's theories had nothing to offer one another by way of ameliorating theoretical shortcomings. For instance, it was Winnicott who noted that the child's drives (Freud) can enhance a child's self-development. While Kohut agreed that the dominance of drive-motivated behavior is evidence of poor self-development, he did not note the potentially positive, productive role of the drives in self-development.

Overall, however, it is perhaps Winnicott's work that benefited more from Kohut's theory of self-development. For example, Winnicott's notion that a False Self protects the True Self when an individual develops in an unempathic environment was phenomenologically problematic. It implied that the child develops two selves, one manifest and one hidden. This idea has a dualistic quality that raises just as many questions as it answers about unhealthy self-development, as the nature of the True Self in its hidden state is ambiguous. Winnicott did not adequately address how a self can be considered a True Self if it is fundamentally weakened, constricted, and buried beneath a False Self. Both selves were held to be in tact, with the False Self acting in the role of protector. However, protecting one's True Self, even if it is done at the price of overriding the spontaneity of the True Self, is not a wholly dysfunctional, disingenuous project. Thus, the preferable alternative to the schema of multiple selves was the simpler notion of self-depletion put forth by Kohut. Rather than a dualistic theory of parallel True and False Self co-existence, one may legitimately consider Winnicott's "False Self" as the self in its depleted or fragmented form.

Kohut's work was also used to make up for Winnicott's less elaborate conceptualizations of the self as well. While Winnicott showed how the self begins development in early infancy, he did not articulate the nature of the healthy self in as much depth and detail as Kohut. Kohut's ideas about ambitions, values, and skills, his various descriptions of the self as an independent center of experience, and his insistence that the self is not a part of a mental apparatus all significantly add to a humanistic understanding of selfhood. Moreover, Kohut was explicit about the fact that there are multiple opportunities for self to form and repair (i.e., between the second and fourth years and then again between the fourth and sixth years of life). Though it may not be incompatible with Winnicott's ideas, this sort of idea is not addressed by Winnicott. Since even Freud believed that a later stage of development (i.e., the oedipal period) could repair or worsen the preceding course of development, it is reasonable to assume that Winnicott would have been open to the idea that the self has multiple opportunities to form and repair. Indeed, his belief in the role of psychotherapy supports this claim. Further, while Winnicott remained focused on describing the nature of the False Self, Kohut brought to psychoanalytic theory an understanding of the various self-pathologies that can arise from a lack of adequate mirroring.

Finally, rather than relying on Winnicott's concept of the "body-ego" to refer to the developing child's earliest psychological organization, Kohut's "nascent self" was preferred. By relying on the term "ego," Winnicott's concept of the body-ego is more closely aligned with Freudian psychic apparatus psychology than Kohut's notion of a nascent self. Kohut, like most humanists, was explicit in his desire to remove the self from the strictures of Freudian psychology. Moreover, Winnicott spoke of infantile experience as a time where the child has no self, but rather an ego that has not yet come to perceive the mother as a separate being. Kohut's notion of a nascent self emphasizes an emerging self in infancy and is thus preferable to the concept of a body-ego on that basis as well.

Despite the complementary nature of Winnicott's and Kohut's works, there was one facet of their conceptualizations of selfhood that were not entirely compatible. There were Cartesian elements to both Winnicott's and Kohut's notions of selfhood that were quite different, despite the fact that they shared the characteristic solipsism of a dualistic philosophical anthropology in common. Winnicott saw the self as ultimately isolated from the world. Kohut, utilizing causal-empirical terminology, saw the self as a tension arc. However, these elements of Winnicott's and Kohut's theories of self development were deemed unnecessary in synthesizing the current perspective. Moreover, they pose unproductive barriers between psychoanalytic psychology and more humanistic approaches to development. There is no need for a conceptualization of the self as ultimately isolated from everything and everyone in the surrounding world (i.e., Winnicott's self) or a conceptualization of the self that relies on a physicalistic metaphor such as a nuclear tension arc (i.e., Kohut's self). Thus, these ideas did not appear in the preceding narrative.

Critical remarks on the theory presented here.

The developmental framework derived from Winnicott and Kohut has certain shortcomings that suggest areas of potential growth for an analytically inspired theory of self-development. First, there is a hidden element of drive-theory regarding the relationship between the self and others in the current viewpoint. Despite their respective emphases on object-relations, both Winnicott and Kohut constructed theories that emphasized the needs of the individual self above all else. Thus, neither Winnicott nor Kohut adequately described the important role of other people in the life of the individual self, the interpersonal or social context of the child's selfhood. While both Winnicott and Kohut were quite cognizant of the important role of others in the formation and maintenance of a healthy self-structure, the language and overall thrust of both Winnicott's and Kohut's work is unmistakably analytic in its focus on the needs of the individual above all else. Other people are objects or self objects whose importance tends to lie primarily in their ability to fulfill the needs of the individual self and his or her movement toward self-actualization.

Second, though Winnicott and Kohut provided much insightful data about the nature of mother-child interactions, one has to question the degree to which their focus on the mother-child dyad made their theories neglectful of other forces influencing child development. Neither thinker spoke about the wider societal, cultural, and historical forces that can influences a child-rearing environment. Issues such as these ought to be addressed if an analytic-humanistic approach to self-development is to flourish and continue to provide a viable theoretical alternative to traditional approaches to child development.

Strengths of the current approach.

Irrespective of these shortcomings, the theory of self-development presented here has certain obvious strengths. First and foremost, this theoretical framework is quite clear and explicit about the kinds of mother-child interactions that set the stage for strong, healthy self-development. The analytic-humanistic approach covered in this explication and analysis provides a wealth of information about the nature of good mothering, from Winnicott's detailed descriptions of holding and handling, to Kohut's ideas regarding the formation of nuclear and ambitions and values.

The other major strength of this approach is that there are a wealth of specifics regarding the nature of weak self-development and the ways in which self-pathology can manifest due to unhealthy developmental conditions. Winnicott and Kohut made a significant contribution to psychoanalytic thought and developmental theory in general via their novel account of symptom formation, descriptions of depleted or False Self-development, and their ideas regarding self-pathology in general. The theory presented here provides an alternate view of the traditional (Freudian) psychoanalytic conceptualization of symptom formation. A child that becomes fixated on a region of the body as a locus of need-gratification is demonstrating the effects of a disintegrating self-structure. This is not to altogether reject the explanations of psychopathology from Freudian drive-theory. Both Winnicott and Kohut saw the id and the self as developing in a parallel manner. Thus, both considered the structural neuroses as more or less comprehensible in Freudian terms, but insisted that there was more to human psychopathology that needed to be articulated in the language of a self-styled psychology.

KEY TERMS AND CONCEPTS

Ambitions
Blank tablet view of childhood
Creative impulse
Ego-support
Empathy
Facilitating environment
Going-on-being
Handling
Holding
Idealized goals
Identification
Impinging anxiety
Mental apparatus psychology
Mirroring
Nascent self
Need satisfaction
Object-presentation
Object-relations theory
Omnipotence
Optimal frustration
Self
Self-pathology

Self-psychology
Selfobject
Structural neuroses
The False Self
The good-enough mother
The not-good-enough mother
The nuclear self
The optimal mother
The True Self
Unempathic mother
Unhealthy self

CHAPTER 4

AN EXISTENTIAL-HUMANISTIC THEORY OF SELF-DEVELOPMENT: CHARLOTTE BÜHLER*

The theorist whose work is covered in this chapter is Charlotte Malachowski Bühler (1893–1974), an existential-humanistic psychologist (Bühler, 1968d, 350; Yalom, 1980, 20). There are two reasons for Bühler's inclusion. First, Bühler's work is relatively unknown in comparison to other major humanistic and developmental theorists despite her important contributions to psychology:

> Charlotte Malachowski Bühler's contributions to the field of psychology are immense. Her major contributions lie in the areas of life-span development and humanistic psychology.... She came to know psychologists such as Carl Rogers, Gordon Allport, and Abraham Maslow, whose humanistic psychology was very much in accordance with her own. Although Maslow is often credited with being the "father of humanistic psychology," a review of her early work indicates that her ideas actually predate his. (Gavin, 1990) (Ragsdale n.d., pars. 2, 15)

Thus, presenting Bühler's work can make a contribution to the literature on development and stimulate an interest in her work in general. Second, Bühler's thoughts on childhood and adolescence have yet to be brought together to form a single, organized schematic for interpreting child and adolescent development.

This chapter will begin with a general introduction to Bühler's theoretical orientation, comparing and contrasting her work with other theoretical models relevant to the area of child development. This will be followed by a summative account of what she considered to be the four basic tendencies of human life and development. Next, the specific developmental sequence of childhood and adolescence according to Bühler will be schematized, including an articulation of the issues

---

* This chapter is based on an article entitled, "Charlotte Bühler's Existential-Humanistic Contributions to Child and Adolescent Psychology." *Journal of Humanistic Psychology*, Volume 46, No. 1, 48-76 (Copyright, 2006, Sage).

Bühler observed to be integral to each period of growth. Finally, there will be a brief overview and some critical remarks regarding Bühler's child psychology.

Global Characterization of Charlotte Bühler's Existential-Humanism

Bühler and Freudian theory.

For Charlotte Bühler, being an existential-humanistic psychologist means adopting a holistic view of human beings. Specifically, she referred to the importance of utilizing "the whole person as a model" for psychological inquiry (Bühler & Allen 1972, 26). This approach to the study of human beings contrasts with the reductive conceptualizations of human existence that continue to be presented as fundamental psychological theorizing in child psychology texts. The persistent tendency to begin chapters on developmental theory with Freud's developmental insights illustrates this contrast.

Within the traditional or "orthodox" Freudian scheme, human awareness is divided into layers, the major division being the chasm between the conscious-preconscious interplay of awareness and the unconscious mind. For Freud, personality development is first and foremost driven by unconscious urges, primarily the sexual and aggressive tensions produced by the id. The issue here is not that Bühler denied the usefulness of concepts such as unconsciousness or id for psychological theorizing. Quite the contrary, she acknowledged the usefulness of such concepts (Bühler 1968c, 18–19). However, Bühler's theory is holistic in comparison to Freud's in that unconscious hedonistic drives and the homeostatic pleasure principle are not given sovereignty in Bühler's work (Bühler 1964). Bühler considered the notion of an id to be useful, but only as integrated within the total nexus of human motivations rather than seeing people as relentlessly driven to reduce physical tensions generated by a repository of animal drives (1968c, 18–19). To quote Viktor Frankl (1986, xxiv–xxv) on the matter:

> Certainly man has instincts, but these instincts do not have him. We have nothing against instinct, not against a man's accepting them. But we hold that such acceptance must also presuppose the possibility of rejection. In other words, there must have been freedom of decision. We are concerned above all with man's freedom to accept or reject his instincts.

Bühler consistently maintained that humans do not act totally or even primarily on behalf of tension reduction. As opposed to the "closed" organismic system revolving around the satisfaction and reduction of its biological urges, Bühler saw humans as "open" organisms, open to the world of possibilities available to them for experiencing and growing (Bühler & Allen 1972, 33). Rather than maintaining the materialistic thesis that matter tends toward entropy, she noted, "One of our tenets in humanistic psychology is that the human being tends toward higher degrees of order over the course of his life, allowing for temporary disorders in the process" (34). Inspired by Goldstein's (1939) concept of "equalization" and Bertalanffy's (1950) notion of the "steady state," Bühler viewed healthy personalities as motivated to maintain an optimal level of arousal for the performance of acts and ultimately the realization of their unique potentials for growth and development (Bühler & Allen 1972, 35–36).

Here again, it is not that Bühler denied the existence of the homeostatic tendencies emphasized in psychoanalytic theory, but that she felt it necessary to surpass its myopic focus by articulating and highlighting human growth-oriented strivings in order to render an accurate description of the whole human person (Bühler & Allen 1972, 26). In order to counterbalance the Freudian influence on child psychology, Bühler focused her work on healthy development. For her, healthy humans seek comfort and accomplishment, maintenance and change, homeostasis and growth (Bühler 1968c, 17, 24). Humans strive to fulfill biological needs, psychoemotional needs, and spiritual values alike (1968d, 341–342).

Bühler and behavioral theory.

Bühler's adoption of a holistic perspective also entailed a concerted attempt to study what she called the "total action-perception process" (Bühler & Allen 1972, 26). Struggling against the reductive behavioral interpretation of human action as determined by environmental contingencies, Bühler insisted that humans do not merely react to the environment, but perceive the world and take action based upon the values that structure their perceptual field (28–29).

For Bühler, a person's perceptions are integral components of goal-setting (Bühler & Allen 1972, 26). This was her way of attending to the experiential dimensions of human action that were neglected by behaviorism. For Bühler, the meanings and values that people attach to the objects, events, and people in their lives are significant motivating factors initiating and guiding their particular repertoire of behaviors. Hence, she proposed a psychology grounded in "a theoretical model of man as positive, active, and purposive" (43). In other words, human beings are thus always to a greater or lesser degree active mediators of their own existence (52). In Bühler's view, it was the job of a humanistic psychology to emphasize this aspect of human existence, the degree to which humans are spontaneous and creative creatures rather than "reactions to sensory stimuli" (28–29).

Charlotte Bühler saw human life as a project, a work in progress. Life is always a becoming, a forward-moving process, but the circumstances of one's existence do not make it completely readymade (Bühler 1968c, 16). A human being must make choices in life and set the goals that will frame the context of one's future development (1968d, 340). Setting and pursuing goals facilitates the dynamic interaction between person and world that allows one to learn all about oneself and one's significant relations. Thus, through goal-setting, one has the potential to strive toward a higher level of personality integration and optimize one's conditions for future growth, health, and fulfillment (341).

Bühler on the context of development.

This is not to say that Bühler believed that human agency and decision-making are without context or limitation. To be sure, Bühler understood the meanings and values that guide one's choices and goal setting as influenced by one's particular genetic endowment, the demands of one's cultural-ideological age, maturational factors (i.e., opportunities for growth that appear during any of the various phases of development rather than growth caused solely by biological maturity), and especially one's emotional dynamics (1968c, 12; 1968d, 342; 1968b, 38). Moreover, Bühler held that a developing child's emotional dynamics were most intimately tied to his or her parental relations. In particular, she felt that parents optimize a child's conditions for emotional growth by providing a loving, caring emotional atmosphere without "spoiling" the child, by tempering the severity of discipline, by displaying pro-social models of behavior, and by gauging their demands and expectations against their child's gifts and inclinations (1968a, 180–186). For Bühler, a plethora of varied and subtle forces influence the life of a particular developing person, but these influences do not mean that freedom of the will is excluded as a possibility inherent within his or her existence (1968c, 12–13). In her words, "The relative freedom of individual exploitation of … gifts and aims depends on what use the individual makes of himself and his circumstances" (12). Thus, due to both the sheer complexity of the factors involved in determining a child's decision-making and the mediating role of individual freedom, "prediction of the goal-setting behavior of a growing individual can only be very tentative" (1968a, 180).

Bühler and the self.

Charlotte Bühler viewed decision making as always intimately tied to the unique structure of one's individual existence. The choices one makes are always particular to one's own life and circumstances as a matter of course. In order to properly conceive of human existence as carried out via the making of these personally significant choices, Bühler referred to the human being as a self. Bühler called the self the "central core" of the individual, the seat of personal creativity and the originator of one's goal setting (Bühler & Allen 1972, 44, 50).

Viewing the individual human being as a self represents the final major facet of Bühler's holistic perspective. Selfhood protects "the whole person," as it were, from being deconstructed and fragmented into impersonal component parts (Bühler & Allen 1972, 26–27). In stark contrast to the highly conflicted neurotic person, an individual with a strong sense of self is able to "pull himself together and to function in a unified manner" (Bühler 1968d, 334). Thus, elsewhere, Bühler referred to the self as the "core system which organizes, selects, and integrates the multitude of motivational trends" (1968c, 18). For Charlotte Bühler, therefore, selfhood implied not only the agency inherent within subjectivity, but also the uniqueness of an individual agent, and the personality integration sought in his or her striving toward health (20; Bühler & Allen 1972, 26–27).

Bühler's self is a volitional subjectivity, perceiving, valuing, and making choices in life (Bühler 1968d, 331). This self stands in contradistinction to the self of traditional psychoanalysis, which she believed to be a mere objectification, a "built up" mental representation generated by the ego (Bühler & Allen 1972, 44). Thus, praising the neoanalyst Karen Horney for her more adequate understanding of the self, Bühler noted, "It is to Karen Horney's great credit that she emphasized the 'self' as a 'whole' person against Freud's subdivided personality" (Bühler 1968c, 19).

Bühler and ego psychology.

Like Horney, Bühler did not see the concept of the ego of either Freudian psychoanalysis or ego analysis to be adequate for a genuine understanding or appreciation of the organizing and integrating work of the self. There are three reasons for this. First, the concept of ego strength as denotative of psychological resilience in certain psychoanalytic circles is a half-truth that does not fully recognize the total repertoire of functions that the ego performs, defenses being among these functions. Ego strength can lead not only to strong adaptational qualities, but also to strong defensiveness. In such an instance, ego strength does not necessarily strengthen the self. Rather, ego strength may actually alienate one from one's truest self due to the veil of self-deceptions generated via the mechanisms of defense (1968d, 349).

Second, Bühler considers "the ego, to which modern ego psychologists ascribe the role of integrator, as primarily a conscious, organizing agency within the realm of reality" (1968d, 349). The self, in contrast, is primarily "subconscious" in nature, according to Bühler (349). While a self engages in periods of conscious effort and reflection, thoroughly conscious selfhood is phenomenologically revealed to be maladaptive, as the bending back of reflective mental activity would constantly interrupt the flow of life-world experience. This is not at all to imply that being reflective and self-conscious is univocally negative, but rather that the primordial disposition of genuine selfhood is a prereflective engagement with things and others.

Thus, as primarily conscious, the ego does not do justice to the depth and complexity of the self's orientation toward the world. For Bühler, the self's agency is recognizable on all levels of awareness, from conscious to unconscious. As she put it, "Unconsciously or consciously, the individual decides which of the various directions is to predominate at a given time" (1968c, 19). Bühler repeatedly used the words *subconscious* and *unconscious* to indicate that there are dimensions of human experience other than those that are thematic, spelled out, and made explicit in consciousness. She did not detail subtle differences between the terms *subconscious* and *unconscious* (e.g., 18–19), nor did she seem concerned over the fact that Freud considered the term subconscious as misleadingly implying that humans have two consciousnesses (Laplanche & Pontalis 1973, 430–431). Rather, Bühler used both subconscious and unconscious in a very general way to note that the human self displays subtle and varied gradations of awareness in its decision making and goal setting. In this sense, Bühler's use of the term unconscious is broader than Freud's, including elements of prereflective experience, what Freud would consider preconscious awareness.

Third and lastly, the ego is primarily an adaptational system of the personality that responds to the demands of the environment. However, the self, as Bühler understands it, actively strives toward personality integration through creative effort. If development proceeds in a healthy manner, decision making and goal setting are increasingly done under the auspices of the self's efforts toward co-constituting a personally meaningful, creative existence, one imbued with values and a sense of purpose-in-life (Bühler, 1968b, 38–39). These aspects of experience surpass the more mundane level of adaptation to one's surroundings. Remaining at a functional-adaptational style of life, for Bühler, would be a distortion and truncation of self development. In her words, "Sometimes a person may stifle his creative self development in favor of adaptation to his surroundings" (Bühler & Allen, 1972, 47). For Bühler, a personality that is guided by its ego would lack depth, because its self-direction would not come from its "core" (i.e., the self) (Bühler 1968c, 20). Hence, she noted, "Since the ego is only a manifestation of the individual's reality interests, it is hard to see how it can do justice to the personality as a whole with its sometimes reality-transcendent orientation and its subconscious depths" (18–19).

Bühler's self and healthy development.

In Bühler's view, the healthy development of an individual is facilitated under conditions that are not only conducive to adaptation (the domain of the ego), but also conducive to the development of a sense of hope, curiosity, conscience, a sense of purpose, creativity, identity, and a sense of meaning-in-life (the domain of the self) (1968d, 331–333; 1968b, 38–40). Under optimal conditions, a child would have inherited and learned skills and talents that have adaptational value in one's cultural milieu and experienced parental intimacy, adequate love, and affectionate care as well (1968b, 37; 1968a, 174). Such conditions serve to empower the self to act as the "integrating system" of the person, creating a personality that revolves primarily around spontaneity and constructive, pro-social goal setting rather than calculative and managerial functions or destructive tendencies (1968d, 330–331; 1968b, 35–36).

Of all of the self's characteristics, Bühler ultimately saw the desire to make one's life personally meaningful to be especially significant for maturity. Her way of speaking about the inherent human desire for meaning, purpose, and value in life was "intentionality" (Bühler & Allen 1972, 45). Intentionality is the "phenomenon of people wanting 'to live for something'" (Bühler 1968c, 21).

This aspect of Bühler's humanism contrasts with the humanistic orientations of Carl Rogers and Abraham Maslow, for example, where the ultimate aim of personality development is that of self-actualization and brings her closer to Viktor Frankl's existential psychology where an overriding "will-to-meaning" is considered to be indicative of health. Having loyalties to both humanistic and existential thought, Bühler thoughtfully recognized the value of both self-actualization (by which she means the achievement of an abundantly creative and independent identity in particular) and intentionality (1968d, 350; 1968b, 32–34). Consequently, she used the term self-fulfillment to refer to self-actualized living that is simultaneously characterized by tendencies toward "reality-transcendence" (i.e., intentionality, the need to live for something). In Bühler's words, "If we were to name a top goal, it would have to be something as general as fulfillment. The goal of self-realization, which has been favored recently, can only then be identified with fulfillment if self-realization includes living for others, doing right, etc." (1968d, 344). Elsewhere, Bühler noted more emphatically and directly, "What is human life all about? ... The give and take of love and dedicated creative accomplishment." These are the "two endgoals that promise self-realization and fulfillment" (Bühler & Allen, 1972, 48). The mature and healthy self, in Bühler's view, represents the dynamic striving of the person toward higher levels of personality integration via the pursuit of fulfillment (Bühler, 1968d, 332, 349).

The Four Basic Tendencies of Human Life Span Development

Charlotte Bühler maintained that four "basic tendencies of life" are involved in the self's integrating efforts (Bühler & Allen 1972, 48; Bühler 1968d, 332, 349). Bühler calls these need satisfaction, self-limiting adaptation, creative expansion, and the upholding of internal order (see Figure 4.1 below). Need satisfaction includes the satiation of physical needs (e.g., water, food, elimination of waste, sex). Also included under the rubric of need satisfaction are emotional and intellectual needs, such as ego recognition, self-esteem, education, and the need for personal satisfaction in love (Bühler & Allen 1972, 48; Bühler & Marschack 1968, 93). Self-limiting adaptation denotes the need to adjust, to cope, to fit in with one's surroundings and to attain a sense of security in the world. Self-limiting adaptation also includes the desire to belong and participate in society (Bühler & Allen 1972, 48; Bühler & Marschack 1968, 93). Creative expansion refers to the human striving to become industrious, enterprising, productive, and self-expressive. It also includes the desire to master the environment and assume positions of authority and leadership (Bühler & Allen 1972, 48; Bühler & Marschack 1968, 93). Finally, upholding internal order represents the inherent human tendency toward consistency, constancy, organization, and unity in one's own personality (Bühler & Allen 1972, 48; Bühler & Marschack, 1968, 93).

All of these tendencies are evident in healthy human development, according to Bühler, from infancy onward (Bühler & Marschack 1968, 94). Moreover, the four basic tendencies form the general structure of the human developmental course of life. As she put it:

> Infants are predominantly need-satisfying. Self-limiting adaptation predominates during the later childhood years and creative expansion is preeminent in adolescence and adulthood. The tendency toward upholding order prevails during the climacteric age, together with that period's concern for self-assessment. The period of old age finds many individuals regressing to infantile need satisfaction, while others try to accept in self-limiting adaptation restriction which are forced upon them. Some persons are able to continue their creatively expansive activities. (94–95)

Elsewhere, she noted along similar lines:

> Thus, normatively speaking, we find fluctuating degrees of predominance in the various stages. The growing child develops his self-limiting adaptation during the learning process, the adolescent and adult move into a widening world during a period of predominant creative expan-

sion, the adult begins to assess his past and himself in the climacteric age, probably because he wants to restore his inner order, and the old person either regresses to need satisfying tendencies or continues to follow his previous adaptive or creative drives. (Bühler 1968c, 17–18)

Figure 4.1 Schematic Representation of the Self and Its Four Basic Tendencies

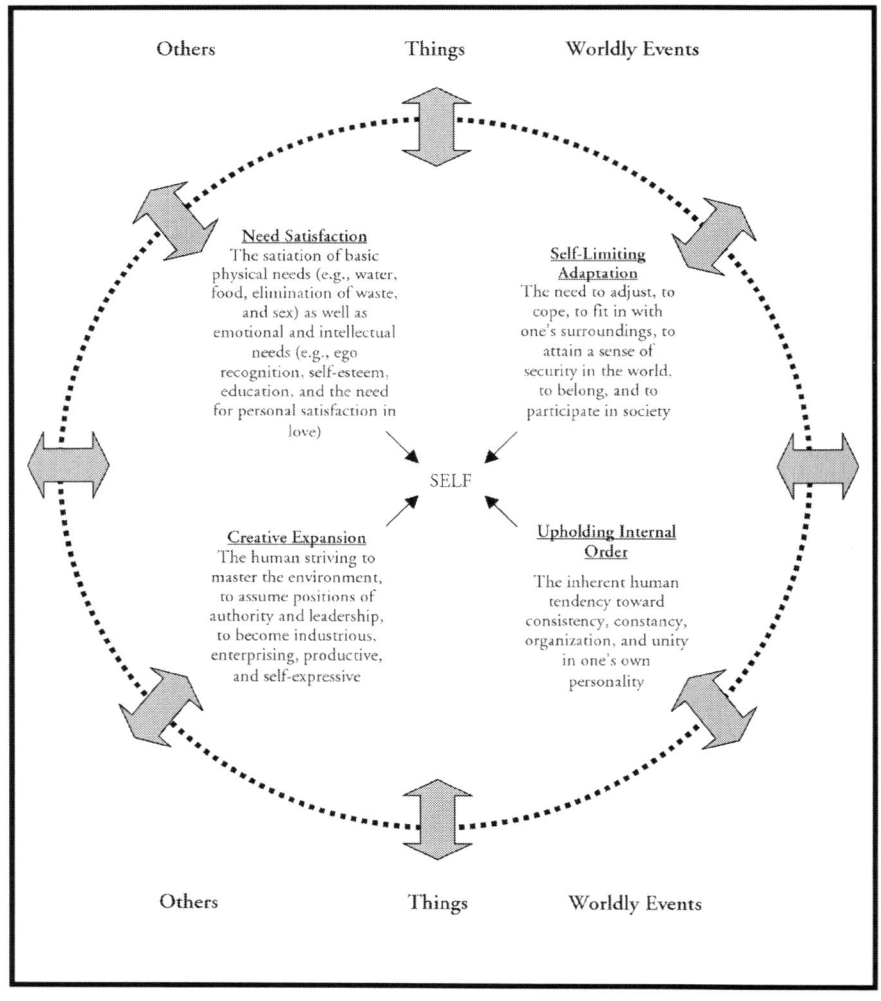

Summarizing, while order-upholding tendencies remain active throughout the lifespan, Bühler found need-satisfaction, self-limiting adaptation, and creative expansion to predominate infancy, childhood, and adolescence respectively. Hence, these basic tendencies of life will characterize the humanistic theory of childhood development outlined here. This theory is a stage theory. While Bühler acknowledges that phase divisions are conceptual devices for interpreting a continuous process, she maintained the need for them, because she believed in their usefulness for describing and understanding developmental dynamics and metamorphoses (1968c, 14).

Charlotte Bühler's Four Phases of Child Development

Infancy (birth to two years old).

In Charlotte Bühler's view, the primary motivational tendency of infancy is that of need satisfaction (Bühler & Marschack, 1968, 94–95). During this time period, the child's life tends to revolve around physical needs, such as the need to incorporate nutrition and eliminate waste. Thus, Bühler noted that within the first 4–5 days of life, newborns display selective perception in an active effort to facilitate feeding (Bühler 1968b, 28). This selectivity of perception, according to Bühler, "forces us to assume the existence of a primary individuality, even a singularity of personality" (28–29).

The infant also seeks to satisfy basic cognitive needs, such as his or her need for sensory stimulation and novel experience. Bühler noted that an infant will not only turn away from unpleasant stimulation, but also actively turn toward stimuli and take an interest in the perceptual world from at least the first ten to fourteen days (Bühler, 1968b, 28). This early in infancy, children display spontaneous curiosity and explore the world around them to the extent that their sensory capabilities allow (e.g., playing with their fingers or trying to imitate sounds) (28). Thus, Bühler remarked, "Primary creativeness, i.e., when an individual engages in an activity which results in the discovery of new potentials, is observable from about the infant's second week of life" (Bühler & Marschack 1968, 93).

Within just a few months, infants begin more sophisticated attempts to coordinate and organize sensory and motor activity. Bühler considered these attempts to be beginning efforts toward integration (i.e., order-upholding tendencies) (Bühler, 1968d, 331; Bühler & Marschack, 1968, 94). In her words:

> The experienced observer of infants may note that even in the second half-year of life some children seem to concentrate on certain of their

pursuits. They may watch and manipulate a toy, grab for their bottle, coo, or move toward a person in what appears to be a determined manner. They seem at such moments to act with a unifying intent. (Bühler 1968d, 331–332)

At around the same time, Bühler observed that infants' social and emotional development becomes somewhat more sophisticated. Infants can use their heightened sense of coordination to facilitate social relations. As a consequence, infants begin to take an active social interest in those around them by approximately five to six months of age (1968b, 31). By establishing contacts with those around them, infants find the means to satiate their basic emotional needs, such as the need for attention and affection. This stage is summarized in Table 4.1.

Table 4.1
Infancy (birth to two years): The Primary Motivational Tendency Is Need Satisfaction

- Within the first four to five days of life, newborns display selective perception in an active effort to facilitate feeding (the selectivity of their perception being the first sign of their individuality).
- Infants will actively turn toward stimuli to satisfy their need for sensory stimulation from at least the first ten to fourteen days.
- Infants display spontaneous curiosity and explore the world around them to the extent that their sensory capabilities allow (e.g., playing with their fingers or trying to imitate sounds).
- Primary creativeness (i.e., activity resulting in the discovery of new potentials) is observable from about the second week of life.
- In the second half-year of life, infants begin more sophisticated attempts to organize and integrate sensory and motor activity (e.g., watching and manipulating a toy, grabbing for their bottle, cooing, or moving toward a person in a determined manner).
- Infants begin to take an active social interest in those around them by approximately five to six months of age, facilitating the satiation of their basic emotional needs, such as the need for attention and affection.

Early childhood (two to eight years old).

Bühler saw the time period of early childhood as spanning the second to approximately the eighth year of life and found it to be primarily characterized by new efforts at self-limiting adaptation. According to Bühler, at about two years old, children begin to utter the phrase, "I want to ...," marking "the first exercise in choosing" and experimenting with goal setting (1968a, 187). The child has established a sense of will evident in his or her efforts at "having say," making requests, even making demands (1968d, 331).

Though the child has entered the domain of volition, however, he or she must first come to terms with the discrepancy between what he or she wants and what he or she can actually have in life (Bühler 1968b, 31). The child must learn the boundaries of propriety regarding their wants, wishes, and desires in the context of a civilized society with rules, norms, and mores. For example, as the child proceeds through early childrearing into preschool and kindergarten, he or she is required to learn and adjust to more sophisticated standards of etiquette and social norms. Amid increased social interaction, the child must learn a great deal more about how to fit in with others (1968c, 17–18). While this process of adjustment is sometimes difficult and painful, the challenges that are posed to the adapting child provide him or her with opportunities to feel a sense of accomplishment. Thus, Bühler noted, "The experience in the area of mastery begins with 'I can' or 'I cannot'" (1968b, 33).

In Bühler's view, children in early childhood eventually surpass mere imitation and conformity to social norms and begin to develop their own personal interest in "rules and other organizing principles" (1968a, 183). Children wish to gain some basic understanding of these organizing principles and how they might relate to their own development. Thus, Bühler asserted that between the second and fourth years of life, children have already begun to seek answers to the question, "who am I?" (1968b, 31).

In essence, these children are beginning to develop tendencies toward self-actualization or self-realization, as she also called it. In Bühler's words, "The child with a creative potential begins his first attempts toward self-realization when he is between two and four years old. A more or less creative little girl may have already have ideas of how to set up her identity" (1968b, 32). To be sure, at such an early age, children's attempts at self-actualization are not necessarily conscious or well thought out. As Bühler noted, "They are not exactly sure ... but they know vaguely that there is something to be realized in some distant future" (33). Moreover, the dominant motivational tendency of this phase remains self-limiting adaptation, not self-actualization. Nonetheless, Bühler found the period of early childhood to be marked by a definite beginning investment in the realization of one's inherent potentials for creative and independent living (31).

In addition to the burgeoning of will and identity, Bühler saw children during this phase as beginning to develop a sense of conscience (1968d, 333). As she noted, children of three or four years of age will begin to question issues that they deem unfair and find them emotionally upsetting. Bühler interpreted this to be an indication of these children's involvement in the development of values and ethical principles. By beginning to be invested in the domain of values, Bühler thus saw these children as manifesting the first sign of the intentionality that will eventually act as the principal unifying force of their personalities (Bühler 1968b, 33; Bühler & Marschack 1968, 98–99). Still, self-limiting adaptation continues to remain the dominant force governing children's behavior, not intentionality. This stage is summarized in Table 4.2.

Late childhood/early adolescence (eight to twelve years old).

Charlotte Bühler called the third general time period of child development by two names: late childhood and early adolescence. For Bühler, this phase of development spans from the eighth to approximately the twelfth year. Bühler held that self-limiting adaptation and creative expansion simultaneously dominate this phase because it is a transitional period between childhood and adolescence.

According to Bühler, the early adolescent begins "to have an overview of his various personal relationships as well as his competence in life" (Bühler 1968b, 37). Overall competence and the social efficacy of the child become vital issues of this period. He or she is seeking to adjust to his or her social surroundings in a more radically adaptive way. In seeking a superior style of adaptation, the child employs his or her creative capabilities. As Bühler noted, "The eight-to twelve-year-old child develops ideas, methods, and directions of his own" (35). Through this process of becoming increasingly industrious with regard to his or her personal direction within society, the child begins to develop a sense of his or her ability to achieve his or her desired life goals (i.e., his or her sense of competence). In Bühler's words, "In the eight-to twelve-year period, all foregoing experiences of being able to master things and situations and to overcome failures converge to generate an attitude toward a concept of achievement" (36). Bühler's way of speaking about a child's sense of efficacy and desire to achieve was constructiveness, and she tended to use these two words synonymously (1968d, 335). In late childhood/early puberty, the individual decides whether he or she wants to live in a constructive or destructive manner (335). As she described it, constructiveness is a "basic orientation of one who ... for himself and others ... pleases, educates, or contributes to any kind of growth and development" (1968b, 35–36).

Table 4.2
Early Childhood (two to eight years): The Primary Motivational Tendency Is Self-Limiting Adaptation

- At about two years of age children begin to utter the phrase, "I want to …," marking their first exercise in choosing and experimenting with willful goal setting.
- The discrepancy between what children want and what they can actually have in life becomes an adaptational challenge that provides them with opportunities to feel an early sense of accomplishment.
- Between the second and the fourth year of life, children have begun to seek answers to the question "Who am I?" evident in their interest in rules and other organizing principles.
- These children are beginning to pursue self-actualization, though not necessarily in a conscious or well thought out manner; adaptation nonetheless dominates the child's personality.
- Children of three or four years of age begin to find issues that they deem unfair emotionally upsetting (burgeoning conscience).
- By beginning to be invested in the domain of values, children manifest the beginnings of intentionality in their behavior; still, adaptation continues to dominate the child's personality.

Along with the child's sense of competence, Bühler considered his or her values to be another critical determinant of the child's style of achievement. During this phase of development, the child is more actively and deliberately involved in coforming his or her values and belief systems within his or her sociocultural context (1968d, 332–333). He or she is forming an increasingly established set of "ordering principles," as Bühler put it (1968b, 37). Bühler observed, the older child (or early adolescent) is "known to debate with others … such issues as honesty, fairness, popularity, power, the importance of being an accomplished person, or just being the best in everything" (37). Consequently, the child's striving to achieve certain goals not only depends upon whether he or she believes in his or her abilities to succeed, but also upon his or her belief in the worth, significance, or importance of the goals in question. This stage is summarized in Table 4.3.

Adolescence/early adulthood (twelve to twenty-five years old).

The fourth and final phase of this exposition is the transition between childhood and adulthood, adolescence. Bühler saw adolescence as beginning at approximately twelve years of age with an outside envelope of twenty-five years of age. Because the time frame is so liberal in extending to the mid twenties, Bühler sometimes referred to this period as early adulthood. Creative expansion is the preeminent tendency of life during this time (Bühler & Marschack 1968, 94–95).

Table 4.3
Late Childhood/Early Adolescence (eight to twelve years): The Primary Motivational Tendencies Are Self-Limiting Adaptation and Creative Expansion

- Overall competence and the social efficacy of the children become vital issues of this period.
- Children are seeking to adjust to their social surroundings in a more radically adaptive way by employing their creative capabilities (i.e., they develops ideas, methods, and directions of their own).
- Through the process of becoming increasingly industrious with regard to personal direction within society, children begin to develop a sense of their ability to achieve their desired life goals (i.e., their sense of competence).
- Experiences of being able to master things and situations and to overcome failures generate an attitude toward achievement (i.e., they decide whether they want to live in an essentially constructive or destructive manner).
- Children are more actively co-forming values and belief systems within their sociocultural context, and these influence children's achievement style along with their sense of competence.

Thus, Bühler spoke of the adolescent world as "a widening world," where adolescents normally begin to develop a heightened, more self-conscious interest in their futures (Bühler 1968c, 17–18, 25). In particular, Bühler noted that healthy adolescents have "a fully established self-awareness" (1968b, 33). The significance of this self-awareness is that adolescents begin to become somewhat more cognizant of the fact that their life has a beginning and an end. This, in turn, increases the perceived value or gravity of their decisions and choices relative to previous phases of development (1968d, 333). Thus, Bühler also noted that adolescents' increase in self-awareness also allows for burgeoning "independently self-responsible identities" (1968b, 33).

The development of an independently self-responsible identity, as it were, proceeds via the adolescent's efforts at committing to values and meaningful goals (1968b, 40). Bühler held that values and beliefs are possibly the single most important factors involved in "holding a person together and keeping him going" (38). Among the first places that the adolescent's efforts at committing to values becomes manifest is in his or her personal relationships. In Bühler's words, "The adolescent discovers and aspires to two new goals of human relationship: intimacy and commitment ... defined as voluntary chosen bonds. To achieve this is one of the most, if not *the* most, essential aims of the maturing person" (37). In addition, the adolescent makes his or her first concerted attempts to create and discover a sense of direction, purpose, and meaning for life (i.e., a fully active intentionality) (1968d, 333). He or she forms his or her first conception of the different kinds of fulfillment that life has to offer (333). It is during this time of life that an adolescent begins to construct his or her first "philosophy of life" as an organizing principle (333).

At the same time, however, Bühler also noted that, "Generally speaking ... adolescents have only vague and tentative life goals" (1968b, 41). While the adolescent is moving increasingly toward dedication, devotion, commitment, and responsibility, Bühler considered adolescent life goals to be "conceived tentatively and experimentally" (1968d, 333). Once the adolescent has moved beyond the tentativeness of experimentalism regarding life goals, then he or she can be said to have entered the domain of adult existence. This stage is summarized in Table 4.4.

Table 4.4
Adolescence/Early Adulthood (twelve to twenty-five years): The Motivational Tendency of Creative Expansion Facilitates the Overriding Drive Toward Self-Fulfillment

- Healthy adolescents have "a fully established self-awareness," making them more cognizant of the fact that their life has a beginning and an end and increasing the perceived value or gravity of their decisions and choices.
- The development of an independently self-responsible identity proceeds via adolescents' efforts at committing to values.
- Among the first places that adolescents' efforts at committing to values becomes manifest are their personal relationships.
- Adolescents make their first concerted attempts to find direction, purpose, and meaning for life (i.e., a fully active intentionality), though goals tend to be vague, tentative, and experimental.
- They develop their first concept of the different kinds of fulfillment that life has to offer.
- Adolescents begin to establish their first "philosophy of life."
- The course of the individual lifespan is elevated above a focus on need satisfaction or adaptation in the drive toward self-fulfillment.

Overview: Charlotte Bühler's Stage Theory of Self-Development

The above discussion highlighted Charlotte Bühler's thoughts and observations regarding development prior to adulthood. Bühler described what she perceived to be the characteristic style of life that children display at each of her stages of development. While describing the issues of each stage, Bühler made a concerted attempt to include observations regarding the developing self along the way. In this respect, her work can be viewed as analogous to the stage theories of Freud, Erikson, and Piaget. Rather than articulating the stepwise developmental changes that occur with regard to the id, ego, or rational mind, however, Bühler's work provides a frame of reference for viewing child and adolescent psychology that emphasizes the evolution of the self throughout the lifespan. This self is not an isolated organism, but rather an always-involved matrix of personally significant projects and meaningful relations with other people.

In order to highlight and clarify the evolution of the self, a brief overview of the self's stage-related development within Bühler's theory is in order. Although the period of infancy is dominated by need-satisfying tendencies, Bühler maintained that the origins of selfhood are evident nonetheless. During infancy, Bühler noted three primary factors indicative of self-development. First, the infant's selectivity of perception is evidence, according to Bühler, of a primary individuality of personality. This is the first evidence of the self's uniqueness, making the particular child in question distinguishable from all others. Second, the infant engages in activities in order to discover new potentials for experiencing and moving from about the second week of life, in Bühler's view. She referred to this as the infant's "primary creativeness," another aspect of the self, one that contrasts with the ego's adaptive nature. Third, the infant eventually begins to make efforts toward sensorimotor organization and coordination, which indicate that the self's integrative tendencies have begun:

> Though the establishment of a self is glaringly obvious in the 2 to 4 year old's statement of "I," The experienced observer of infants may note that even in the second half year of life some children seem to.... act with a unifying intent. (1968d, 331–332)

During early childhood, self-limiting adaptation is the primary motivation of the child. Again, however, more evidence of the developing self can be found in the second year of life with the child's first attempts to assert his or her will. By exercising choice and beginning to experiment with goal setting, the child has begun to learn what it means to be a volitional agent. Bühler also asserted that between the second and the fourth year of life, children have begun to seek answers to the question, "Who am I?" In this first apparent interest in identity formation, Bühler saw the child as beginning to develop tendencies toward self-actualization. Finally, at around three or four years of age, the child begins to question the fairness of certain kinds of behavior. For Bühler, this was an indication of the child's involvement in the development of values, ethical principles, and ultimately early intentionality.

During the transitional period of late childhood, a more radical style of adaptation is sought via the use of the self's creative potentials. In particular, Bühler noted that between the ages of eight and twelve, the child develops ideas, methods, and directions of his or her own. Thus, more of the self's individuality comes into being. The child also begins to develop a sense of his or her ability to achieve life goals, his or her competence. Through experiences of being able to master things and situations, the child develops an attitude toward achievement. That is, the level of self-efficacy that the child has developed becomes a factor determining whether the creativity associated with the self will be dedicated to constructive or destructive purposes in life. Finally, Bühler found the child to be more actively and deliberately involved in co-forming his or her values and belief systems at this time. Bühler saw these values and belief systems as more evidence of the self's intentionality and integrative efforts.

Through the creative expansion that characterized adolescence, the course of the individual lifespan was at last elevated above the child's focus on need satisfaction or adaptation. Creative expansion facilitated the convergence of self-actualizing tendencies (toward a creative and independent identity) and intentionality (toward living for something that would make one's life appear meaningful or purposeful) in the drive toward self-fulfillment. This phase is marked by "the adolescent's first commitments of love, friendship, and ... the different kinds of fulfillment life may offer" (Bühler 1968d, 333). For Bühler, the desire for self-fulfillment remains the sovereign motivation of healthy human growth from adolescence onward. This is not to say that need satisfaction and adaptation dissolve or no longer exist. It is rather that these tendencies become enveloped within a higher order of personality development. From adolescence on, they are all integrated within the self's overriding pursuit of fulfillment. All four of Bühler's basic human tendencies remain with the person throughout the entirety of the lifespan.

Strengths of Bühler's Approach and Critical Remarks

I hope to have shown through the preceding discussion that there is a viable and perspicacious humanistic theoretical framework for interpreting child and adolescent development within Charlotte Bühler's writings. This theoretical approach emphasizes the development of the self in its meaningful relations to the world-with-others. Bühler was emphatic about the need for a theory of self-development as a part of her dedication to viewing the developing human person as a whole. She was not unaware that others had similar developmental interests, especially in psychoanalytic circles (1968c, 18–19). However, Bühler was not convinced that enough had been done to describe the nature of self-development in psychoanalysis. In her words:

> It is to Karen Horney's great credit that she emphasized the "self" as a "whole" person as against Freud's subdivided personality. Horney's "real self" is inborn, while Carl Jung's self is achieved. However, this real self and its workings were not clearly defined, a fact that Ruth Munroe (1955) termed a weakness of the nonlibidinal schools, together with their lack of concern for the genetic process. Only Harry Stack Sullivan

concerned himself with developments, but, as Munroe says, the nature of the self-realizing self remained obscure. (19)

Bühler's work may be seen as an attempt to compensate for these shortcomings. Bühler sought to apply basic humanistic ideas to the area of development and provide a stage theory of self-development to be considered alongside other stage theories emphasizing different vectors of growth (e.g., Freudian theory, Eriksonian theory, Piagetian theory).

Charlotte Bühler displayed an originality of approach in her conceptualization of development as a humanistically oriented psychologist. This originality is best seen in her treatment of self-actualization (or self-realization), a fundamental concept in humanistic psychology, as well as her treatment of intentionality, a concept denotative of the existential will-to-meaning. Those familiar with the works of Goldstein (e.g., 1939) and Maslow (e.g., 1954, 1967, 1968) may have already noted that Bühler deviates from the typical conceptualization of self-actualization as a sovereign drive or primary motivational force in humans. For both Goldstein and Maslow, the drive toward self-actualization is already present in infancy. When an individual satiates basic biological and adaptational needs throughout development, he or she is understood to be displaying the initial expressions of self-actualization (Goldstein, 1939, 323; Maslow 1967). While Bühler believed that selfhood begins to emerge in infancy (e.g., the infants "acting with a unifying intent"), she did not see the child as beginning to strive toward self-actualization until the conclusion of infancy (i.e., early childhood):

> The child with a creative potential begins his first attempts toward self-realization when he is between 2 and 4 years old. A more or less creative little girl may already have ideas of how to set up her identity.... These tentative early goals show us the beginning of the child's conscious attempts to identify with certain persons and objectives in the humanistic perspective of values of which the child has become aware. (Bühler 1968b, 32)

Moreover, despite the fact that children begin to pursue self-actualization, Bühler regularly qualifies her discussions of self-actualizing tendencies during this time period. For example, she stresses the "tentative" and "vague" nature of the child's self-actualizing efforts during this time and holds these efforts in contradistinction to the "independently self-responsible identities" of adolescence (Bühler 1968b, 32–34). What appears to be more significant to Bühler about children in the second stage of development is their self-limiting adaptation.

Bühler doesn't stress the issues of self-actualization (i.e., the issues of identity) as an overriding priority until adolescence, with the third stage of development being a transitional period between an adaptational lifestyle and a more creatively oriented, self-actualizing lifestyle. In this particular regard, Bühler relies more heavily on her conceptualization of the self and its four basic tendencies than self-actualization for her understanding of development. For Bühler, the healthy child qua self selects what kind of general orientation toward life will be the primary organizing principle of each stage of development (e.g., need-satisfaction, then adaptation, and so on). As the healthy child matures, he or she develops a more complex personality structure; a new integrative tendency dominates and the prior tendency becomes outmoded (see Figure 4.2 below) (Bühler 1968c, 19; Bühler & Marschack 1968, 93–94).

Figure 4.2 The Primary Integrative Tendencies of Bühler's Stages of Development

PHASE OF LIFE	Infancy (0–2 years)	Early Childhood (2–8 Years)	Late Childhood/Early Adolescence (8–12 Years)	Adolescence/Early Adulthood (12–25 Years)
PRIMARY INTEGRATIVE TENDENCY OF THE SELF	*Need satisfaction*	*Self-limiting adaptation*	*Self-limiting adaptation and creative expansion*	*Self-fulfillment via creative expansion*

To be sure, Bühler's notion of self-actualization as gradually developing and coming to fruition with the advent of creative expression is similar to Maslow's understanding of the self-actualization process. However, that Bühler saw the overall growth process of the whole child as somewhat independent of the self-actualization process rather than identical to it makes her closer to Carl Rogers than Maslow in this respect, as Rogers (1959) saw human development as governed by both an actualizing tendency and a self-actualizing tendency.

In actual fact, Bühler's theory is original, and not to be identified with Maslow, Rogers, or any other humanist. That Bühler did not address the details of how and why her use of the concept of self-actualization differs from Goldstein's or Maslow's use of the term was at best an oversight, at worst a theoretical shortcoming. The benefit of Bühler's interpretation of the role of self-actualization in development may be that her theory can interface and dialogue more readily with the psychoanalytic theories of development that she admired and took seriously. By interpreting the drive toward self-actualization as gaining strength slowly amid the predominantly need-satisfying and adaptational tendencies of childhood, Bühler sought a more dialogical developmental theory than most developmental psychologies. Whereas theorists such as Adler (1930) and Goldstein (1939) relegated older psychoanalytic concepts such as those in Freud's work to the status of being nothing but primitive attempts to express a more global motivational principle (i.e., self-actualization), Bühler felt that there was potential insight to be gained by leaving alternate conceptual frameworks intact. Theories that emphasize need-satisfaction (e.g., Freudian psychoanalysis) and adaptation (e.g., ego psychology) are given a well-respected place within Bühler's theoretical scheme. Nonetheless, as the person grows, the more primitive motivational schemes do eventually become integrated within the newer, more complex personality structure guided by a different primary motivational force. Thus, Bühler notes:

> My definition of the self and my assumptions about its development (1962) are as follows: the motivational parameters of need satisfaction, self-limiting adaptation, creative expansion, upholding of internal order, as well as those of the id, ego, and superego represent vectors with certain inherent ends and potential goals. (1968c, 19)

Bühler's treatment of intentionality as a reality-transcendent striving toward meaning, value, and purpose was also novel. The reader who is familiar with Viktor Frankl's work on this topic may recall that Frankl essentially did not look at the will-to-meaning from a developmental perspective. On one particular occasion Frankl addressed the development of the will-to-meaning by noting that it emerged with particular urgency during adolescence (1986, 27–28). Here, Frankl's thoughts on the topic were similar to Bühler's. However, elsewhere (1969), Frankl stated, "In the earliest stages of development there is no indication of a will to meaning" (41). For Bühler, this statement would be unquestionably false. Thus, another indication of Bühler's originality was her concerted effort to describe the development of intentionality prior to adolescence.

While Bühler's notion of self-fulfillment as a way of reconciling the humanistic concept of self-actualization and existential concept of intentionality also represents a highly original dimension of her theory, this very same notion of self-fulfillment may be the most striking theoretical difficulty of her work. To be sure, this is not because the idea of reconciliation is impossible. Viktor Frankl (1969) maintained that self-actualization was a possibility in human existence as a by-product of self-transcendence (38). Frankl believed that self-actualization was a natural occurrence when an individual lives in a self-transcending manner. Moreover, he believed that his thoughts and observations on self-transcendence were compatible with Bühler's theory:

> Now let us turn to the concept of a will to meaning. This is an assumption which is very compatible with Charlotte Bühler's basic tendencies. For according to her theory, fulfillment is the final goal, and the four basic tendencies serve the goal of fulfillment, provided that which is meant by fulfillment is the fulfillment of meaning rather than fulfillment of the self, or self-actualization. (37–38)

Despite the fact that Frankl felt a certain kinship to Bühler in this passage, in another context, Frankl speaks more hesitantly about the relationship between their theories. In particular, Frankl disapproved of Bühler having asserted that Frankl's logotherapy "joined" the ranks of humanistic psychology (Bühler & Allen 1972) on the basis of the fact that humanists tend to view self-actualization as the fundamental principle of psychological health and maturity (Frankl 1978, 72).

Frankl's criticism could have gone farther. Though Bühler insisted that self-actualization could only really be achieved if a self-transcendent will-to-meaning came to fruition within a person's life, Bühler tended to make comments that gave an overriding priority to self-actualization in development. For instance, in one passage she wrote:

> It becomes increasingly evident that in dedicating himself to a self-transcending goal, a person feels his life to be meaningful. But for the goal to be meaningful and at the same time to fulfill a basic existential human need, it must be chosen in accordance with a person's best potentialities. (1968b, 40)

This is a style of thought that Frankl sought to correct. As Frankl saw, there is no compelling reason why it is imperative that a person chose goals to pursue that are "in accordance" with his or her "best potentials" in order to be meaningful or fulfilling (1967, 46). Assuming, for instance, that a person is not a particularly talented guitar player, does this then mean that he or she cannot achieve intense and impassioned fulfillment from learning and playing guitar? Is it not possible that the achievements that a less talented guitar player might gain from the struggles involved in reaching higher levels of skill and accomplishment could conceivably make playing the guitar more meaningful to him or her than a person for whom guitar playing comes more naturally? Taking the argument further, what if a person has an outstanding talent for murder? Does this then imply that he or she ought to actualize that talent? Here, it seems that Bühler's understanding of the dynamics of meaning in a person's life is left wanting.

This theoretical difficulty is pervasive in Bühler's work. She often used the words *self-actualization, self-realization,* and *self-fulfillment* interchangeably, noting that fulfillment was an end result of self-realization (e.g., Bühler & Marschack 1968, 93; Bühler, 1968d, 332). Yet, at other times, she would admonish that the "top goals" of self-realization and self-fulfillment entailed doing right, living for others, and commitments of various sorts (344; Bühler & Allen 1972, 45, 48). Moreover, the developmental prioritizing of self-actualization, as it were, never appears in her descriptions of children's progression through the various developmental phases.

Still elsewhere, Bühler spoke of self-actualizing tendencies and self-transcending tendencies as being equiprimordial. In her words, "Thus, the healthy person will ... strive for a balance between pursuit of his own needs and dedication to self-transcending contributions" (Bühler & Allen 1972, 49). Bühler seems to have taken the complexity of the relationship between self-actualization and self-transcendence for granted, leaving the reader to continually ponder about her exact position on the matter. She never found it necessary to grapple with the possibility that her conceptual scheme might lean in an erroneous direction. That is, one may make a formidable argument, as Viktor Frankl does, that self-transcendence is the precondition for self-actualization. In Frankl's words:

> Self-actualization is not man's ultimate destination. It is not even his primary intention. Self-actualization, if made an end in itself, contradicts the self-transcendent quality of human existence. Like happiness, self-actualization is an effect, the effect of meaning fulfillment. Only to the extent to which man fulfills a meaning out there in the world does he fulfill himself. If he sets out to actualize himself rather than fulfill a meaning, self-actualization immediately loses its justification. (1969, 38)

Another aspect of Bühler's work that may be viewed as a shortcoming is her lack of interest in the self-styled developmental ideas of some of her predecessors and contemporaries. While Bühler was critical of Horney and Sullivan for not going far enough in their descriptions of self-development, Bühler appears to have been uninterested in seriously dialoguing her ideas with those of Alfred Adler

(1935, 1939), Carl Rogers (1951, 1959), and D. W. Winnicott (1965). Perhaps if Bühler had made more of an effort to dialogue with these thinkers, her works may have been given more recognition in developmental theory or psychology in general. Bühler's ideas have gone relatively unnoticed in comparison to the theories of self-styled developmentalists prior to and subsequent to her efforts (e.g., Kohut 1977; Stern 1985).

Despite any shortcomings, the fact remains that Bühler's work on self-development is a significant contribution to developmental theory. Bühler generated an innovative humanistic theory that can further our understanding of the self, the dynamics of personality integration, and healthy human development. In short, she is an important, yet neglected female figure in psychology.

KEY TERMS AND CONCEPTS

Adaptation
Adolescence/early adulthood
Becoming
Context of development
Creative expansion
Early childhood
Ego strength
Four basic tendencies of human life span development
Goal setting
Growth-oriented strivings
Homeostatic pleasure principle
Independently self-responsible identity
Infancy
Intentionality
Late childhood/early adolescence
Need satisfaction
Self
Self-actualization
Self-fulfillment
Self-limiting adaptation
Steady state
Total action-perception process
Upholding of internal order
Whole person

CHAPTER 5

AN EXISTENTIAL-ANALYTIC THEORY OF SELF-DEVELOPMENT: RICHARD KNOWLES

Richard T. Knowles's work *Human Development and Human Possibility: Erikson in the Light of Heidegger* (1986) is a point of convergence between psychoanalysis and existential-phenomenology. In his book, Knowles used his understanding of the existential-phenomenological philosophy of Martin Heidegger to reinterpret Erik Erikson's developmental ego psychology. Knowles's approach provided a more humanistic alternative to traditional psychoanalytic theories of development due to his existential-phenomenological perspective and his emphasis on self-development. To begin this chapter, I will briefly review Erikson's reinterpretation of Freud's stages of development to provide a context for the discussion of Knowles's reinterpretation of Erikson's work.

Erikson's Stages of Psychosocial Development

Erik Erikson grounded his approach in the psychosexual theory of development put forth by Sigmund Freud. For Freud, all experience and behavior were ultimately in the service of satisfying the animal drives of the id. In the end, human existence could be reduced to its biological substrate. Far from recognizing the centrality of the social aspects of human development, Freud's interpretation of human beings focused on individuals' will-to-pleasure (Frankl 1986). Erikson (1963) sought to go beyond Freud by integrating a more profound respect for the role of the ego and its attempts to come to grips with the demands of its social milieu into the psychoanalytic theory of child development. Thus, Erikson placed more emphasis at each stage on the importance of interpersonal relations in the development of personality. As a result, he modified the time ranges for the stages somewhat and called his theory a psychosocial theory of development.

At each stage of development, Erikson saw the child as needing to resolve a particular ego "crisis" in social and emotional development. He used the term crisis to refer to a radical turning point in development. A successful resolution of any of these crises means that the child will begin to develop new ego qualities and psychological strengths that allow him or her to advance to a new stage of development (1961). Should a failure to resolve an ego crisis occur at any stage, the child will become fixated at that stage or regress to issues of the previous stage.

The Eriksonian stages that are most relevant to the present text are the first five. In Freudian terminology, these are—from first to last—the oral, anal, phallic, latency, and genital stages. These stages cover development from infancy to adolescence.

For Freud, the child's id seeks libidinal satisfaction via the mouth during infancy (i.e., licking, sucking, biting, chewing, and swallowing). As is the case at each psychosexual stage, the child requires gratification, but not to excess. Moreover, the child cannot be traumatized, abused, neglected, or in any other way denied adequate satisfaction. If the child is overindulged or undersatisfied, then the child is liable to develop a fixation. At this stage, fixations come in the oral-aggressive and oral-receptive varieties. Whereas Freud emphasized the child's oral pleasure seeking during this stage, Erikson chose to highlight the extreme dependency that the child experiences during this time. Due to this extreme sense of vulnerability, the child's ego seeks out consistent, predictable nurturance from caregivers. Starting with Freud's emphasis on the role of feeding, Erikson noted that while the id needs oral pleasure, the child's ego is in need of a sense of the mother's caring dedication to feeding (and his or her needs in general) (1963, 249). Should the child find his or her caregivers to be responsive and committed, he or she will develop an adequate sense of trust in himself or herself, others, and the world. In addition, he or she will develop a sense of hope. Thus, Erikson saw the first stage of development as a time where the child must resolve the ego crisis of basic trust versus basic mistrust. However, should psychological maltreatment (i.e., some form of abuse or neglect) or other trauma prevent the child from developing a basic sense of safety in the world, he or she will come to rely heavily on attempts to withdraw from shared reality in order to attain a sense of security. For Erikson, an example of the kind of pathology that results from a fixation at this stage is infantile schizophrenia (248).

In the event that the child successfully resolves the first stage ego crisis, he or she will move on to stage two. Erikson called the ego crisis of this stage autonomy versus shame and doubt. During this stage, Freud emphasized the child's attempts to obtain an adequate sense of pleasure via the anal sphincter muscles despite parents' attempt to enforce potty training. Fixations due to inadequate parenting at this stage included the anal-retentive and anal-expulsive types. What Erikson chose to focus his attention on during this stage of development was the fact that potty training revolves around the issue of control (an ego quality). With bodily maturation, the anus becomes one of the first major things in the child's life that he or she can have control over. However, as soon as parents see this potentiality becoming actualized, they seek to use their own authority and will to teach the child the socially acceptable way to regulate bowel movements. If the child comes to feel that the parents are not trying to dominate him or her, but are ultimately attempting to help him or her develop self-control, the child will develop a sense of autonomy. In addition, the child will develop a sense of will. However, if parents are psychologically abusive in their child-rearing tactics, the child will not develop a sense of personal authority. Rather, the child will develop feelings of shame and doubt. For Erikson, an example of the kind of pathology that would be the result of a fixation at this stage is obsessive-compulsive neurosis (1963, 252). Alternatively, if the psychological maltreatment that the child undergoes during this stage proves to be overwhelming enough, the child may regress back to problems of the previous stage. Such is the case with every new stage.

Erikson saw the ego crisis of the phallic stage as one of initiative versus guilt. During this developmental period, the region of the body that comes into focus is the genitals. Freud showed us that the oedipal dream manifests itself. The child needs to feel like the beloved mommy's boy or daddy's girl for a time and then have this dream manageably come to an end by identifying with the parent of the same sex. If this fails to occur, the child may develop a host of difficulties revolving around relationships and sexuality. Moreover, failures from the previous stages will become pronounced in the personality. At the same time, however, the child is developing a new sense of mobility. The child is developing new mental and physical skills that give him or her the ability to envision and undertake projects of his or her own planning. According to Erikson, if the child is allowed to enjoy these new abilities under the caring direction and guidance of his or her parents, then he or she will develop a sense of initiative. Moreover, the child will develop a sense of purpose. However, should abusive or neglectful parents rely excessively on punishment and guilt rather than involvement in their child rearing, initiative will not develop. Rather than being motivated to become involved in projects and relationships, the child will be burdened by a looming sense of guilt over acts that are contemplated and undertaken (e.g., the forbidden Oedipal wish). For Erikson, an example of the kind of pathology that results from a fixation at this stage is hysterical neurosis (1963, 257).

During the latency period, the ego crisis that arises for the child is industry versus inferiority. For Freud the latency period was a time when the instinctual urges of the id were sublimated. The child is spending his or her time learning how to be like mom or dad, practicing the skills needed to become a young man or woman. Erikson believed that during this time the ego is attempting to attain a sense of mastery in using the body as a tool to for building an identity via work and play activities. According to Erikson, the child requires encouragement and sometimes sensitive instruction or "coaching" to accomplish this task. If the child finds that he or she can successfully identify with his or her physical and mental abilities and feel at home in his or her body, then he or she will develop a sense of industriousness. In addition, he or she will develop a sense of skillfulness. However, if the child encounters some difficulty during this period, especially in the presence of psychologically abusive caretakers, industry will not develop. Rather than becoming enterprising and diligently involved with tasks, the child will develop a sense of inferiority.

Finally, Erikson characterized the stage five ego crisis as one of identity versus role confusion. Freud saw this stage as the time when the genital region is rediscovered, only now in a more adult fashion. Adult sexuality comes into focus and genital maturation brings about a radical change in priorities and lifestyle. With the advent of sexual relations, the child must integrate all of the identifications and other ego qualities that he or she has developed in order to maintain stable interpersonal relations. Thus, Erikson saw the child as searching for a sense of devotion in life. In particular, a constant sense of identity is sought.

As an adolescent, the child is now preparing for adulthood. In order to do so he or she requires a stable sense of identity in order to accept the responsibilities of adult life. However, Erikson notes that the task of achieving a constant sense of identity is dependent upon the success of past stages. As he put it, "In puberty and adolescence all sameness and continuities relied on earlier are more or less questioned again.... Adolescents have to refight many of the battles of earlier years" (1963, 261). Thus, psychological maltreatment throughout development increases the probability of role confusion in adolescence. If, however, there is a successful resolution of the ego crisis of identity versus role confusion, a sense of fidelity will arise. The chart in Table 5.1 outlines both the Freudian psychosexual stages and the Eriksonian psychosocial stages of development.

Knowles's Reinterpretation of Erikson in the Light of Heidegger

While Erikson went beyond Freud by integrating the ego and social aspects into his developmental theory, Knowles (1986) contended that Erikson's work can also be integrated into a more fully developed articulation of the meaning of child development. In an effort to reinterpret Erikson's work, Knowles used his interpretation of Heidegger's (1962) ontological framework called the Care Structure. According to Knowles, the Care Structure is comprised of three elements: facticity, fallenness, and existentiality.

Table 5.1
Two Psychoanalytic Theories of Child Development

Freud's Psychosexual Stages and Corresponding Fixations				
Oral (0–2 years)	Anal (2–3 years)	Phallic (3–7 years)	Latency (7–Puberty)	Genital (Puberty–)
Oral-aggressive	Anal-retentive	Vanity	Unspecified	Unspecified
Oral-receptive	Anal-expulsive	Flirtatiousness		
		Promiscuity		
		Sexual Frigidity		
		Sexual Confusion		

Erikson's Psychosocial Stages (Ego-needs, Ego-crises, and Corresponding Fixations)				
(0–1 years) Consistent, Predictable Care	(1–3 years) Self-control	(3–5 years) Direction	(5–11 years) Identification with one's physical and mental abilities	(11–18 years) Devotion
Basic Trust vs. Basic Mistrust	Autonomy vs. Shame and Doubt	Initiative vs. Guilt	Industry vs. Inferiority	Identity vs. Role Confusion
Infantile Schizophrenia	Obsessive-Compulsion	Hysteria	Inferiority Complex	Delinquency
				Over-identification with Heroes & Cliques
				Stereotyping

Facticity denotes those things in life that we do not simply choose of our own freewill. Knowles refers to this as the limited aspect of our existence: "Facticity ... refers to the fact that the person finds himself or herself already in a situation, already within limits, having a past, having been born into a certain tradition, family, social class, being male or female, and so forth" (Knowles 1986, 8–9). Fallenness, for Knowles, refers to the fact that we are often preoccupied with our day-to-day activities in a way that truncates or constricts our ability to openly discover and create possibilities for existing. It denotes the kind of habitual involvement with the here and now that makes us forgetful of our individuality. In essence, we interpret our lives in the way that everyone and anyone would, as a part of an anonymous collectivity (16). Humans are fallen, when they live in a way that is passive and conforming, sacrificing conscientious worldly involvement and decisiveness for the status quo, sacrificing active participation in our affairs for withdrawal or mere wishfulness. Fallenness is also evident in the opposing extreme, living in a way that is essentially controlling, calculative, and managerial rather than spontaneous and affective (6, 10–11, 37). Finally, humans can also be described as existential. According to Knowles, existentiality refers to the times when humans are most themselves (17). Existentiality denotes both the distinctly human dimensions of development and the unique aspects of an individual's becoming. What is distinctly human is not the fact of having a body, nor the act of conforming to a social order, nor the act of engaging in calculative thought processes. Humans are most themselves when they develop unique styles of projecting themselves toward future possibilities within their social milieu (13). This is both the existential dimension of development and an existential-phenomenological description of selfhood.

According to Knowles, Freud emphasized the biological aspect of human existence. In terms of the Care Structure, Freud can be said to have done an articulation of certain of our factical aspects. Namely, Freud articulated the primarily sexual and aggressive aspects of human existence. Temporally speaking, Freud was interested in the past. He wished to show that personality was determined by how the id was or was not satisfied during our psychosexual development.

Parallel to Freud, Erikson's focus on ego functions places his work as an articulation of certain of our fallen aspects. For Erikson, what was critical in our psychosocial development was the development of various rational and managerial qualities to deal with present social realities. In particular, healthy development rested upon the development of a sense of consistent care, self-control, direction, identification with one's bodily capabilities, and a sense of devotion.

However, Knowles contends that a full articulation of the meaning of child development requires still more than an articulation of Freud's factical and Erikson's fallen aspects. Knowles contributed to the developmental theory put forth by

Erikson by making contributions to the factical, fallen, and existential dimensions of human development. He showed that there are other significant dimensions of factical-bodily existence that have remained unexplored by psychoanalysis, but which nonetheless illuminate child development. He also showed that there are significant dimensions of ego development (i.e., the fallen aspect) that have not been fully articulated by Erikson. Finally, Knowles brought the existential dimension of human existence into the Eriksonian developmental framework.

Phenomenology of Embodied Facticity as a Developmental Progression

Knowles's contribution to the factical-bodily dimension consisted of a phenomenological description of how the child lives his or her body during particular stages of development. His descriptions of embodiment extend to the fourth analytic stage. The first of these, horizontality, refers to the fact that the child is in a reclined position during the earliest portion of his or her life (1986, 23). Since he or she cannot walk or stand or even sit up independently, the child is in what Knowles referred to as a prone position. This is meant to highlight the major psychosocial themes of infant life, especially the child's limited repertoire of behavior, his or her vulnerability, and the anxiety that accompanies this vulnerability. With limited vision, both in the sense of not possessing 20/20 vision and in the sense of having limited mobility, the child is in a situation where the appearance of the mother's face is of prime importance. The child can scan the environment and search for the mother. However, the mother must be willing to show herself and do so with affection and welcoming. When done consistently, the mother's warm, inviting appearance within the child's limited field of vision contributes to his or her ability to manage feelings such as fear and anxiety. In other words, he or she is assisted in the task of developing emotional stability in a life and death situation. In the absence of care, the consequence is death. The absence of a mother's caring, welcoming appearance means an absence of hope for future growth and development.

During the second stage of development, embodiment gives rise to the phenomenon of "taking a stand" (Knowles 1986, 50). It is at the second stage that mothers begin to use the phrase "the terrible twos." Such a phrase is indicative of the fact that the child is now attempting to have some say in what happens to him or her in day-to-day life, especially in the form of protests against the mother's wishes. The burgeoning desire to enforce his or her will goes hand in hand with the experience of standing up on two legs, which occurs during this time. Standing up and facing the world provides an enhanced feeling of distance and distinction from everything and everyone in the surrounding world. Being upright and "at" the world in this way provides the impetus for the objectification of the world, which can ultimately bring about a more complex and insightful relationship with the world than what is possible in the animal kingdom. Moreover, being face-to-face with others increases the level of complexity and intimacy possible in interpersonal relations as well. The child can now have a "face off" with mother, so to speak. Later in development, the face-to-face relationship will bring about issues of responsibility, accountability, ethics, and so on. For now, however, the issue is a primitive sense of empowerment. The child must come to perceive that he or she is a significant subjectivity whose volition matters in the world.

The third stage of development is a time when the child is experiencing a vastly improved sense of movement and deliberate action. Mental and physical abilities are now refined to the point where the child is planning and carrying out activities that are the product of his or her own imagination. Will is not as tied to acts of defiance and the child is "on the move," as it were. Knowles noted that being on-the-move in psychoanalytic circles has traditionally meant being "on the make" in the sense of interest in psychosexual aims. However, from a broader view, improved mobility during this stage means that the child is increasingly developing a sense of the "social body" (1986, 78). Being a member of any culture entails a slow but sure process of learning the social customs, norms, mores, and values that are attached to certain forms of behavior. Some of these social customs are taught, such as the impoliteness of pointing or staring. However, many of these are not learned through explicit instruction, but developed over time through direct social contact, like how to behave in an elevator, for example.

It is in and through the fourth stage of development that a child approaches puberty and the development of an adult body. While the analytic descriptions of adult embodiedness, therefore, can be seen as more or less adequate, the nature of embodiment during the latency stage is still left wanting. For Knowles, embodiment at this stage means developing a sense that the body is an adequate instrument for engaging in work and play (1986, 105–106). During this time, it is not enough to know that movement is possible. The child is now in search of a sense that he or she can do some things especially well. He or she is in search of a sense of mastery over tasks. If developed, this fundamental sense of kinesthetic competence will be evident in skillful activity unhampered by self-consciousness.

Ego Development Outside of Analytic Strictures

For each stage of development, Erik Erikson brought up critical issues relating to ego development that must be resolved in order for the child to continue moving in the direction of healthy development. At the same time, Erikson stayed close to traditional Freudian themes in his articulation of the significance of each ego issue. Just as Erikson expanded on Freud's theory, Knowles expanded on Erikson's descriptions of ego development. However, Knowles's use of the term *ego* and his descriptions of ego development at each stage do not remain firmly attached to psychoanalytic metapsychology and its notion of the "psychic apparatus."

Knowles noted that he used much of Erikson's language, but that the ego in more common, contemporary usage does not have to imply the psychology of the mental apparatus associated with psychoanalysis. The ego is a term that is loosely used to refer to identity or self, especially within cognitive psychology. The more common usage of term *ego* (and thus the typical notion of selfhood in much of psychology) identifies the person with technical, functional, managerial qualities. Knowles spoke of such qualities in terms of rationality, calculation, and strategic thinking (1986, 28). However, as a fallen mode of being, the ego dimension also implies various forms of passivity as well.

These were not a part of Erikson's scheme. For Erikson, the managerial ego functions that were vital at each stage were consistency and predictability, self-control, direction, identification one's physical and mental abilities, and devotion. Knowles takes Erikson's lead and refers to the general ego issues of each stage in the following slightly modified way: consistency and predictability, control, direction, method and technique, constancy. Moreover, Knowles shows how these general ego issues can manifest themselves in more pronounced active and passive ways in day-to-day life (i.e., in our "everydayness").

As is obvious, most of the terms used by Erikson and Knowles are identical. Moreover, there is much overlap in their use of these terms, as Erikson tended to stretch his understanding of the ego beyond what is typical for psychoanalytic psychology (Knowles 1986, 6). During the first stage, the infant picks up on the consistent, reliable care of the mother. This puts him or her in a position where he or she is relaxed and open to reality and can begin to perceive regularities in the surrounding physical world. He or she learns to look for and eventually habitually expect regularity, consistency, predictability in life in general. Hence, radical change and upheaval tend to be experienced as upsetting or stressful even in adulthood (28). The more active, controlling ego manifestation of consistency is fear (45). Rather than being relaxed, open, and courageous in the face of vulnerability or the unknown, one may live in the ego mode of being tense, anxious, and worried as a form of pseudocontrol over one's predicament. When this nonhopeful, nonopen mode of active ego involvement fails, the alternative is the passive manifestation of fantasy. In Knowles words:

> When I am afraid, I experience a tightening of the body, an increased alertness to the situation, and my interpretation of the situation, if not completely wrong, is narrowed. Since I can't sustain such an attitude of tightness and alertness for long, I may daydream or fantasize about the situation and surrender myself to the fantasy in a tension-free irresponsibility. In both instances, the way I am to the future shapes my present and my past. In fearing the future, I narrow not only my future but my past, remembering only fearful events, and in the present I am immobilized. (46)

Knowles moves away from Erikson's focus on self-control at the second stage to the idea of control in general. *Control* as an ego quality signifies manipulation, exerting force, being in command of situations. It is not quite inspired action, but instead entails applying conscious, calculative, deliberate effort to reach goals. Control is a cognitive orientation toward the world that includes both self-control and control over others and things (Knowles 1986, 56). Knowles called the more extreme manifestation of control willfulness (71). Willfulness is not to be confused with genuine willing, which is a more open stance toward the world that allows for receptivity. Willfulness is a mode of being in which there is a rigorous effort to manufacture the energy needed to accomplish tasks. Willfulness is not inspired and mobilized into action due to the call of something or someone of value in the world, but by active effort to "do," to "overcome," even if it means being aggressive or violent. Willfulness is the result of pep talks and "psyching oneself up" (72). The opposite of willfulness is wishing. When one's self-manufactured energy runs out, the result is an exhausted, passive condition of wishing one's goals were accomplished (72).

Direction is a term that is used by Knowles to denote very much the same things that Erikson meant by the term for the third stage. The child internalizes an understanding of the processes involved in directing behavior toward productive aims. The child perceives the value of maintaining action in the services of creative goals. However, the directing is not the creating itself. It is not the imaginative thrust of the child's motivation, only a steering wheel of sorts, so to speak. Nonetheless, direction, like all the ego qualities, is needed for healthy development (Knowles 1986, 84). Knowles considered boredom to be the magnified version of direction (96). In a state of boredom, one mistakenly feels as if he or she must supply all of the energy needed to initiate and maintain behavior due to a lack of worldly inspiration. In the state of boredom, what is covered over is the fact of begin a boring person. The individual looks at his or her situation, finds it to be of no help in terms of achieving a level of excitation or arousal, and resigns to the notion that becoming interested or energized is not feasible at that time. One is not, therefore, open to situations in such a way as to discover something new, fresh, or inspiring. Boredom, in this light, is almost a form of stubbornness. The reverse ego mode is enthusiasm (97). In a state of enthusiasm, the person is all-too-quick to inspiration, with little of substance from the world around. Enthusiasm is a sudden blast of pseudo-inspiration that runs is course fast. Being enthusiastic is a normal phenomenon that is nonetheless no substitute for genuine imagination and creativity.

Method and *technique* are the terms that Knowles used to describe the ego quality of the fourth stage. According to Knowles, in order to for a person to be industrious, he or she must develop a certain level of methodological understanding and technical skillfulness for whatever task is being pursued. Method and technique are what individuals master when they are first beginning to learn a task, whether it be swinging a bat or trying one's hand at counseling, for example. At a certain point the methodological and technological talents that one adopts are transcended, integrated into a non-self-conscious engagement with the task at hand. Nonetheless, method and technique are necessary beginning requirements for the mastery of skills and are thus important developmental achievements (Knowles 1986, 108). At one extreme of everyday, fallen behavior, individuals can be described as living out a technological mode. In the technological mode, the person is quite taken by method and technique. Such preoccupation manifests itself in a managerial, calcultative attitude toward projects with no real identification with the task at hand. One can think of a people as using their technical skills by "going thorough the motions" in this regard. On the other extreme are the anti-technological individuals who shy away from labor and the process of developing skills. (120). Such individuals would sooner have others take care of certain needs rather than enhance their own abilities and get their own hands dirty, so to speak.

Constancy is the ego issue of the fifth stage and the counterpart to Erikson's notion of devotion. Constancy refers to being regular, "on schedule," steady, dependable, and faithful. This does not imply a deep, impassioned sense of loyalty on the part of the person, just an unwavering stability of action (Knowles, 1986, 147). Like the other fallen modes of relating to the world, constancy is a cognitive quality. The pronounced forms of constancy in everyday life are fanaticism and faintheartedness (152). The fanatic soothes his or her need for constancy by becoming identified with a group or movement that provides a ready-made identity. Groups such as "dead heads," the KKK, gangs, cults, and the like all provide a relatively clear set of instructions about how to behave. The opposing tendency is to forgo the process of developing an identity and the risks involved therein by never really pursuing life goals with conviction and determination (153). By remaining faint-hearted, the individual is shying away from the difficult process of growing up, with all of the perseverance, accountability, and self-sacrifice that becoming an adult entails. All of the ego modes as articulated by Knowles are detailed in Table 5.2 below.

Table 5.2
Knowles's Ego Issues for Each Stage and Additional Ego Manifestations

General Ego Issue	More Active Attempt to Control One's General Orientation to World	Essentially Passive Orientation to World
Consistency And Predictability	Fear	Fantasy
Control	Willfulness	Wishing
Direction	Boredom	Enthusiasm
Method and Technique Constancy	Technological Mode Fanaticism	Anti-Technological Mode Faintheartedness

Phenomenology of Self-Development

As a humanistic approach to child development, Knowles's most important contribution to developmental theory is the inclusion of the existential or self-dimension. According to Knowles, existentiality, or the uniquely human dimension, provides the integrating theme of each stage (1986, 13). Another way of saying this is that the self is the integrator of the personality. Knowles called the self the "core" of personality (26). In other words, the term *self* is used to describe the person when he or she has integrated the bodily and ego dimensions (active and passive) of existence into a relaxed, resilient orientation toward future growth and development. Self-modes are thus modes of perception, not physical states, moods, or cognitive processes (29). For Knowles, selfhood is a holistic developmental concept. From the perspective of selfhood, mind, body, and world are not perceived as three separate entities, nor are past, present, and future. The person, in those infrequent times where he or she has risen above the average everyday ego modes, displays self-qualities when un-self-consciously living in and through past, present, and future with-others-alongside-things. The diagram in Figure 5.1 illustrates the nature of the self according to Knowles.

According to Knowles, Erikson alluded to the existential dimension when he spoke of certain strengths derived from a successful resolution at each stage. In particular, Erikson referred to hope, will, purpose, skill, and fidelity (1961). However, Erikson presented these as afterthoughts or positive by-products of a successful resolution of each stage's ego crisis. For Knowles, these strengths were the most human and healthy outcomes of the developmental stages. Thus, these strengths provide a more solid basis for self and identity than Erikson's ego qualities. As he put it, "I would submit that these experiences are the most central for the various developmental stages and that the bodily, rational, and social aspects accompanying them are less central, although necessary" (1986, 5). As an existential thinker, Knowles admonished that the goal of development is not merely normality. Normality belongs to the realm of ego development. Rather, the goal of development is a growth orientation, a forward moving evolution toward maturity and personal fulfillment. This is the domain of health and self-development.

Although Knowles chose to emphasize the strengths that Erikson spoke of, however, Knowles did modify the way they first appeared in Erikson's work. For Knowles, the strengths are as follows: hope, will, imagination, competence, and fidelity. The implication of this aspect of Knowles's approach is that the nature of a difficulty at any stage in development is broadened to include the critical importance of existential concerns. In contrast to Erikson's approach, the focus of attention no longer remains on our fallen aspects. A failure to progress to a new stage of development due to some kind of psychological maltreatment or other environmental deficiency is more than a failure to develop an ego quality, but ultimately a crisis of hope, will, and so on. For Knowles, these are the qualities that foster the integration of one's factical and fallen aspects into a relaxed openness to the future. Psychological suffering arises due to a constriction of this openness.

Figure 5.1 Representation of the Self According to Knowles

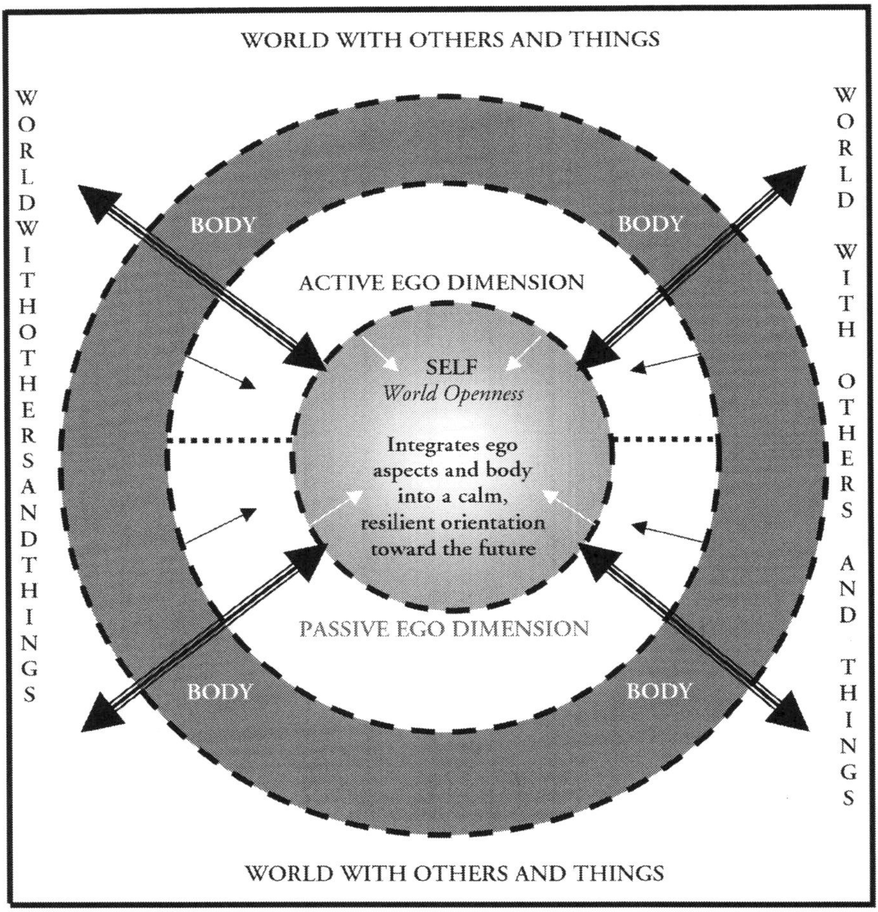

```
                    WORLD WITH OTHERS AND THINGS

W                                                                    W
O                                                                    O
R                                                                    R
L           BODY                            BODY                     L
D                                                                    D
W                                                                    W
I              ACTIVE EGO DIMENSION                                  I
T                                                                    T
H                                                                    H
                       SELF
O                   World Openness                                   O
T                                                                    T
H                    Integrates ego                                  H
E                    aspects and body                                E
R                    into a calm,                                    R
S                    resilient orientation                           S
                     toward the future
A                                                                    A
N              PASSIVE EGO DIMENSION                                 N
D                                                                    D
T           BODY                            BODY                     T
H                                                                    H
I                                                                    I
N                                                                    N
G                                                                    G
S                                                                    S

                    WORLD WITH OTHERS AND THINGS
```

Before reviewing the self-qualities of each stage it is important to note that in Knowles's view, the particular struggles of each stage are never simply left behind with the advent of new stages (1986, 54). Children continually deal with each developmental task during future stages in the context of new opportunities for growth (122–123). At the same time, this does not imply that Knowles is a historical determinist. In other words, the past does not affect the present in a simple, linear way. As an existential-phenomenologist, Knowles's view of time was less causal and natural scientific than both Freud and Erikson. For Knowles, the temporal focus of the self (and of self-development) is the future (12). Past stages set a context for future development and they are contextualized by that development as well. In other words, the future has a primacy in terms of perception in that each developmental struggle is remembered and appropriated within the context of the child's orientation toward the future (92). Thus, from the perspective of self-development, the child is forward moving and future focused, but not at all ahistorical. Past and future co-determine one another, with the primary focus of self-development being the child's orientation toward his or her future.

Hope is the self-quality to be developed at the first stage. Above and beyond the issues of feeding and predicting, the issue of trust was introduced by Erikson. For Knowles, the kind of trust that characterizes self-development is the ability to trust in others and one's future while simultaneously being unable to predict exactly what the future will bring. This kind of trusting is hoping (Knowles 1986, 31). Hope is not a physical characteristic, a mood or feeling, or even a cognitive process, though all of these aspects of human functioning are involved in hoping. Physical calm and the mental assessment of one's situation are necessary, but hope is at all stages a quality of the person which enables world openness despite one's vulnerability and inability to predict and control one's fate. Hope is thus a fundamental or primordial openness to the world and the future at the core of selfhood.

Will is the self-quality to be developed at stage two. Genuine will is distinguished from the sustained effort of control and willfulness as well as the passive state of wishing. Like all the self-qualities, will is neither a primarily active nor passive orientation toward the world, but rather a state of openness that allows for active effort or receptivity as needed. Will is a primordial sense of empowerment, a basic and firm sense of being able that is the vital directing energy for the child's intentions (Knowles 1986, 60). A child who has developed will has moved beyond self-government (i.e., autonomy) to a state of being where he or she experiences himself or herself as a significant and potent subjectivity. One may think of will by its other name, freewill, to see its importance for a humanistic theory of development. According Knowles's reading of Erikson, it is at the second stage of development that freedom of the will becomes a significant factor in the development of a child.

At the third stage, the self-quality to be developed is imagination. While Erikson spoke of the importance of developing initiative, Knowles noted that envisioning and carrying out tasks is something that is done in an imaginative way in healthy circumstances. The healthy child is not content with initiating and directing activities. Action is also the product of the creative mind. This product, as inspired by the imagination, is something that the child identifies with and considers meaningful. Imagination is more than learning, intelligence, and action; it is an inspired, creative integration of the child's physical and mental abilities. The imaginative, creative impulse of the healthy child projects him or her toward future opportunities for experiencing, learning, and growing (Knowles 1986, 86).

To complement the ego quality of industry, Knowles referred to competence as the self-quality to be developed at the fourth stage. Aside from being industrious, a healthy child experiences moments when diligent involvement with tasks is unself-conscious and exceptionally energized. Teachers talk about being "on" in their lectures, athletes speak of being "in the zone," and these are concrete manifestations of competence. It is a state of being wherein the person is open to the world, so much so that he or she is closely identified with the task and experiences no disruptive self-consciousness or nervous preoccupation with success or failure. The competent person feels at home in his or her body and derives a feeling of enjoyment and vitality in tasks. The body is perceived as reliable and capable of achieving future goals and accomplishments (Knowles 1986, 113).

Fidelity is the self-quality to be developed at the fifth stage. Building upon the strengths of the prior stages, the healthy adolescent does more than just remain constant. While constancy and regularity are advancements in the direction of fidelity, they are not sufficient to constitute the full development of fidelity. According to Knowles, there are several interrelated aspects to fidelity (1986, 150–151). Fidelity requires a personal presence to the project or relationship that is the object of one's dedication. This distinguishes fidelity from constancy. One's dedication comes about spontaneously, as a result of genuine inspiration and care, not mechanically, as if "going through the motions." The person hears the call to commit oneself. This invitation to commitment is met by the making of commitment, the giving of one's word. Fidelity is finally achieved with the keeping of that commitment, keeping one's word. It is only through the completion of this process (i.e., the keeping of commitment) that a person can truly come to understand who he or she is, the content of his or her character.

Deviations from Healthy Development

Aside from bringing the existential dimension of child development into focus, Knowles expanded upon the kinds of pathology that could occur due to difficulties developing each self-quality. Again, a failure to progress to a new stage of development due to some kind of psychological maltreatment or other environmental deficiency is more than a failure to develop an ego quality; it is a failure of self-development. Knowles characterized the problems associated with each stage of development as fallen or factical, depending on the characteristics of the suffering involved.

According to Knowles, truly pathological consequences (i.e., in the sense of neurotic or psychotic disorders) due to failures along the developmental path are only related to the first three stages of development. For Knowles, once the child has developed the fundamental strengths of hope, will, and imagination, the development of fallen or factical pathologies is no longer likely. The forms of fallen pathology associated with the first three stages are paranoia, compulsive and impulsive character, and hysteria and neurotic depression respectively. The factical pathologies associated with these stages are schizophrenia and advanced addiction, psychotic compulsion, and psychotic depression respectively. The chart in Table 5.3 below correlates each stage of self-development with the pathological fallen and factical modes of that stage.

Table 5.3
Pathological Deviations from Healthy Self-Development According to Knowles

Existential/Self Issue	Potential Pathological Fallen Manifestations	Potential Factical Pathological Manifestations
Hope	Paranoia	Schizophrenia Advanced Addiction
Will	Compulsive Character Impulsive Character	Psychotic Compulsion
Imagination	Hysteria And Depression	Psychotic Depression

Knowles spoke of paranoia as a fallen manifestation of a failure of hope due to the paranoid person's preoccupation with consistency. For the paranoid person, inquiring into the activities of others and the checking up on them to predict their behavior is consonant with the ego qualities of the first stage (predictability and fear). The person, suffering from embattled hope, compensates with hyper-vigilance (Knowles 1986, 43). A similar situation is found in compulsion relating to the second stage. The same lack of openness, preoccupation with detail, lack of relaxation, lack of inspiration, and lack of spontaneity permeate both styles of behavior. However, in compulsion, the focus is on the checking out and ordering things in line with the ego issue of control (66).

The other fallen pathology of the second stage of development, impulsive character, represents the opposing, more passive deficiency of the will (66). In this instance, there is a striking absence of will, as seen in the impulsive person's inability to contain urges, wishes, and desires. The individual finds himself or herself at a loss when it comes to controlling behavior.

At the third stage, hysteria and depressive neuroses are the fallen deficiencies of imagination (93). The hysteric character type is impressionistic and impressionable, not moved by genuine will and authentic creative desires. He or she becomes preoccupied with whatever whim appears from moment to moment. Fantasy is the primary orientation toward the world and takes precedence over imaginatively projecting oneself toward a realistic future. Depressive neurosis, by contrast, is an affliction that makes the moment to moment existence of the person in the present feel like an endless monotony. The present weighs heavy on the person and the future fades to the background of experience. The ego is seen as having to supply all of the energy needed to propel the person into inspired, creative action. As such, the call of inspiration from the world is lost and the notion of spontaneous activity and enjoyment is cannot be envisioned. The individual feels continually overwhelmed and sluggish in the face of the tasks of the day.

Like all factical disorders, schizophrenia and advanced addiction involve a focus on the past and the body (1986, 38, 41). In instances of infantile schizophrenia and schizophrenia in general, one notices a pronounced difficulty living in one's body. As a result, self-mutilation may occur. Moreover, many schizophrenic individuals experience their bodies as uncomfortably animal-like or machine-like. The strong emphasis on the past goes hand in hand with the sheer inability to openly project oneself toward a hopeful future. A preoccupation with the past is evident in the person's desperate attempts to maintain a sense of security, overriding any ability to be fully present to anything or anyone. Hence, the paranoia of paranoid schizophrenia is more severe than that which is found in paranoid character. The individual in the throes of advanced addiction is also at odds with his or her body in that physiological needs take precedence in his or her life (41). There is a similar inability to be in the present as having or not having the chemicals to which one is addicted is the overriding focus of behavior. In psychotic compulsion, which is more severe than compulsive neurosis, the person's will is so embattled that attempts to over compensate with control dominates all behavior (64). Rituals are set in stone, and in the most severe cases, individuals cannot complete these rituals. They get stuck in the ritual, with no recourse to being present to anything or anyone else. The emphasis on the body is evident on the compulsive's obsession with cleanliness. In psychotic depression, the depressed person cannot imagine a future that is enjoyable and fulfilling (89). The future is more radically blocked than in depressive neurosis, and the individual remains preoccupied with a guilty past. The focus on the body is seen in the feeling of lethargy and general lack of energizing vitality.

In Summary: Strengths of Knowles's Approach and Critical Remarks

Richard Knowles built a very complex, humanistic system of interpretation for understanding child development. A major strength of Knowles's theory is that it provides a place for the future in development. The existential/self dimension of development is characterized as an orientation toward the future, meaning that the child is developing various ways of being open to possibilities for new experience and growth (i.e., via hoping, willing, imagining, and so on). By using the works of Freud, Erikson, and Heidegger, Knowles characterized child development as a multifaceted process of evolution involving the factical, fallen, and existential dimensions of existence. This framework is depicted in Figure 5.2 below.

Figure 5.2 Schematic of Knowles's Existential-Analytic Developmental Theory

	STAGE 1	STAGE 2	STAGE 3	STAGE 4	STAGE 5
EXISTENTIAL	*Hope*	*Will*	*Imagination*	*Competence*	*Fidelity*
	Trust	Autonomy	Initiative	Industry	Identity
	Consistency And Predictability	Control	Direction	Method and Technique	Constancy
FALLEN					
	Laying Down	Standing	Being on the Move	Skillful Activity	Reproductive Maturity
FACTICAL	Oral	Anal	Phallic	Latency	Genital

Knowles's theory of development, though stage-like, does not propose a developmental determinism. The past does not determine future development in a linear, causal way. It is for this reason that the lines demarcating each stage are broken lines. The multidirectional arrows further signify the two-way traffic between the stages. In Knowles's words, "Because development is a cycle or a growing spiral rather than a straight line, and because we understand time as lived rather than as clock time, the issues reappear in later crises also" (1986, 54). Developmental experiences are a source of strengths and limitations that are continually worked on throughout the lifespan. The developmental tasks that took center stage at earlier developmental phases are brought into the context of the challenges of each new stage and continue to be worked on in new forms (i.e., with new content) (54). Issues of the past, in Knowles's view, are never merely left in the past, but continue to be reworked in progressively refined and mature ways when the child's development is future-focused, forward moving, and healthy. Correlatively, the degree to which he or she is called forward via the development of self-qualities co-determines how the issues of these past stages are viewed and dealt with. In healthy circumstances, the self-qualities developed at each stage (i.e., the existential aspect of the person) integrate the factical and fallen dimensions laid out by Freud, Erikson, and Knowles into a relaxed, resilient openness to the world, others, and the future. Where the child's orientation toward the future becomes embattled or constricted, the present and past take on varying degrees of negative significance and psychological suffering ensues. "Negative significance" in this context means that the child's psychological development is no longer experienced within optimal conditions for health and fulfillment. In milder instances, common everyday-fallen experiences such as fear or boredom may result. In more severe instances, neurotic-fallen developments such as compulsive character or depressive neurosis manifest. In the most severe cases, factical disorders arise, such as psychosis, where the growing person's freedom is the most constricted and emotional pain is the most pronounced.

Knowles's use of Erikson's developmental ideas is at once a strength of Knowles's model and a limitation of it. Using psychoanalytic theory as a springboard limited the scope of Knowles's theory in that his observations remained tied to Erikson's stage-ordered approach throughout his description of development. Thus, Knowles may have missed aspects of child development that might be seen outside of the stage-like progression laid out by Freud and Erikson or outside of stage theory altogether. Nonetheless, Knowles successfully used Freud and Erikson to produce an insightful, existential view of child development.

It is unfortunate that Knowles's reinterpretation of Erikson provided no new insights into the nature of parenting or pedagogy. Knowles rarely discussed parenting skills and their relation to developmental outcomes. To be sure, he may have avoided such discussions to protect his work from the charge of developmental determinism. However, it seems more likely that the relative lack of material on parenting was due to his reliance on Erikson's work. Knowles never addressed the issue of good parenting or inadequate parenting from a fresh, new perspective. Rather, he assumed that Erikson's thoughts on the nature of parenting were adequate and assumed that the reader was already familiar with the Eriksonian perspective. This is not to imply that Erikson's view of parenting was somehow fundamentally flawed. To the contrary, his notion of what constituted good parenting is quite consonant with a humanistic point of view. The following quote illustrates the humanistic tone of Erikson's perspective: "Parents must not only have certain ways of guiding by prohibition and permission; they must also be able to represent to the child a deep, an almost somatic conviction that there is a meaning to what they are doing" (1963, 249). Still, Knowles brought nothing new to this critical aspect of developmental theory from the perspective of existential-phenomenology.

Perhaps the greatest shortcoming of Knowles's work is its strict interpretation of the present as an ego or fallen mode of existence. Knowles never discussed the role of the present in positive, growth-promoting terms (e.g., the "here-and-now"). A different interpretation of the present will be presented in future chapters. For now, it will suffice to note that Knowles made a positive contribution to child psychology by allowing a place for the future in developmental theory.

In addition to including a place for the role of the future in development, Knowles made a major contribution to child psychology by providing a detailed description of selfhood from an existential-developmental perspective. Knowles was careful to never describe the self in ambiguous Cartesian terms. Instead, the self is simply a begin-in-the-world-with-others-alongside-thing, or more simply, world-openness. The self, as the "core" of the person, carries out its role as integrator of the personality through the development of hope, will, imagination, competence, and fidelity. These qualities, especially the first three, are the characteristics of the self up to and including adolescence.

KEY TERMS AND CONCEPTS

Advanced addiction
Anti-technological mode
Autonomy versus shame and doubt
Basic trust versus basic mistrust
Being on-the-move
Boredom
Care structure
Compulsive character
Consistency

Constancy
Control
Depression
Direction
Ego crisis
Ego development outside of analytic strictures
Ego psychology
Ego qualities
Embodied facticity
Enthusiasm
Existentiality
Existential-phenomenology
Facticity
Faintheartedness
Fallenness
Fanaticism
Fantasy
Fear
Freudian stages of development
Hope
Horizontality
Hysteria
Identity vs. role confusion
Imagination
Impulsive character
Industry versus inferiority
Initiative versus guilt
Libidinal satisfaction
Method and technique
Oedipal dream
Paranoia
Phenomenology of self-development
Psychoanalysis
Psychological strengths
Psychotic compulsion
Psychotic depression
Puberty
Schizophrenia
Self

Self-consciousness
Stage of development
Taking a stand
Technological mode
Will
Willfulness
Will-to-pleasure
Wishing

CHAPTER 6

DANIEL STERN'S ANALYTIC-DEVELOPMENTAL SELF-THEORY

Stern's Theory and Existential-Humanism

Before bringing the developmental self-theory portion of this book to a close, a final theory of self-development needs to be mentioned: Daniel Stern's analytic-developmental theory. Stern's theory is the most modern of the theories covered thus far. His approach to development is the product of self-oriented psychoanalysis (e.g., Winnicott and Kohut) and direct observations of infants from developmental psychology. By using findings from developmental research, Stern sought to free analytic-developmental theory from its skewed focus on clinical issues (e.g., trust, separation-individuation, guilt, and so forth). At the same time, Stern maintained that empirical research in the area of developmental psychology stood to gain just as much from psychoanalysis' emphasis on understanding how early experience is organized and structured (1985, 4). It is for this reason that Stern chose to use the self as the central theme of his developmental framework (5). For Stern, understanding the nature of the self means illuminating how children "bring together separate sounds, movements, touches, sights, and feelings to form a whole person" (3).

According to Stern, infants tend to develop in "quantum leaps" (1985, 8). Within months, infants make such developmental progress that they look and act qualitatively different. These qualitative shifts in the way the child looks and acts in relation to others are what Stern uses to anchor his self-theory. Thus, Stern held that the self "serves as the primary subjective perspective that organizes social experience" (11). Each new way of being in relation to others signals a new sense of self that has developed. Each new way of being is a new way that the child has learned to integrate his or her various mental and physical skills and abilities in the service of relating to the world.

Like Winnicott, Stern's focus was on early infancy, especially the preverbal period. While this time of life is not typically thought of in terms of selfhood, Stern insisted that there are preverbal senses of self that precede the verbal sense of the self of later development. He held that there is an "organizing subjective experience" that is "the preverbal, existential counterpart of the objectifiable, self-reflective, verbalizable self" (1985, 7). In his words:

> There is the sense of self that is a single, distinct, integrated body; there is the agent of actions, the experiencer of feelings, the maker of intentions, the architect of plans, the transposer of experience into language, the communicator and sharer of personal knowledge. Most often these senses of self reside out of awareness, like breathing, but they can be brought to and held in consciousness. We instinctively process our experiences in such a way that they appear to belong to some kind of unique subjective organization that we commonly call the sense of self. (5–6)

Stern's reliance of the concept of selfhood gave his theory a holistic quality that is consonant with an existential-humanistic view of development. His discussions of developmental progress focus on what he called the child's "presence" to others and his or her social "feel," which he insisted was "more than the sum of … acquired behaviors and capacities" (8). Each of Stern's four "senses of self" will be outlined below. This is followed by some critical remarks regarding his theory and its relationship to other self-styled approaches to development.

Four Senses of Self

A sense of emergent self.

While developmental theorists have traditionally viewed the child's earliest experience as disorganized and lacking in distinctions between self and other, Stern disagreed. For Stern, the first two months of a child's life are characterized by an increasingly sophisticated sense of mental organization. Rather than a confused state of undifferentiation, Stern saw the young infant as developing a feeling of relatedness to the world and others. The sense of emergent self is a time in infancy when mental organization as a means of relating to the world is in the process of forming (Stern 1985, 38). The formation of self and other in terms of mental organization occurs via the child's searching for structural invariants in his or her experience. The child naturally searches for aspects of his or her experiences of self and other that tend to be present with enough regularity that they are looked upon as primary characteristics of these phenomena (42). These highly regular characteristics thereby become mentally prominent and relatively distinct from the more fleeting secondary characteristics of self and other.

According to Stern, a child displays his or her unique individuality very early in life by the particular way that sensory and motor experience are integrated (1985, 63). Many distinct experiences of oneself moving and sensing are brought together over time to form an increasingly holistic experience of self. When the feeling of self is unified enough to constitute a strong reference point from which to perceive others and interact with them, then the child has developed a core self (46). For the first two months, however, the child is building larger and larger partial organizations of sensorimotor experience (i.e., the self as it is emerging) (45). The integrating efforts of the emergent self are made possible due to several factors. First, affect and cognition are not experienced by the child as indistinct (42).

The infant's perception and knowledge of the world is thoroughly emotional rather than conceptual. Far from maintaining a dualism of thought and feeling, Stern held that the child's mind is innately holistic, tending toward a unification of its various capacities. Whatever knowledge the child has of his or her mother, for example, is intimately connected to the affect evoked from past interactions with mother. Second, children have an innate ability to transfer perceptual information across sensory modalities (48). Stern noted that even as infants, humans have a mysterious ability to abstract shapes, intensities, and temporal patterns from the world in one perceptual system and re-present them in another system (51). In his words, infants are "predesigned to forge certain integrations" (52). For instance, an infant has an innate capacity to form a mental connection or perceptual unity between the look of a smooth nipple and how it ought to feel in his or her mouth.

Finally, infants are capable of experiencing vitality affects, which are forms of feeling or styles of emoting (54). In other words, there is always a specific manner in which all emotions, thoughts, and behaviors are felt to come into being. For instance, a person might become agitated to anger slowly over time or experience a "sudden rush" of strong, vile hatred. An idea can be generated slowly over time and much rumination, it might be a "fleeting" thought, or it might come as an "intense moment" of insight. For the infant to be able to experience the particular way in which he or she is sad, joyful, or any other emotion furnishes him or her with the broader array of perceptual data relating to the specific nature of his or her relations with the world and others.

A sense of core self.

Stern characterized the second to the seventh month of life as the time of core self-development. During this time, Stern noted that children appear more wholly integrated and experience themselves as coherent bodies distinct from others (1985, 69–70). Moreover, the child is able to consolidate "core others" by identifying experiential invariants within the exaggerated movements and vocalizations typically made by caretakers (i.e., *parentese*) (74–75). Thus, Stern did not view the infant as existing in a symbiotic relationship with the mother. Instead, he insisted that children between two and seven months consolidate a sense of self that is felt to be a separate, cohesive, bounded, physical unit with a sense of intent, agency, personal affectivity, and continuity in time (26).

According to Stern, the sense of core self is characterized by coherence, self-agency, affectivity, and history. Coherence denotes the child's feeling of having a physical form in space (Stern 1985, 87). Coherence further denotes the fact that the infant feels himself or herself to be in only one place at a time, a unity of spatial locus (82). Coherence also refers to the child's sense of coherent movement and self-synchrony (i.e., the fact that all of his or her individual parts tend to move at roughly the same time and thus belong together) (83). Finally, the child experiences coherence via the matching of feelings of intensity in different parts of the body to different states of emotion, pain, pleasure, and so on. (87).

The infant's sense of self-agency refers to the child's sense of volition. Self-agency means that the infant has developed a strong impression that he or she can have an impact on others and the world through movement and deliberate intention. The child has developed a sense of cause and effect that invites participation (Stern 1985, 81).

The infant's affectivity facilitates the feeling of unity due to the fact that each time the child experiences a certain emotion, there are entire constellations of physiological changes that consistently reappear (Stern, 1985, 89). This continual reappearance imbues the child with a feeling of physiological predictability, stability, and consistency over time.

For the infant to have a feeling of oneness and identity over time, the child must have a feeling of history. To speak of the child's history is to refer to the issue of memory (Stern 1985, 90). This final feature of the child's now core self is the key to his or her integration of self-invariants and the consolidation of various other features of experience (94). Through memory, the child is able to identify both experiential invariants across situations and the general kinds of interactions that typify his or her relations with significant others in his or her social milieu.

A sense of subjective self.

In the seventh to the fifteenth month of a child's life, Stern spoke of the sense of subjective self. This sense of self is more sophisticated in that the child's relations with others have become more complex. At this time, the infant develops a sense that he or she has a "private" mind. This is the most primitive developmental beginning of a "theory of mind." The child starts to feel that he or she can conceal feelings and intensions or share them. In essence, the child has now become a more full-fledged participant in affective attunement, sharing empathic states with others (Stern 1985, 139).

In Stern's view, this time period is devoted to both individuation and to establishing an intersubjective union with others (1985, 10). The child is not only becoming more autonomous, but he or she is repeatedly seeking to share a focus of attention with the mother (129). The child attributes intentions and motives to others, attributes the states of feeling to others, and senses whether or not they are congruent with his or her own feelings (27). Knowing that her child is pursuing a bond, the (normal) mother uses the child's burgeoning affect attunement to establish attachment security (142). The child is attuned to his or her mother in and through the various modalities of perception. Data can be received through one modality, such as the gentle, smooth sound of a mother's humming, and integrated with data from another modality, such as the gentle, smooth strokes that the mother applies to the child's skin (152). In this way, the child learns about the various dispositions and emotional intensities that he or she is capable of, setting the stage for imitation and deferred imitation (158).

Emergence of the verbal self.

From the fifteenth to the eighteenth month, the final sense of self comes into existence: the sense of verbal self. During this time, most children have become symbol users, representing their experiential world in a system of sounds and signs, held together in a particular grammar. Language provides the child with a symbolic storehouse for knowledge which can be used for examining experiences in self-reflection or communicating the meaning of those experiences to others (Stern 1985, 11, 162). Language facilitates the co-construction of meanings with others, which includes the construction of the child's own life narrative (162). With the advent of symbol usage, the child is now capable of symbolic forms of play (163). In addition, he or she develops better long-term memory and recall (164).

Among the more important skills derived from the use of language is the ability to reflect upon oneself and one's place in the world. The child is now capable of making his or her self the object of reflection (Stern 1985, 165). He or she can transcend immediate experience and open up to the world of possibilities. As Stern put it, "Interpersonal interaction can now involve past memories, present realities, and expectations of the future based solely on the past" (167). At the same time, however, Stern warned that language can be used to narrate or objectify, meaning that language opens up the potential for the child to misrepresent his or her experience (174). As he put it, language can "drive a wedge" between the personal and abstract (163). The problem with concept formation, in Stern's view, is that abstract classifications and categories can take mental precedence over specific details of people, places, things, episodes (177). Verbal messages can mask nonverbal experience (180). In short, language can be used to distort the true nature of the child's perception of himself or herself (182).

In Summary: Strengths of Stern's Approach and Critical Remarks

Despite the stage-like appearance of Stern's approach, he did not consider his developmental framework to be a stage theory. Stern argued against conceptualizing self-development in a phase-like manner. He did this for a variety reasons. First, Stern felt that the term "stage" denotes a time period where an issue comes to the forefront of development, is resolved by the end of the stage, and subsequently moves into the background of the child's developmental progress (1985, 20, 29). For Stern, however, no sense of self that arises in the course of development simply gets "resolved," and recedes in developmental significance (29). This objection to stage theory provided Stern with a means for contrasting between his self-styled developmental theory and other kinds of theories (e.g., psychosexual, psychosocial, and so on).

However, it is also possible to look upon self-development in a stage-like manner without assuming that stage issues are left behind or essentially eclipsed by new stage issues. Years before Stern, Charlotte Bühler maintained that all four of her developmental phases (so designated by the rise in predominance of each basic human tendency) are evident and remain vitally important throughout the entirety of the lifespan (Bühler & Marschack 1968, 94). Knowles (1986, 54) held that developmental issues are never simply resolved, but continually arise and become increasingly elaborated throughout the lifespan despite the fact that he was utilizing a stage approach. Thus, while Bühler and Knowles espoused stage theories, their stages do not bear the characteristic feature of "stage completion" as criticized by Stern.

To be sure, Stern was aware of the potential to look upon development as stage-like without holding to a theory of strictly "time-locked" phases:

> Those who are persuaded that there do exist basic clinical issues, time-locked specific phases, would argue that all clinical issues are of course being negotiated all of the time, but that there is still the feature of predominance, that one life-issue is relatively more prominent, at one life period. (1985, 22)

In fact, Stern himself utilized the idea of predominance for his own theory: "Since there is an orderly temporal succession of emergence of each domain during development—first emergent, then core, then subjective, then verbal—there will inevitably be periods when one or two domains hold predominance by default" (31–32). Nonetheless, Stern maintained that self-development is not stage-like and rejected stage theory. Though he was not abundantly clear on this matter, it appears that he felt that stage theories tended to be too developmentally segmented even when the stages are meant to indicate loosely structured periods of predominance. Rather than following through on a strong, clear argument against stage predominance, Stern shifted to a second, culturally based argument.

Stern's second major objection to stage theory was that the phase-like appearance of issues such as autonomy is a socioculturally determined phenomenon rather than an inherent part of child development. In other words, it is not so much that the development of autonomy is naturally a part of the child's development, but rather that autonomy issues to become pronounced during a certain time frame due to cultural values and societal pressures. For Stern, the stage-like appearance of any developmental issue is due to the caretakers' interactions with the child, both the child and the parents co-constituting a time in development where a certain issue or issues take precedence over others. Thus, he noted, that the "terrible twos" associated with the autonomy phase in Western cultures are not so terrible in all societies (1985, 23). At the same time, however, Stern makes the social and contextual argument for his own theory:

> Organizational change from within the infant and its interpretation by the parents are mutually facilitative. The net result is that the infant appears to have a new sense of who he or she is and who you are, as well as a different sense of the kinds of interactions that can now go on. (9)

Thus, for Stern to hold that developmental stages are unfounded due to the inherently social, cultural, and historical nature of child development appears somewhat contradictory.

A third reason why Stern objects to stage theory is that there is no reliable evidence of predictable effects from having been traumatized at a developmental stage. According to this argument, if developmental issues appear in a strictly stage-like manner, then having been abused, neglected, or otherwise poorly treated at a certain stage should have some kind of predictable outcome or syndrome. Stern noted that longitudinal research has yet to provide a consistent body of data proving that trauma at certain stages predictably and reliably results in specific developmental outcomes (1985, 23). The difficulty with this argument is that quantitative research in the area of child abuse has traditionally ignored the very aspect of the child-victim's life that Stern himself finds so important to understanding development: the child's subjective experience. Quantitative research in the area of child abuse and neglect has not made a concerted effort to grapple with the vital issue of how the child's maltreatment is experienced by the child. This issue is only starting to attract serious attention in the area of psychological maltreatment, as we will see later in this text. Thus, the objective fact that child maltreatment has occurred is simply not the singular determining factor that would allow one to predict child abuse sequelae. The child's interpretation of the maltreatment and the various other bio-psycho-social forces (i.e., aside from the issue of developmental stages) that influence the interpretation of the maltreatment are all grossly unaccounted for by the research on child abuse and neglect.

Stern's final and most substantive objection to traditional stage theories of development is that they are clinically driven. Issues such as autonomy and individuation, for example, are viewed as developmentally relevant for certain time frames due to their status in psychotherapeutic interpretive frameworks (Stern 1985, 23). Stage theories thus tend to be biased in favor of the particular theorist's therapeutic schema (20–21). In other words, phase theories in general appear to suffer from a clinically oriented theoretical bias in their reconstruction of childhood experience (33). The history of this bias is most pronounced in psychoanalysis. The strongest push for a stage approach to development has traditionally been from psychoanalytic thinkers, as psychoanalysis has always been a therapeutically oriented form of psychology. Freud's interest in developmental stages arose from his need to account for the problems he was encountering in psychotherapy. The Erikson-Knowles model reviewed in this text belongs to this clinically focused child psychology as well. As Knowles (1986) noted of his own work:

> This text is intended primarily for a developmental psychology course for practitioners ... for those intending to go on to become clinical psychologists. Because of its therapeutic orientation, it would seem especially appropriate for ... applied fields such as social work, pastoral counseling, school psychology, counseling psychology, guidance and counseling and so on. (xiii)

Stern's final argument does not have strong application to Charlotte Bühler's approach to development, however. Almost twenty years before Stern, Charlotte Bühler not only discussed of child development in terms of the development of the self, but also critiqued the notion of psychological phase divisions in a much more direct and succinct manner:

> The main arguments against describing the life cycle in terms of psychological phases have been that (1) psychological development is continuous and lacks distinct steps, and (2) there is no exact parallel between biological and psychological development. Both arguments, of course, are correct. (1968c, 14)

Aside from not wanting to adopt analytic theoretical strictures, Bühler chose not to schematize development in the manner that Erik Erikson did for the above reasons. Like Stern, she believed that the selection of stage divisions was too arbitrary in traditional stage theories (Bühler 1968c, 15). Moreover, she doubted the notion of a strong parallel between biological, psychosexual, and psychosocial development. Thus, it is doubtful that Bühler would have opted for Knowles's approach to self-development due to his grounding in psychoanalytic developmental theory. She would have viewed Knowles's approach as too rigid, overly segmented, and subject to the charge of arbitrary phase distinctions due to its basis in the Freudian-Eriksonian developmental framework. Yet, Bühler went on with her critique of developmental stages as follows, "Both arguments, of course, are correct, but only partially so. I do not think, therefore, that they eliminate the necessity for phase divisions" (14).

As was noted in the Chapter on Bühler's theory, she did not wish to eliminate the idea of stage divisions altogether. She did not create a stage theory that only allows for developmental issues to arise at certain designated sensitive periods, nor did she believe that these issues fade in significance or become relatively inert after having been "resolved." However, she did maintain the idea of issue predominance during a developmental stage that Stern halfheartedly rejected. In all likelihood, Bühler would have found Stern's complete elimination of phase distinctions relating to self-development too dismissing of stage theory.

Like Stern, Bühler believed child development to be an intensely social process. She viewed the process of child development to be a socioculturally and historically situated phenomenon. However, whereas Stern saw the cultural forces that contribute to the demarcation of developmental stages as evidence that stages are "illusory" (1985, 23), Bühler (1968c, 15) saw the same forces as justification for making broad based, general phase distinctions:

> Society, more than the individual, assigns roles according to age.... Because this holds true for societies all over the world, it must be explained ultimately by the developmental changes of human attributes and aptitudes with which society interacts. These changes do occur. And no matter how slowly they evolve, they bring out new directions....

> Because many different roles begin and end during a person's life-time, phases may be distinguished from a variety of viewpoints. It seems arbitrary to decide on specific turning points. Yet, if we see the human being not simply by himself but as a member of society, we find that practically everywhere society assigns differing roles to the child, the youth, the young adult, the middle aged, and the aged. These changing roles go hand in hand with changing abilities and aptitudes, functions and interests, motives and goals, and accompany the changing relationships with other individuals and groups.

Thus, for Bühler, phase distinctions can be observed by describing how the child's evolving physical and psychological capacities interface with the demands that issue from his or her social and historical situatedness (i.e., social roles, values, expectations, etc.). The meeting ground of the child's evolving capacities and the demands from his or her social milieu are the four basic tendencies of human life. The skills and abilities that the child develops facilitate the pursuit of each basic tendency in a manner consonant with (or at odds with) the child's social context. The tendencies that come to the forefront of development at each stage characterize the nature of self-development as it unfolds during that time of life.

Stern's aim in creating a theory of development was to foster a holistic understanding of the child's experience and relations with others. Rather than focusing on abstract conceptualizations regarding developmental progress or isolated skills and abilities relating to development, Stern wanted to articulate the dynamic forces behind the qualitative shifts in social relatedness that the child displays. Consequently, Stern turned his attention to the domain of selfhood. Bühler had done this years earlier in her own way without the benefit of the developmental literature that Stern had at his disposal. Bühler observed that increases in physical and mental abilities (i.e., quantitative changes) facilitate the transformation of motives and goals as the child develops within his or her sociocultural context (1968c, 16). As the child grows, changes in the motives and goals that he or she pursues create qualitative changes in his or her experience and relations with others. This was Bühler's way of talking about the developmental changes in the child's self, because she described it as the originator of one's goal setting and (like Stern) the "integrating system" of the person (Bühler 1968d, 330–331; Bühler & Allen 1972, 44, 50). Bühler defined the self as the "core system which organizes, selects, and integrates the multitude of motivational trends" (1968c, 18). For Bühler the four basic tendencies of life are always intimately involved in the self's integrating efforts (Bühler & Allen 1972, 48; Bühler 1968d, 332, 349).

Both Stern's "senses of self" and Bühler's "four tendencies" are concepts abstracted from the experiential world of the developing person. However, Stern's focus was narrower than Bühler's. A primary difference between Stern's senses of self and Bühler's basic tendencies is that each sense of self is meant to point to the nature of the infant's "subjective experience," the different ways in which the infant comes to perceive himself or herself in relation to the world and to others. While Bühler was also describing how childhood experience evolves with each of her stages, the four basic tendencies do not refer exclusively to modes or styles of an infant's experiences. Rather, the four basic tendencies are conceptual generalizations (e.g., Bühler 1968c, 14) that refer to the existential projects that move to the forefront of healthy development at each general phase of life and act as the context within which the child's experience and behavior are framed. In this sense, one might say that Stern was attempting to be somewhat more phenomenological (though he was not a phenomenologist), while Bühler was attempting to be more somewhat more existential. Thus, her basic tendencies have a somewhat more abstract sounding character about them than Stern's senses of self.

The difference between Bühler's and Stern's approaches to self development can be better understood through a consideration of the ways they conceptualized selfhood. Stern defined selfhood in a narrower, more conservative way than Bühler. To be sure, Stern's conceptualization of the self is the most conservative approach covered thus far. Specifically, Stern was interested in the self insofar as selfhood was indicative of normal human functioning (1985, 7). In his words, "I am mostly concerned with those senses of self that are essential to daily social interactions.... I will therefore focus on those senses of self that, if severely impaired, would disrupt normal social functioning and likely lead to madness or great social deficit" (7). Stern's refusal to look at development in pathological terms gave his work a humanistic thrust. However, his steadfast focus on "normal functioning" as a counterpoint to severe psychopathology prevented his work from fulfilling its humanistic potential.

Of all the characterizations of selfhood covered in this text, Stern focused only on normal development rather than healthy development. Each self-styled theorist covered thus far has had a particular way of characterizing healthy development. Rogers, Horney, and Kohut each spoke of self-actualization or self-realization in their own ways. Winnicott spoke of the development of the True Self. Bühler conceptualized healthy development in terms of self-fulfillment. Finally, Knowles (1986) referred to the existential dimension of human growth, contrasting it with the biophysical and the ego and cognitive domains of development. As he put it:

> The ideal for a psychology of the self is not normality; this is the ideal for an ego psychology.... Freedom from pathology [i.e., normalcy] opens up a greater possibility for authentic action but it is no guarantee. And there are also cases where people have realized great possibilities despite the presence of pathology. Because the limits are more narrow, possibilities are fewer but they may still be realized. Too often traditional psychology has posed normality as the ideal without sufficient criticism of it. (96)

A humanistic approach to development does not view a healthy self as merely conforming to psychological norms. Without an articulated notion of psychological health, Stern's theory does not sufficiently emphasize aspects of self development such as the child's creative longing, his or her striving and thriving, the sense of meaning and fulfillment, and so on.

From a specifically phenomenological perspective, Stern's work is problematic in that he appears to have created a theory that is grounded in a Cartesian-empirical philosophy. Stern never spoke of subjectivity and objectivity as poles or dimensions of experience, despite his insistence that childhood is thoroughly interpersonal. Rather, he conceives of the interpersonal world of the infant as somehow mysteriously traversing two worlds: the subjective and objective. In his words, "Somehow the infant registers the objective experience with self-regulating others as a subjective experience" (1985, 104). Even though Stern's work counts among the more holistic interpretations of childhood experience to date, the subject-object dichotomy is implicit in his observations. Thus, Stern also noted:

> When the infant is around nine months old, however, one begins to see the mother add a new dimension to her imitation-like status as a potentially intersubjective partner. (It is not clear how mothers know this change has occurred in the infant; it seems to be part of their intuitive parental sense.) She begins to expand her behavior beyond true imitation into a new category of behavior we will call affect attunement. (140)

Stern admonishes that the infant-mother relationship as such is primary in the development of the self, but his implicit Cartesianism resurfaces in his observations regarding the maternal perspective. Rather than engaging in a phenomenological description of maternal experience or calling for such a description, he can only speculate that the mother's "intuitive parental sense" accounts for her close emotional contact with her child. The infant's subjective world and the mother's subjective world are wholly separate, but somehow mysteriously establish interpersonal contact.

Irrespective of these shortcomings, Stern's work makes valuable contributions to a humanistic theory of self-development. Stern reemphasized the important point that self-development begins early in infancy, and not in early childhood or thereafter. Early self-development is not characterized by symbiotic relations between the mother and child. Rather, the child's experiential world begins to form and congeal almost from birth. Moreover, Stern's work reemphasized what Bühler had noted years earlier: that one ought to be leery of stage theories of development, as they are adult creations to account for the child's qualitative shifts in childhood experience.

KEY TERMS AND CONCEPTS

Affectivity
Analytic-developmental theory
Coherence
Core others
Core self
Direct observation of infants
Emergent self
Four senses of self
History
Individuality
Language
Mental organization
Parentese
Preverbal period
Preverbal senses of self
Quantum leaps
Self
Self-theory
Self-agency
Sensorimotor experience
Sensory modalities
Subjective self
Theory of mind
Verbal self

CHAPTER 7

EARLY CONTRIBUTIONS TO THE PHENOMENOLOGY OF CHILDHOOD EXPERIENCE: KURT KOFFKA AND ERNEST G. SCHACHTEL

As is evident, self-styled developmental theories have a variety of origins (e.g., American humanistic psychology, psychoanalysis, existential psychology, and so on). Despite their varied origins, all of the self-styled theories discussed in this text had an implicit or explicit (as in the case of Richard Knowles) phenomenological thrust. Thus, there appears to be an intrinsic harmony between self-theory and phenomenology with regard to development. Still, these self-styled theories did not have an overriding focus on phenomenological description. This holds true for Knowles's work as well, as his theory relied equally on the Eriksonian-analytic developmental framework and existential-phenomenology.

With this chapter, phenomenology as a method of describing childhood experience comes into focus. The discussions that follow all revolve around the phenomenology of childhood existence. This chapter introduces the phenomenology of childhood perception utilizing the ideas of Kurt Koffka and Ernest G. Schachtel. Ironically, Koffka and Schachtel were among the earliest contributors to a phenomenological approach to child development. The irony here is that neither Koffka nor Schachtel were "pure" phenomenologists. Koffka was a Gestalt psychologist. The phenomenological aspects of his major developmental work, *The Growth of the Mind* (1931), are the result of the fact that the early development of Gestalt psychology as a school of thought was influenced by phenomenological philosophy, especially Husserl. Schachtel was also very much influenced by phenomenology. However, he was equally influenced by psychoanalytic thought and humanism (e.g., Goldstein), and he distanced himself from the mainstream of phenomenological psychology at the outset of his primary text on development, *Metamorphosis* (1959, vi).

Kurt Koffka

The current discussion aims to briefly explicate the most prominent phenomenological themes embedded within Koffka's work on development before examining Schachtel's work and the phenomenological descriptions that follow. For Koffka, outlining a phenomenologically styled approach to development was necessary due to the uniquely human issues that arise when discussing child development. In Koffka's view, transferring our knowledge of the principles that govern all animal behavior onto human development meant continually risking an oversimplification of developmental issues and arriving at a distorted understanding of human development. In his words:

> This, therefore, is our problem: To discover the evolutionary principles of child-psychology. But although we must depend for assistance upon comparative psychology, we must not confine ourselves merely to transferring the principles of comparative psychology to our own filed; instead, we must first test the value of these principles, and where necessary we must be ready to recast them. (1931, 3)

Thus, Koffka's fundamental position with regard to the nature of human development was that it contains elements that diverge from the development of all other natural organisms. This gives his work an unmistakably humanistic quality.

Koffka's respect for the possibility that the phenomena of human development may reveal meanings not contained within the scope of comparative psychology gave his work an equally phenomenological quality since phenomenology is a method of observation that highly values the unprejudiced description of worldly events. Koffka believed that while experimental and quantitative research had value, it was ultimately a phenomenologically styled method of observation that would empower psychological researchers to access the full qualitative significance of experience and behavior for individuals living through the issues of human development. As he put it:

> We must also introduce a term for those facts which can be established only by a single person; these we shall call *experiences*, or *phenomena*. In order to prevent misunderstanding, it should at once be noted that the employment of these terms does not imply that experiences are unreal—that they are illusory or of inferior rank as compared with real events. On the contrary, experiences have just as true an existence as so the processes we have chosen to call "real." (1931, 8–9)

However, one should not infer from this quotation that Koffka was an introspectionist who studied "inner life" to the relative neglect of behavior. Koffka studied both behavior and experience. Further, Koffka held that the term "behavior" encompassed conduct and experience (i.e., "inner" and "outer" behavior) rather than only the "outwardly observable behavior" of behaviorist psychology (11).

Koffka considered child development to be a product of both nature and nurture (1931, 42). While he acknowledged the powerful influence of a child's genetic endowment (especially as regards physical growth or "maturation"), he nonetheless considered childhood to be a "period of learning *par excellence*" (40–43). He considered the role of learning in a child's life to be the primary distinguishing factor between the world of childhood and the adult world (42–43). Koffka held that learning was the distinguishing feature of childhood for two reasons. First, due to their sheer inexperience in comparison to adults, children have to continually develop new skills, master new tasks, and adapt to situations that are novel. The younger and more inexperienced the child is, the more learning is a central part of daily life. Thus, Koffka noted of infancy that, "the extent and the intensity of the learning that goes on at this time far exceed the amount of learning in all the later epochs of an individual's life-history" (43). The second reason why Koffka saw learning to be the hallmark of childhood was his observation that human offspring are poorly equipped to handle the demands of the environment for a long period of time in comparison to other organisms in the animal kingdom. Human evolution has sacrificed instincts, fixed action patterns, and rapid physical maturation. In exchange, human development has become particularly suited to learning the means for adapting to various environments and surviving in an array of adverse conditions. In short, human development has been freed from instinct in order to master the environment in a more radical and profound way than is found in other organisms.

Koffka saw child development as highly individual in nature. Accordingly, he observed that "normal" children learn at such varying speeds that identifying constants with regard to the speed of development is a very difficult if not impossible goal. He considered variations in the speed of development to be partially the result of inherited traits (meaning both individual biological and psychological characteristics) and the innate neural plasticity of human offspring (i.e., the adaptability inherent to our species) (1931, 137). He considered the other primary determinant of learning speed in childhood to be the particular sociocultural context of development. For Koffka, both what is learned and the rate at which it is learned are the result of the manner in which children's inherited traits interface with the demands from the environment. In his words:

> Thus, for some individuals the rate of development is very rapid, while for others it is very slow; furthermore, some individuals show a greater regularity of development than do others. A slow rate of progress at the beginning may be followed by a period of very rapid development, and, conversely, an accelerated development may suddenly be arrested, as illustrated by infant prodigies who fail to live up to their early promise. In general, these differences may be attributed to inherited disposition, though an environment which constantly offers strange and unchildlike problems may also contribute to hasten a child's development and early maturation. On the other hand, an environment which offers no appropriate stimulation to activity may be a serious check to development. (51–52)

Perhaps Koffka's greatest contribution to the phenomenology of childhood experience was his observation that children's earliest experiences are organized perceptual forms. As Koffka put it:

> We are speaking of the earliest beginnings of consciousness; and that it is the very first experience of the child that we are attempting to characterize. Our characterization then, is this, that the first phenomena are *qualities, or figures, upon a ground*. Introducing at this point a new concept, we add that they are the simplest *mental configurations*. (1931, 145–146)

For Koffka, order is present from the beginning of the child's psychological life and does not come wholly from the accumulation of experience as is thought in traditional, mainstream, positivistic psychology (i.e., psychology derived from British Empiricism) (146). Koffka saw childhood experience to be the result of active, creative effort. Children actively synthesize the data furnished to them by their sensory systems and create whole perceptions.

Perception for Koffka is an immediate presence and reality in the child's world. A child's mind is not completely "blank" at first, proceeding through a period of utter sensory chaos, only to be ordered at some later period of development. The child experiences, according to Koffka, qualities emerging from uniform grounds (1931, 158). Koffka further observed that the child's expressive movements can be "connected" to their perceptual world, some as evidence of undifferentiated, ground perceptions; some as evidence of figure perceptions. For instance, he considered rest and contentment to be essentially ground reactions, where no particular "figure" stands out in the child's experience. Rather, the child's attention is dispersed; in their state of need satisfaction, he or she experiences no tensions of any kind, nor does he or she feel compelled to attend to any particular sensory quality emanating from within his or her body or from the environment. On the other hand, Koffka took crying in reaction to localized pains, pursing the lips, eye movements, and turning the head toward or away from stimulations to be examples of figure perception on the part of the child. In other words, he believed these reactions clearly showed that the child does experience and respond to "something in particular" rather than nothing or sensory chaos (158–159).

Koffka's descriptive work dovetails with self-theory in that he saw the task of a child's development to be the integration of his or her psychological and physical attributes. The traits and skills that a child inherits are utilized for the purpose of meeting the demands of his or her sociocultural, historical, and familial situation. Specifically, Koffka noted that a child's mind grows through the integration of his or her sensory, motor, sensorimotor, and situational configurations (1931, 160–166). Sensory integration refers to the child's growing ability to synthesize relatively primitive sensory qualities into increasingly complex objects of perception (161). Motor integration refers to the child's refining and sharpening his or her fine and gross motor skills (160–161). Sensorimotor integration refers to the fact that sensing and moving are not separate abilities, but rather a unified whole that evolves throughout early development. For example, in order for a child to perfect his or her visual perception, the movement of the eyes is a requirement. Over time, the child gets better and better at developing motor control over his or her eyes for the purpose of scanning and focusing on the environment (162–163). Finally, situational integration refers to the incorporation of intellection into behavior. Rather than reacting in a knee-jerk fashion, the developing human develops an ever-increasing ability to pause and reflect, to maintain a distance from his or her immediate surroundings, to contemplate the manifold meanings inherent to the situation and produce "ideational behavior," as Koffka called it (166).

It should be mentioned, however, that while Koffka insisted that perceptions (as organized, formed, configured experiences) are present at the outset of psychological life, he did add the caveat that they were of the most primitive order. He called these perceptions "primitive qualities arising off of uniform grounds" and noted that they are nothing like adult perceptions of objects, events, and situations:

> Again, it should be emphasized that the configurations, which we have assumed to be the first phenomenon of mind, must be thought of as very simple indeed—merely as a quality emerging from a uniform ground. Accordingly, we must not think of these phenomena as being at all like the experiences we adults have; at the beginning, only the

slightest degree of complexity and definiteness can be ascribed to them. (1931, 158–159)

Still, this line of thinking differs from Freudian thought on the topic of perception, as psychoanalytic thought has traditionally upheld the notion of a "stimulus barrier" that protects the child from unwanted stimulation from the environment. Koffka maintained that infants perceive external reality. His notion that early perception consisted of primitive qualities only is taken up more fully by Schachtel.

Ernest Schachtel

Autocentric and allocentric perception.

Ernest Schachtel went much further in describing the nature of childhood experience than his predecessor, Koffka. Schachtel's approach to childhood experience rests upon phenomenological descriptions of perception that apply to all humans, young and old. For Schachtel, human perception can be described as autocentric or allocentric in nature (1959, 83). Autocentric perceiving refers to "subjective" experiencing, meaning that perception revolves around the vital, corporeal self. Specifically, in the predominantly autocentric mode, perceptions refer primarily to pleasure or unpleasure, comfort or discomfort, attraction or repulsion (90). In other words, autocentric perception is feeling-bound and localized to the area of the sensory organs involved in the particular perception in question (90). In autocentric perception, it is the feeling states of the perceiver that have primacy over the characteristics and traits of worldly things. Taste, smell, and proprioception (i.e., pain and thermal sensation) are the characteristic autocentric senses proper (89). They are highly localized and are typically experienced as "feeling-bound." Schachtel avoided using the term egocentric, presumably to ensure that his work would not be confused with transcendental egoism, psychoanalytic ego psychology, or Piagetian rationalism.

The allocentric mode of perception refers to "objective" experiencing. Here, objective perception does not refer to the so-called "pure" objectivity or total neutrality sought after in the natural sciences (Schachtel 1959, 83*n*, 85). Rather, Schachtel uses terms like "objective" and "objectification" in a more phenomenological way to mean perception that revolves around objects, events, situations, and others as such. Thus, perceptions in the predominantly allocentric mode of perception do not primarily refer to the feeling subject. Rather, the perceived is experienced as having an independence that allows for examination from different angles, profiles, or perspectives (272). The primarily allocentric senses include touch, hearing, and vision when these senses are employed for the purposes of examining the properties of things as such (rather than contact aimed at deriving pleasure) (99). The allocentric mode is the distinctly human mode of perception.

Autocentricity and allocentricity are both ever-present modes of communication with the world, as all subjectivities are inextricably bound to a world in which they are caught up. The person always has a world. The mind is always intentionally tied to things even when it is highly introspective. Schachtel's phenomenologically inspired view allows for no strict subject-object dichotomy. In his words, "This difference is not a matter of absolute alternatives, but rather of the relative predominance of objectification in the allocentric senses and of pleasure-boundedness and felt organ localization in the autocentric senses" (1959, 97–98).

At the same time, however, Schachtel believed the primary difference between infantile experience (meaning the first year of life in particular) and perception in later development to be that infants perceive the world in a primarily autocentric manner. Early on, experience is essentially "sensory-motor-affective" (Schachtel 1959, 126). As children near the end of the first year of life they relate to the world in a more decidedly "distanced" conceptual manner (126).

Schachtel disagreed with Freud's concept of a stimulus barrier that shields infants from all external stimulation and protects them from overwhelming stimulation. Similarly, Schachtel would not have supported the notion of an autistic phase of early development. He insisted that newborns do experience the world around them and derive pleasure not only from tension reduction and recoiling from stimulation (as in traditional psychoanalysis), but also from turning toward stimulations that they find pleasing (Schachtel 1959, 117). Schachtel observed that pleasure and reality are not diametrically opposed (117). According to his view, behavior that psychoanalysts have traditionally interpreted as evidence of an aggressive drive is often children merely deriving pleasure from their contact with the environment:

> There is nothing inherently aggressive in banging the rattle against a blanket or the side of a crib, or the spoon against the table, or in tearing paper. All these and many other vital sensations or fused perceptions which occur in the course of motor activity leading to the infant's pleasurable contact with environmental objects are essential steps in the infant's self-actualization; they furnish an important link in the infant's motivation for the continued exercise of its muscles and senses, its motor coordination, and its exploration of the environment as well as of its own body and physical capacities. (133)

Schachtel disagreed with Freud's idea that neonates withdraw from stimulation and avoid perception altogether (1959, 122). For Schachtel, autocentric perception of the world dominates early experience. Autocentricity is the norm of early experience due to the slow development of fine motor skills, focal attention, and the child's poorly developed allocentric senses, particularly vision. He considered vision to be the chief allocentric sense, the "highest and most objectifying" of the senses (144). He believed that children see in an autocentric manner, gazing at pleasurable color qualities, shades, movements, and so forth long before they can perceive the clarity of form that would allow for objectification (144). In his words, "From interested looking at the changing images which appear and disappear in the infant's visual field it is still a long way of many months to the perception of objects with distinct forms and detailed articulation of structure" (147). Slowly, over the course of the first year, children's vision improves, allowing them to see things via manifold perspectives (i.e., allocentric vision) (130). Until sensorimotor improvements allow for allocentric perception, infants experience would-be "objects" in the manner of what Schachtel called "fused syncretic activity" (145). That is, infants attend to objects in as much as they produce pleasing feelings, but do not have substantive being over and above the pleasurable sensations they produce.

For Schachtel, infant perception develops in gradual, loosely demarcated phases. Neonates turn toward stimulations with increasing frequency over the first two weeks of life (Schachtel 1959, 122). At this point, their gaze is very general and, according to Schachtel, does not offer up objects, only vague, general qualities like color. Around the end of the first month, infants gaze in a more interested, steady manner. However, images still "have neither depth nor articulate form" at this time (145). Rather than a figure standing out against a background, Schachtel (like Koffka) held that the infant experiences a total situation in which an indistinguishable "something" is prominent rather than a full-fledged object (148). At around ten weeks, the infant stares at objects for a prolonged period of time. They can follow moving objects with their eyes and keep them in focus (256). Near the sixteenth week, infants can focus on not-too-small objects, but motor development is still too primitive for the child to manipulate objects and explore them from multiple perspectives (140). From approximately eight months on, infants' visual acuity has improved to the point where they can focus their attention on small objects (257). Beginning around the same time (i.e., between thirty-two and fifty-two weeks), perception that is primarily allocentric in nature finally comes into being. During this time, motor coordination of the fingers improves and permits the fine manipulation of objects.

In Schachtel's view, the development of allocentric perception is an evolving, ongoing process. Toward the close of the first year and throughout the second year, children display an ever-improving allocentricity of perception through symbol usage (i.e., thinking in words and images) (Schachtel 1959, 141). Symbol usage allows the child to more fully experience the world of shared perceptual meanings. For better or worse, abstract conceptualizations like "within me" and "outside of me" can now come into being (126). Prior to the second year, Schachtel noted that childhood experience is intensely holistic, particularly in comparison to the perceptual world of older children and adults (260). From the second year forward, children begin to focus not only on objects, but their relationships to those objects, giving rise to a burgeoning self-concept:

> The child's reflective focusing on his own feelings and experiences constitutes the last step in the development of focal attention, and accompanies the development of the idea of "I" and the autobiographical memory—that is, the concept of the continuity of the self. (258)

While children move beyond the domination of autocentric perception they enter their second year, autocentricity is never left behind. Both autocentricity and allocentricity coexist throughout the lifespan. Moreover, the ability to approach things, situations, worldly events, and one's relations with others from both a multiperspectival (allocentric) and a felt (autocentric) perspective is a hallmark of healthy child development (Schachtel, 1959, 158). In Schachtel's view, children's parents play an all-important role in the development of allocentricity and the facilitation of healthy development.

For Schachtel, loving, supportive parents bond with their children and encourage them to explore their environments. They encourage them to indulge in their natural curiosity and desire to explore their worlds. Moreover, these parents assist in the gradual process of learning that there is more to the world that the feeling-qualities that it produces. Healthy parents do this, in part, by allowing their children to observe their many roles and states of mind, eventually leading to an increased awareness that the parents have richly varied lives that can be viewed from manifold perspectives. In essence, healthy parents who support their children emotionally encourage their curiosity and facilitate the discovery of the complex nature of social interactions (Schachtel 1959, 275). Consequently, the child's experiential world continually evolves and complexifies throughout development. Thus, for Schachtel, a child's emotional development is by no means separate from their perceptual and cognitive development.

On the contrary, Schachtel saw emotional development and cognitive development as closely intertwined.

Emotional development: embeddedness and activity affect.

Schachtel developed his ideas concerning affect by first critiquing Freudian thought on the topic. Freud saw affect as purely subjective and devoid of any positive communicative purpose, as he held that affect is most closely tied to childhood traumas and evidence of frustration (i.e., an excess of libidinal energy) (Schachtel 1959, 20–23). His accounts of development revolve around drive reduction and the flight from sustained contact with "reality" (8–9). Thus, Freud conceptualized pleasurable affect as the reduction of bodily tensions and the return to a tensionless or excitationless state of homeostasis. On the whole, Schachtel believed that Freud focused too strongly on the "conservative forces" in emotional development and neglected the "progressive forces" (7).

In Schachtel's view, Freud was negligent of the fact that children also actively explore the world and maintain stimulation for things that they find pleasurable and interesting (1959, 5). To be sure, Schachtel did not deny the existence of pleasure in the form of tension reduction and the striving to recoil from contact with the world in childhood. Schachtel termed this sort of affective predisposition "embeddedness affect" and contrasted it with the growth-oriented strivings inherent in child development, which he referred to as "activity affect" (6). Like Freud, Schachtel was a conflict theorist. However, rather than focusing on the conflicts that arise between the id, ego, and superego, Schachtel believed that the primary conflict in human development was between the striving toward embeddedness and the desire to explore the world for new experience and knowledge (i.e., activity affect) (13). Infants in a state of relative helplessness and distress, turning away from stimulation, are displaying embeddedness affect or the desire to return to the safety they once enjoyed in the womb.

In contrast, the child who is actively coping, relating, and striving is displaying activity affect, which leads the way to individual growth and resilience (Schachtel 1959, 29). Activity affect comes about because some activity and the stimulation that it produces are enjoyable in and of themselves. Activity that is pursued for its own sake does not elicit emotion in the sense of "emotional discharge," but rather activity affect, which is focused, directed, deliberate, and pleasurable due to being sustained (28). In other words, activity affect is not emotion that is the result of conflict and frustration (24). As Schachtel noted, eating can be both a relief from hunger and the enjoyment of food (25). Activity affect denotes positive tension that is due to children manifesting their innate capacities for striving (25).

Schachtel noted that both embeddedness affect and activity affect are involved in child development and remain active throughout life (1959, 29). He considered joy to be the quintessential activity affect for human beings. For Schachtel, authentic joy is rooted in an "ongoing openness toward and affirmation of others and the world" (42). Joy is an "activation of a feeling of being related to all things living" (42). Since joy entails the enjoyment of sustained contact with the world, it is an activity affect. True joy is much more than mere enjoyment. While intense enjoyment can be a pathway to the more global phenomenon of joy, enjoyment and joy are not synonymous. Joy is a feeling of heightened aliveness and relatedness to the world wherein the person is focused on the activity of the moment and the delight over being a willing part of creation (43).

Schachtel considered anxiety to be the quintessential embeddedness affect for human beings and described the psychological meanings of anxiety as they relate specifically to child development. According to Schachtel, anxiety becomes an issue in the lives of humans right from infancy. With birth, newborns are no longer sheltered from direct contact with the outside world (Schachtel 1959, 49). The infant is no longer "embedded" within the womb and must deal with the psychological and physiological demands of this new state of existence. In particular, infants experience a new awareness of themselves as vulnerable and dependent upon others for their survival. Stated differently, infants become aware of the closeness of death as a possibility inherent in their existence (Knowles 1986, 25). Thus, developmentally speaking, anxiety is originally rooted in the experience of vulnerability due to having left the safety of the womb.

While the primordial state of embeddedness is the intrauterine situation, Schachtel also used the term to refer to the security experienced as a result of a mother's tender care (1959, 51). Beyond that, embeddedness refers to any state of habit, predictability, or routine that provides shelter from that which is both potentially dangerous and unknown (i.e., anxiety provoking) (47). To return to a state of embeddedness is to remove anxiety. Thus, remaining in an embedded state of being, for Schachtel, is a way of maintaining present securities at the cost of failing to actualize some new potentiality for growth and development.

In Schachtel's view, parents play a particularly significant role in determining whether children develop in an emotionally mature manner. As he put it, "The significance of the environment's role in the developmental conflicts is not confined to the frustration of instinctive drives; it extends, more importantly, to its encouraging and discouraging influence on the development of the child's potentialities" (1959, 15). For Schachtel, children's drive to explore the environment is dependent upon adequate bonding. Emotionally supportive mothering facilitates the development of allocentric perception and activity affect. Inadequate bonding, however, can stifle the child's desire for new experience:

> They can effectively stifle or inhibit the infant's exploratory drive and turn the pleasure in his expanding and varied contact with reality into anxiety. They play an important, perhaps decisive role in the development of the feeling of disgust, and even more important, they reinforce and very much increase separation anxiety. (135)

Schachtel explicitly addressed the issue of child maltreatment as it applies to anxiety and embeddedness (1959, 49n). He held that activity affect is partially congenital, but nonetheless maintained that an "overanxious, overprotective, or punitive mother" could prevent congenitally active children from coping effectively with environmental demands (30). Schachtel noted that many parents are beset with anxiety. This, in turn, prompts them to maintain a state of embeddedness to shelter them from their insecurities. As a result, these parents are typically resistant to the possibility of their children emerging from the embeddedness of the family unit. Psychological maltreatment becomes a means for breaking the child's will and preventing the development of an independent self. Thus, psychologically maltreated children are made to feel threatened by the potential dangers of opening themselves to new possibilities for existing and experiencing the world. Living with the constant threat of aggression or a lack of emotional support discourages new encounters with the world and others. Rather than actively seeking out new experience and pursuing opportunities for maturation, these children may thus prefer to seek shelter from the threatening, anxiety-provoking world outside of their particular state of embeddedness.

After early childhood, this aspect of abuse often has the effect of evoking anxiety in children over the possibility of not being able to leave embeddedness. In other words, psychologically maltreated children's desire to stay embedded can be experienced as another source of anxiety: the threatening possibility of not being able to escape from embeddedness, develop, and mature. For Schachtel, the most frequent neurotic manifestation of a failure to emerge from embeddedness is using others as a quasimother figure who will serve as a "protective shield" from the world (1959, 52–53). However, attempts to stay sheltered within embeddedness could range from an average, everyday preoccupation with routine to severe psychopathology.

All in all, Schachtel has created a developmental framework that revolves around the phenomenology of perception. According to this view, emotionally supportive and encouraging parents assist in children developing autocentric perception, allocentric perception, and activity affect. These children are emboldened by their nurturing social environments, thus empowering them to sustain the sort of world-openness that allows for the realization of their innermost potentials for existing, growing, and becoming a person (Schachtel 1959, 157). Parents who are not emotionally supportive, however, discourage their children's active exploration of the world. They increase the risk that their children will be autocentrically preoccupied with feelings of threat and vulnerability in the face of the surrounding world. Further, these children would be overly inclined to pursue embeddedness, predisposing them to sacrifice their world-openness and natural striving toward self-actualization in favor of simple drive satisfaction and the return to a homeostatic state of tensionlessness.

Criticisms of Koffka and Schachtel

In spite of their perspicacity, the preceding descriptions of childhood perception are not without limitations. For example, Koffka made productive use of the figure-ground concept by noting that specific infant behaviors correlate with the experience of figures or grounds. Koffka held that contentment is a "pure" ground reaction, indicating that no figure is standing out for the infant during the contented state. However, upon closer consideration of the contentment issue, the possibility of a child being both content and focused on a figure seems compelling. As so many developmental theorists have noted, few issues are as important to an infant as the development of attachment security. It is the infant's primary attachment figure that provides the child with the calm and emotional stability needed to become emotionally mature. In instances where the child's primary attachment figure is not present, anxiety is often the result. Since the presence of this attachment figure provides the means for the infant to experience contentment, it is entirely possible that certain contented states are derived from the child's attending to specific characteristics of the attachment figure, ascertained via visual, tactile, or olfactory means. Thus, the notion of contentment being a pure ground reaction seems extreme and perhaps not necessarily the case at all times.

Ironically, Schachtel's reliance on the humanistic concept of self-actualization seems to have prevented his work from fulfilling its humanistic potential. Schachtel saw the primary conflict of human existence to be the desire to remain embedded and the longing to emerge from embeddedness (1959, 13). Though Schachtel viewed children's behavior as motivated by not only the desire to reduce tensions (i.e., embeddedness affect), but also by the desire for world-openness (i.e., activity affect), his theoretical system tends to place the needs of the self above all else. In the case of embeddedness affect, the child seeks to eliminate his or her own biological tensions. In the case of activity affect, the ultimate outcome of sustained world-openness is self-actualization, which Schachtel interpreted as realizing one's own potentials and "giving birth to oneself" (14). Thus, in the case of activity affect as well, the child is seeking stimulation for the ultimate purpose of fulfilling his or her own potentials for perpetual psychoemotional rebirth. In effect, therefore, both embeddedness affect and activity affect give rise to self-centered aims in Schachtel's system.

A shortcoming of both Koffka's and Schachtel's works is that they underestimated the infant's visual abilities. To be sure, this was seemingly unavoidable as they were creating their theories decades ago, without the benefit of the latest research on infant sensory capabilities. Schachtel, for example, spoke of infants' ability to follow moving objects with their eyes at approximately ten weeks of age (1959, 256). However, more recent evidence from research on infant's visual abilities demonstrated that infant's can follow a slow moving object within just a few days after birth (Fantz, 1965). Nonetheless, Schachtel rightly observed that infant perception is much more holistic and autocentric on the whole in comparison to perception in later periods of childhood, adolescence, and adulthood. Moreover, he was correct in noting that allocentric perception continues to develop throughout later development as a result of refinements in the child's sensory and motor abilities, linguistic proficiency, and cognitive skills overall. To reiterate his phrase, early experience is more "sensory-motor-affective" in comparison to the more conceptual, intellectual perspective of the adult world (Schachtel 1959, 126). While cognitive psychologists like Piaget have looked upon the holistic world of childhood as a world deficient in logic, the phenomenological perspective admonishes that one simply appreciate the differences between childhood perception and adult perception so that a greater understanding of the child may result. Schachtel displayed an unabashed appreciation of both autocentric and allocentric perception, noting that their coexistence is characteristic of healthy, sophisticated mental development (158).

An Introduction to the Phenomenology of Childhood Perception

Despite their different theoretical backgrounds, Koffka and Schachtel each made contributions to child psychology that are fundamentally consonant. Taken together, their works provide an introduction to certain basic principles of a descriptive, phenomenological approach to the study of childhood experience. Koffka predated Schachtel and first brought certain phenomenologically relevant themes to developmental science. Schachtel further articulated these themes, though he did so without explicit use of Koffka's work or Gestalt theory in general.

Koffka admonished that an adequate developmental psychology ought to be mindful of the unique, human dimensions of growth. Schachtel showed that children integrate their uniquely human capacities for allocentric, world-focused perception into their individual autocentric viewpoint. Further, Schachtel observed that children's activity affect is part of a more global striving toward self-actualization.

Koffka noted that human development integrates nature and nurture, genetics and environment. Schachtel maintained that activity affect has a congenital component to it and is therefore given to children via their genetic endowment. At the same time, however, Schachtel held that autocentricity, allocentricity, embeddedness affect, and activity affect are all influenced by parents. Specifically, emotionally supportive parents bond with their children, encouraging and facilitating their children's curiosity, world-openness, and growth-oriented strivings. In contrast, anxious, insecure parents constrict their children's world-openness and truncate their potentials for experiencing newness and pleasurable activity affect. This acts to the detriment of self-actualizing forces that are present from birth.

Koffka described childhood as a time of learning above all else. Schachtel supported this notion in his descriptions of how children's experiential worlds open more and more over the course of the first two years of life. Schachtel's characterization of activity affect and of the development of autocentric and allocentric perception both support Koffka's assertion that childhood is a time of discovery, wonder, and awe (Schachtel 1959, 258).

Koffka saw children as active participants in opening their own perceptual worlds rather than merely passive receivers of sensation. Schachtel agreed that a child's world is the result of both passive, receptive states and more active, attenuated states. Schachtel's insistence on noting how activity affect, sensorimotor development, focal attention, and language co-constitute a child's perception of self and other attested to his belief that a child is more than a passive receiver of sensory data. A child is a participant in the coming-into-being of his or her world.

Finally, both Koffka and Schachtel saw children's worlds as being, for lack of a better means of expression, very worldly. They never viewed children as autistic or univocally averse to experiencing the world around them, nor did they characterize childhood experience as evolving through a symbiotic phase. Rather, Koffka and Schachtel considered the sense of coming-into-being as a unique individual or self to be the result of direct contact with things. Koffka spoke of the integrative process involved in self-development, while Schachtel discussed the burgeoning self-concept in terms of activity affect, autocentric perception, and allocentric perception. In both cases, a lived, felt relationship to the world was considered essential to development. As Schachtel (1959) put it:

> At first, the infant probably has only the vaguest feeling, like: "There is something out there which has to happen, which has to come, to make me feel good." This is different from foetal existence in which there was no *there*—no outside, separate from the foetus. The *something*, at this first postnatal stage, must not be understood as an "object," or a "person," but is entirely vague and nondescript. (255)

While Schachtel's use of the term "entirely" may have overstated the matter, the pertinent point is that childhood experience always has a "there," a world with which to relate.

Koffka and Schachtel both considered the experiential world of childhood to be more feeling-oriented and holistic than conceptual. Especially in the first year of life, they viewed perception as being predominantly lived and felt. Very young children have no notion of "inside and outside," or other abstract ideas. To use Schachtel's term, children's worlds tends to be more autocentric on the whole in comparison to the worlds of later childhood, adolescence, and adulthood. As he put it, "The newborn's perceptions probably are *fusions* of internal feelings (pleasure and unpleasure) and sensory aspects of the impinging ... environment" (1959, 126). However, rather than judging childhood perceptions as logic-deficient versions of adult perceptions (which is the norm in cognitive psychology), Koffka and Schachtel considered perceptions in childhood to be emotionally charged, concrete, felt, figure-ground relations that ought to be examined in their own right. This theme will be further illustrated in the next chapter on the experience of time and space in childhood. For now, a few illustrations will suffice. Consider the image below in Figure 7.1 as an example.

This is a lion made of construction paper that was created by a four-year-old girl named Meghan. Meghan cut out the shape and drew the lion in colored marker by using the teacher's lion as an example. Yet the drawing of the lion deviates significantly from the teacher's example. Certain elements of the lion represent an attempt to portray the features of a lion, especially its shape. However, notice that Meghan was not focused on reproducing comprehensive detail and mathematically correct proportion. Instead, Meghan chose to portray elements of the lion that "stuck out" and made an impression on her. The "w" looking shapes represent the fur of the lion. The lion has strong, penetrating

Figure 7.1 Construction Paper Lion Made by a Child of Four

eyes and hard lines on its face. The teeth are quite present as well. To call this lion, poorly drawn or impressionistic, is to judge it from a logical, adult point of view and miss the felt, lived, concrete viewpoint of the child. One will also notice that Meghan has imbued the drawing with elements that are not objectively present on a lion. She drew hearts, smiley faces, and stars on the lion. A characterization of the lion as "inaccurate" or biased on this basis only has meaning in the world of abstract adult reasoning. If one were to put the world of adult logic aside temporarily, one would see that these aspects of the lion represented Meghan's concrete, vital, lived-experience of creation as she worked diligently within the space of intimacy established by her and her teacher. In other words, to judge the lion as a poor representation of an "objective" lion due to a misrepresentation of proper visual proportions (i.e., what a lion "really" looks like) necessitates the negation of Meghan's worldview.

Figures 7.2 and 7.3 are drawings of pigs by Kristina (age four) and Daniella (age five) respectively. These drawings further illustrate the themes of felt, lived-experience in childhood perception. For both children, the legs of the pig were less impressive than its round, portly body and nose. While Daniella gave some detailed attention to the stocky nature of pig legs and feet, one will notice that she only included two legs rather than four. It was the prevalence of round features and the color of the pig that struck Kristina (the colored portions of her drawing were done in a pinkish hue). She was impressed by the fat body and especially the snout of the pig, which is evidenced by the fact that the pig's snout is quite large relative to the pig's head.

Figure 7.2 Pig Drawing Made by a Child of Four

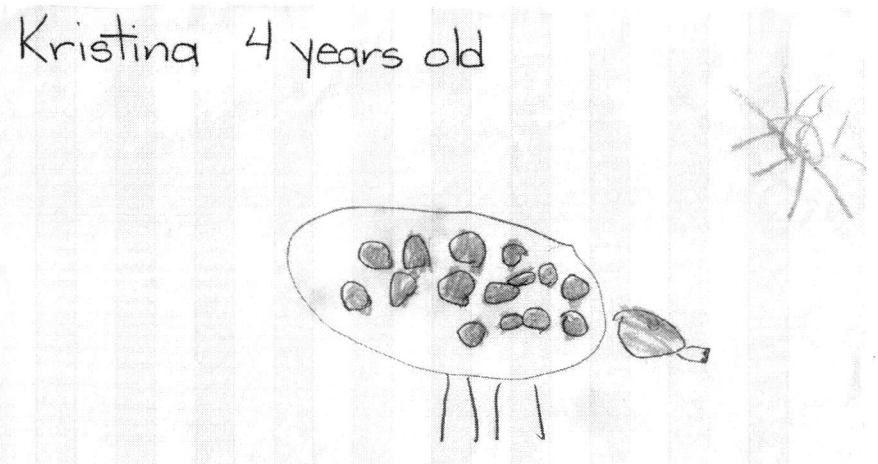

What figures most prominently in Daniella's drawing are the squiggly pig tail and pointy ears. Daniella's pig is also of interest as she was quite careful to imbue the pig with a happy female face (as indicated by the presence of long eyelashes). To see her drawing as evidence of subjective bias projected into her drawing misses the more obvious, concrete fact that Daniella was quite identified with her drawing activity. Her pig reflects her emotional state as she identified with the task of creating the pig drawing. This is not to imply that Kristina was unhappy at the time of her drawing.[3] Rather, the point of these illustrations is to demonstrate the intensely holistic, sensory-affective nature of childhood experience in comparison to day-to-day adult experience.

---

3   It may interest the reader to note that these students' preschool teacher remarked that Kristina was not nearly as personally invested in her drawing as Daniella.

Figure 7.3 Pig Drawing Made by a Child of Five

KEY TERMS AND CONCEPTS

Activity affect
Allocentric perception
Autocentric perception
Comparative psychology
Embeddedness affect
Figure-ground relationship
Gestalt psychology
Humanism
Introspectionism
Learning
Mental configurations
Motor configurations
Neural plasticity
Phenomenological psychology
Psychological maltreatment
Qualitative significance of experience and behavior

Sensorimotor configurations
Sensory configurations
Situational configurations
Speed of development

CHAPTER 8

TIME AND SPACE AS LIVED IN CHILDHOOD

Phenomenological psychology places high importance on the concepts of time and space in attempting to understand human experience and behavior. However, phenomenologists do not interpret time and space in the highly abstract way that natural scientist interpret these topics. For phenomenologists, time and space are first and foremost "lived" phenomena; meaning that the way time and space are experienced by individuals caught up in their worldly affairs has precedence over intellectualized, calculative conceptualizations of time and space. Lived-experiences of time and space are primordial. Mathematical conceptualizations of time and space are abstractions from lived-experience. As Langeveld (1983, par. 44) noted, things are "three-dimensional" because we sit on them, not visa versa.

In everyday life, adults are accustomed to thinking about time and space in rationalistic, mathematical terms. That is, we are used to thinking about time as clock time and space as measurable space. However, it is important to note that these are cultural conventions that depart from the original, lived-experience of time and space. Children do not experience time and space in these quantitative terms at first. Clock time and measurable space have to be taught to them. Children begin life knowing only lived-time and lived-space. Thus, in order to understand childhood experience, an understanding of lived-time and lived-space is essential.

Lived-time and lived-space are covered together in this chapter because they are inextricably related phenomena. Everyday language provides evidence of the inherent connection between time and space. For example, phrases such as, "the distant past" and "the not-so-distant future" contain both spatial and temporal terms. Questions such as, "Where are we?" and "Where am I?" can be read spatially or temporally depending on the context of the dialogue. This is because both lived-time and lived-space are in fact implied in these questions. Ever since Einstein's Theory of General Relativity, natural science abandoned the idea that time and space are separate in favor of the notion of "space-time." Phenomenological psychology holds a similar position, noting that lived-time and lived-space are both predicated upon "a meaningful caring for something or disclosing something"

(Boss 1963, 46). Moreover, as Boss noted, lived-space "can be fully understood only on the basis of temporality. For 'being' always means being 'present'" (45).

Lived-Time

Clock time is public time and is therefore anonymous. It consists of a series of "now-points" that implicate no one and nothing in particular. Lived-time, however, has personal meaning which is derived from one's worldly relations. To "live" time is to actively relate to others and things in the form of meaningful relationships and projects that are sustained over time. The enduring nature of one's relationships and projects implicates past, present, and future alike. As a matter of course, this relating entails the act of interpreting what has been and what may be in some manner of care or concern. As Murray (1986, 226–227) aptly put it:

> It is not the past event, any more [than] it is the future event, that matters in the person's life. It is the way in which the past has been imaginatively picked up, transported, and sustained in the seemingly enduring present that is the critical issue. The events of the past are countless, and most of them will scarcely be remembered in their details. How they have been imaginatively incorporated into the person's scheme of things is something else, and this can prove devastating or inspirational. [In] similar ways the future remains to be unfolded, obviously, but is becomes a powerful factor in human life long before the unfolding ever transpires. It is the manner in which it is imaginatively depicted and brought close to the present that gives experienced, phenomenological and personal time its significance, long before it can be recorded in clock time. As such it could be frighteningly paralyzing or incredibly uplifting.

Though lived-time involves interpretation on the part of an individual, it is not a construct that resides "in the mind" (Lippitz 1983, 176). Lived-time derives from one's meaningful relationship to the world, embedded within the objective and subjective poles of concrete experience (176). The objective pole of lived-time refers to the fact that time adheres to things, as it were, meaning that one can see "brand new" as opposed to antique or young as opposed to old, for example. The subjective pole of lived-time refers to the feeling of temporal rhythm and the particular way one is attuned to past, present, or future (176).

Time in childhood: temporal rhythm.

Prior to understanding measured time, children understand the duration of time on the basis of real events and how long they actually feel (Briod 1986, par. 24). They come to retain a notion of the tempo of events as they repeatedly live through them. Though children do not know the quantitative differences between minutes and hours, they can feel the pace of time (Briod 2002, par. 14). The tempo of their lived-time varies depending on the way they interpret and experience their relationships to things and others at any given moment. Children feel fluctuations in the speed of lived-time that are based on their enthusiasm for the activities of the present as well as those that are anticipated in the immediate future. Children know that certain activities like driving somewhere can feel long. The pace or tempo of such a ride can feel much longer for a child who does not know the difference between "five minutes" and "thirty minutes." Thus, they may continually ask, "Are we there yet?" They may know that going to the bathroom or picking up the toys is not so long, even though they cannot measure and assign a number to "long" or "not long." For example, a five-year-old child who had recently moved to New Jersey once told me that she used to live in Pittsburgh. I asked her how long she lived in Pittsburgh. Her answer to me was an enthusiastic "One thousand!" Since her entire life prior to moving to New Jersey was spent in Pittsburgh, the girl wished to convey to me that her stay in Pittsburgh was long. However, she did not understand calendars as yet. Thus, knowing that public time is numerical, she gave me the largest number she could think of at that moment.

Time in childhood: the focus on the present.

Temporally speaking, children are more attuned to the present than adults. However, the present is nothing like a "now point" for children, but rather a true presence to things in the world (Briod 1986, par. 6). Being "on schedule" and getting things done in the busy, progress-oriented world of adulthood means that adults often cannot exist in and for the moment. They are distracted from the joy of being in and with time. Children, however, stand outside clock time, living for what or who is at hand. Being oblivious to the divisions of clock time gives childhood a more "timeless" feel in comparison to adult experience (Burton 2002, par. 8). Time is lived for the sake of things, people, and events in the here-and-now; schedules are truly of secondary importance. Wasted time to an adult can be creative, productive time to children (Briod 1986, par. 5).

However, by noting that children are particularly present-oriented, it is important to clarify that there are two ways of being focused on the present, depending on the nature of their relationships with the significant adults in their lives.

Under unhealthy conditions, such as living with the threat of abuse, a child lives anxiously in the present. In such instances, the present is uncomfortable and constricting, not allowing for the child to be open to the inviting aspects of things in lived-space. For example, in her phenomenological research on men abused as children, Garrett (2006, 137) observed, "Some participants experienced lives of uncertainty and abuse to the point that day-to-day survival became their life's work." Anxiously living time makes it feel slow and arduous, as the child is continually waiting for an attack that can happen at any minute. The child backpedals away from the dreaded arrival of a potentially painful future. Kirova (2001, 7) obtained similar results when she found that children who experience loneliness and isolation feel as if time is being "stretched out." Of the psychologists covered in this text, Knowles (1986) showed how different sorts of meaningful developmental predicaments create different sorts of emotional states which, in turn, affect the perception of time. Knowles discussed how anxiety, shame, and guilt, for example, can block the future and sometimes create situations where the child remains subject to the factical conditions that characterize his or her life-history (i.e., the past). A central aspect of Knowles's theory was the notion that affect that shuts down the future or present belabors the flow of time. This was most clearly seen in his descriptions of boredom and depression:

> The experience of boredom shares with depressive neurosis the same distortion of time.... In boredom, one experiences time as if one would live forever, as if one had too much time and this is an obvious distortion. There is a falling away of the awareness of past and future or, possibly, an identification of past and future with the boring present. (96–97)

Thus, when time is emptied of captivating content, the child does not swim with the flow of time, so to speak, but impatiently longs to move swiftly while drifting aimlessly in the current.

Under optimal circumstances, however, time is "a pleasure that perseveres in a present" for the child (Burton 2002, par. 3). There is no such reality as "being on schedule." The here-and-now is literally a "present," a gift that often eludes adults because of their functionalized existence (par. 3). When time is filled with captivating possibilities, the immediate future charges the present with excitement, anticipation, and exhilaration. The pace of time is thereby hastened and the child's time "flies," as we say.

Moving beyond the present.

Children eventually arrive at an understanding of clock time as a result of both firsthand experiences and the training of adults. Children grasp the present best at first and gradually move outward more and more toward an understanding of the past and the future. As language and memory improve, so too does the child's imagination and his or her ability to envision temporal modes that are further removed and distant from the present (Briod 1986, par. 12). Language allows a child to transcend the immediate situation. They can reach into the past for ideas as to what may be coming into their lives from the future (Briod 1989, 123–124). At first, however, they are in touch with the immediate past and the immediate future, as these modes of temporality are closest to the present. For example, children may know that in "a little bit" they are going to get ice cream. Similarly, they realize the point at which an event has become part of the immediate past and is no more. Memory ensures that completed events remain or endure on that basis (Briod 1986, par. 12). Through memory and anticipation, then, the past and the future become increasingly relevant to the present. However, children still cannot divide time up into segments. They get closest to being able to segment time by attending to natural phenomena such as the patterns of seasons and patterns of light and dark (Burton 2002, par. 15). Children are also readied for their training in clock time by witnessing the routines, media events, and daily activities structured around adult, public time (Briod 1986, par. 2).

The development of public time.

Usually, by the time children start kindergarten or first grade, adults have begun the formal process of training them to understand our public, collective ordering frameworks for time: calendars and clocks. As Lippitz noted, if the children stray from these ordering systems, there are sanctions (1983, 175). Clock time is enforced as "the" model for understanding time. Improvements in language development facilitate abstract thought, which helps children to better understand the segmented system of public time. By the time children reach early adolescence they have typically become fully assimilated into the objective time tables of the adult world (Burton 2002, par. 19).

Living in accordance with public, clock time has a tendency to draw one's attention away from the experience of personal time. However, clock time is not "all bad," as it opens the door for increased responsibility. Being able to understand and live according to clock time enhances a person's ability to become dependable and reliable to others. Moreover, as Briod (1986, par. 25) noted, clock time invites an interest in the future, as children eagerly anticipate future events by watching the clock. Still, habitually interpreting time in terms of the clock bears with it the danger that children will grow to lose touch with lived-time, time that is personally meaningful, in favor of pragmatic time. As Briod (1986, par. 27) also observed, training children to live by clock time risks imbuing them with anxieties about being "on time" rather than empowering them. Thus, Burton (2002, pars. 16–17) noted that adults ought to educate children about clock time while being sure to avoid "dulling the subjective sense of time inherent within the young." Children should not be trained to grope toward a tomorrow at the expense of the here-and-now.

Time-in-space.

The meaning of the time one spends on projects and relationships amounts to the meaning of one's life. Wasting one's time is wasting one's life. Time well spent is a life well spent. The degree to which one is open to the facts of one's past and present as well as the possibilities of one's future is the degree to which one is open to living one's life. In this sense, temporal openness is the very foundation of human existence, of being-in-the-world-with-others-alongside-things (Heidegger). This implies that temporal openness is simultaneously world-openness. Hence, Boss (1963, 39), who referred to human existence as a world-spanning openness, also referred to human existence as "being the there." The "there" in this context refers to one's world of lived-space. Again, lived-time and lived-space cannot be separated. It is only in-the-world that one finds the meanings inherent to a person's unfolding existence. The manner one lives time is embedded within the way one lives space. As van den Berg (1972) put it:

> If we want to gain insight into another person … we should not inquire fist about his introspectively accessible, subjective account of his observations. This account, although essentially possible, does not as a rule, contain much information. We get an impression of a person's character, of his subjectivity, of his nature and his conditions when we ask him to describe the objects which he calls his own, in other words, when we inquire about his world. Not the world as it appears to be "on second thought," but the world as he sees it in his direct, day-to-day observation. (38–39)

Lived-Space

Lived-space is not to be thought of as a container. Space, in phenomenological literature, does not refer primarily to the geometrical concept that is central to the sciences of nature. Rather, lived-space is a meaningful dimension of experience that facilitates action. Lived-space is the experiential opening or clearing that invites involvement within the concrete world of things and others. Things and others within lived-space are always meaningful and thereby elicit care, interest, and action from the child. Thus, as personally meaningful space, lived-space is always bound to a worldly situation involving embodied perspective and affective investment.

Lived-space and embodied perspective.

Space, as it is actually experienced in one's active relating to things and other people, is relative to one's embodied perspective. Left, right, up, down, big, small, wide, narrow, deep, shallow, near, and far, all take their meaning from qualitatively different experiences of bodily orientation in space. Thus, a child's behavior may vary from an adult's simply on the basis of a different embodied perspective on a situation. This fact is lost on parents who cannot fathom that a toilet bowl (built for the larger bodies of adults) can actually be an intimidating object to a child half their size. In my lifetime, the most striking curiosities of lived, embodied perspective have been experienced upon visiting my old grammar school. I am always amazed at how small everything looks in contrast to my memories of large desks and long hallways. On a more day-to-day basis, I witness the occasional lack of sensitivity to embodied perspective when parents walk hand in hand with young children struggling to keep up with their parents' pace. Sometimes the child falls, dangles from mom's or dad's arm, only to be reprimanded for "daydreaming" or walking too slowly. Such parents are not open to the child's space of action and remain (at least temporarily) ignorant to the fact that the child has to take three or four steps to equal one adult step. Thus, the jaunt down a hallway is experienced quite differently for legs with such different proportions.

Each of our sensory modalities configures space in its own way as well. For instance, with one's eyes closed, the use of hearing alone can make space appear vast and vacuous. Alternatively, hearing a loud, piercing screech can be felt as "going right through me." Hearing, in effect, undoes the boundaries of space and can open up the field of lived-space to horizons that are unfamiliar or unknown. Seeing performs an opposing operation in space. Vision clearly defines the parameters of space and thereby gives one a feeling of empowerment. Our dependence on sight for a feeling of personal power is betrayed by darkness and makes the prevalent fear of darkness and those things that harbor it (e.g., forests, basements, etc.) more comprehensible.

While touch can also delineate and demarcate the parameters of space, it does so primarily by allowing one to gain a concrete sense of proportion. That is, touch allows an individual to uncover the dimensions of things and grasp how one's physical abilities and vulnerabilities complement or conflict with the demands of this particular environment. However, upon closing the eyes to feel one's way around a room, one soon notices how much more empowering it is to fix and organize that room via the use of sight. Feeling a table, for instance, with one's eyes closed can make the table appear somewhat larger than it appears when looked at. Taste and smell can also play a role in determining the nature of lived-space. However, as these senses are so much more autocentric, to use Schachtel's term, they tend to influence the nature of lived-space indirectly through affect and affective memory (e.g., a smell or taste that rekindles a romantic memory and brings one near to the space of intimacy and the actions that it invites).

Movement and especially locomotion constitute another embodied mode of experiencing space. As the child learns to turn his or her head, belly crawl, and crawl on all fours, he or she opens up the horizontal dimension of space common to the rest of the animal kingdom. As he or she sits upright and eventually stands upright, he or she opens the vertical dimension of lived-space that is uniquely human. In walking, the child has his or her first full-fledged experiences of being able to live in the horizontal and vertical aspects of space at once.

The reader will recall that Knowles's (1986) contribution to understanding the factical-bodily dimension of human existence consisted of a phenomenological description of how the child lives his or her body during particular stages of development. Knowles related horizontality to the reclined position of infancy (23). Knowles referred to the horizontal space of infancy as "prone" space. This was meant to highlight the major psychosocial themes of infant life, especially the child's limited repertoire of behavior, his or her vulnerability, and the anxiety that accompanies this vulnerability. Knowles noted that the increasing desire to exert one's will arises simultaneously with the experience of standing up and facing the world (50). Next, Knowles observed, the child is "on the move," developing a sense of the "social body" (78). The child begins the gradual process of learning the social customs and norms that are attached to certain forms of behavior. It is on this basis that groups have come to be referred to as "bodies." Finally, as the child approaches puberty and fine tunes his or her motor skills, embodiment entails developing a sense that one's body is an adequate instrument for engaging in work and play (105–106). The child is now in search of a sense of mastery over tasks.

Lived-space and affect.

To reiterate, lived-space is meaningful space. It is only when things and others within the child's environment take on a personal significance, relevance, or value that the child becomes invested in his or her relation to those things and others. It is only through the infusion of personal meaning that the interpersonal world and object world take on an inviting character, calling the child forth into action. Phenomenologically speaking, emotions are evidence of a child's meaningful investment. Emotions, from a phenomenological point of view, are nonverbal expressions of personal meaning. Where there are no emotions, there is indifference and therefore a lack of significance, relevance, or value. Thus, affective attunement and investment are prerequisites for a child's lived-space to open up and become a clearing for specific forms of interest and action. Each kind of affective attunement, therefore, can be seen as constituting a unique sort of lived-space. Lived-space is not a "location," but an affectively colored milieu that is conducive to certain kinds of action and forbidding of others.

The lived-space between individuals can appear close or distant, depending on the level of intimacy or conflict in their relationship at any given time. Emotional tension can make lived-space appear thick and heavy such that one might feel that the air can be "cut with a knife." On the other hand, "clearing the air" and creating a jovial emotional environment can make lived-space appear to have a light atmosphere. Anger tends to cloud one's perception of the other, while hatred opens up perception to excruciating detail. Depressive states create a feeling of empty space inside oneself such that one may feel the need to "fill the void," with food, alcohol, or dependent relationships. Such "inner" lived-space corresponds to the perception of a dying world, devoid of rich color and movement as demonstrated by the performance of depressed individuals on the Rorschach projective technique. Conversely, happiness, joy, contentment, and fulfillment create a feeling of inner fullness and a corresponding world full of activity and vitality.

Having used hypnotic techniques in therapy, such as guided imagery, I have often been impressed by the fact that when clients fear someone in their lives, they tend to create images of these individuals that are very large, ominous, and animated. Assisting these individuals to overcome their fears involved getting them to shrink the feared person or persons down to a manageable perspective. A similar principle of lived-space applies to children, who revere adults, not only due to their life-experience, savvy, and power to provide, but also due to the fact that adults are literally so much larger than the children. In effect, there are as many manifestations of lived-space as there are potentially meaningful configurations of sensory experience and affective attunement to the world and others around the child.

Lived-space: things and others.

Ellen Benswanger's (1979) phenomenological research highlights the role of one particular kind of emotional issue in the constitution of lived-space in early childhood: the issue of attachment security. Benswanger noted that the principle of Gestalt applies to lived-space. Namely, objects take their meaning in space through their relationship to their contextual backdrop (112–113). For example, a gun takes on very different meanings when it is in a display case in a museum as opposed to when it is in the hand of a masked man in a subway. At the same time, exactly how things are contextually configured is co-constituted by both child and world. The world brings predetermined structure, but the child has to ultimately "put it all together" in his or her own unique and meaningful way. Lived-space as situational and meaningful to a particular child is thus a requirement for things to be significant, relevant, and in some way comprehensible.

According to Benswanger, the invitational nature of things can only be experienced if a child cares for the world in which he or she lives. The child comes to find the world interesting and exciting insofar as he or she is freed to care about the world of things. Through his or her care the child attends to the object world in order to configure it and contribute to its meaningful and evocative organization (1979, 113). However, the child's ability to care for the world is anchored in his or her relations with familiar and trusted caretakers. Having an emotional bond with caretakers constitutes the emotional space of closeness that opens the child to the evocative characteristics of things. Psychoemotional intimacy founds the child's closeness to things (115). Put another way, the security derived from intimate relations with others provides the child with the freedom to explore the world without action-stifling anxiety (118). The "moodedness" of the child's lived-space (i.e., his or her "affective attunement") kindles or constricts his or her potential for engaging the world of things (116–117). When lived-space calls forth in an inviting way, the child's resultant interaction with the environment gives rise to new horizons, new possibilities for behaving, or new apprehensions and anxieties, amounting to an ongoing co-constitution of person and personal space (117).

Personal meaning and self-discovery in lived-space.

Benswanger also noted that children in the space of intimacy not only discover things in the world, but themselves as well. As a being-in-the-world, children do not discover themselves "in their heads," as it were. They find themselves having already been in the world involved with-others-alongside-things. Thus, freedom to discover the world is simultaneously freedom to discover one's self-in-relation to the world and others (Benswanger 1979, 118). "Being-in" lived-space means that a sense of self will emerges through one's interactions with a concrete milieu. Specific actions within the child's environment provide the foundation for an emerging sense of self-in-relation to the particular characteristics of his or her material and social environment (119).

According to Benswanger, the child's discovery of self-in-relation to things and others occurs in lived-space through two primordial modes of relatedness: presence and transcendence (1979, 119). Presence denotes "the attachment of the person to his surroundings" (119). Presence, in other words, refers to the child's interaction with that which is familiar, with that which the child already feels close. Transcendence denotes "those aspects of the self-world relation in which the person is 'over-against' the world. It refers to the proclivity of the subject to move apart and establish distance from [familiar] things, persons, and places" (119). Stated differently, the child establishes a unique sense of self not only by relating to what is familiar, but also by seeking to preserve the alterity of things and others, thereby establishing contact with the strange, the unfamiliar, the alien (119–120). The reader would rightly note the striking similarity between Benswanger's notions of presence and transcendence and Schachtel's notions of embeddedness affect and activity affect.

Benswanger observed that the primordial images of home can become extremely potent, evocative metaphors for attaining a deep understanding of lived-space throughout life (1979, 114). This is due to the formative experiences of lived-space in the home. For example, the image of a home itself, as opposed to what is merely a house, calls forth the feeling of rootedness and stability. Since the lived-space of home is considered the central part of a child's development from a phenomenological perspective, various phenomenological authors have discussed its importance in childhood. Barritt and Beekman (1983), for example, observed that spending time in secluded spaces is an important part of personal growth.

Reminding us that the adult world is often intimidating to the disproportionately smaller child, Barritt and Beekman (1983) noted that the child will use secluded areas as safe havens (par. 18). Adults usually dictate the concrete landscape of the child on a day-to-day basis as they are in control of the child's daily activities (par. 24). However, in secluded areas, the child's will has free reign. This is especially liberating for the child as he or she is also free to experience space without the imposition of common adult interpretations of space. According to Barritt and Beekman, a child's orientation in space tends to be more oriented to persons and activities in the "here and now." Adults, in comparison, tend to be more preoccupied with pursuing practical goals and thus overlook the possibilities of "being present," as it were (par. 24). Consequently, children are much more responsive to invitations to observe and explore objects, to transform their environment into a "sensual, colorful, or frightening landscape of experience" (par. 40).

Langeveld (1983) has also explored the significance of secluded areas, noting that the "secret place" is an important part of healthy child development. The secret place is a space that has not been rigorously structured by adults. In the secret place, things are open to manifold interpretations because their meaning is not predetermined by adults. Experience in the secret place is not prestructured, organized, and made functional or rational by adults. Imagination, creativity, and personal meaning are not constricted by adult "everydayness" (par. 13).

According to Langeveld, children discover secret places around four to five years of age (1983, par. 31). However, they can only discover such places if their wider sense of lived-space is characterized by "a mood of tranquility, peacefulness" (par. 21). A child cannot fully experience the potentials for imagination and creativity of the secret place if he or she is anxious and worried. As the child moves closer to adolescence, he or she no longer makes use of the secret place as such. Rather, what was once the secret place is now transformed into the young persons room, which is not necessarily so secret, but still highly personal nonetheless (par. 35). Both the secret place of the child and the private room of the older child share an important characteristic: both contradict the depersonalized space of the anonymous public in everyday adult life. Thus, both the secret place and the private room are major contributors to the development of personal existence or selfhood (par. 50).

An Illustration: Lived-Space-Time in the Preschool Classroom

I recently had the opportunity to observe preschoolers (ages four and five) in order to develop a sense of lived-space-time in the preschool classroom. About once a week for approximately three months, I visited a class of preschool boys and girls with the permission of the school and the teacher. My visits lasted about an hour so as not to disrupt the class too drastically. The children were not told of my visits in advance. Further, there were no changes in their daily scheduled activities due to my visits.

Upon entering the classroom for the first time, I saw compelling evidence that the children's lived-space was fundamentally altered by my presence: they restricted their range of activity. The children tended to stay in whatever area of the room they were in and minimized their movements. Some children continued to play or color, but at a much slower pace than normal. Some children simply stared at me. Some children would look at me, then look away or down, then looked at their teacher momentarily, and then stare at me again.

It goes without saying that the children were anxious. The present was no longer carefree and fun as they were now preoccupied with the uncertainty of their immediate future. As a result, their space of intimacy had been disrupted. The lived-space that they had established in their classroom was the result of both a familiarity with their teacher and a trust in the safety and security of being in class with her. The future had not been in question. The emotional bond established by the teacher with her students created a warm, inviting atmosphere that freed the children to explore their room without reservation. My entrance into the room constituted a temporary threat to their sense of familiarity and security. I represented the unknown, the alien, and thus, the potentially dangerous. This had the effect of slowing down behavior or stopping it altogether. Within seconds, I reduced the scope of their lived-space within the classroom. Moreover, the things in the room immediately ceased to be inviting. The call of things, the invitation to explore, and the inspiration to play was shut down now that a new priority had arisen: that of being on alert in the presence of a potential threat.

To be sure, my large size relative to their small bodies was a factor in the change in their lived-space. When unfamiliar children entered the classroom, the children's behavior did not change as radically as it did when I first entered. Eventually, over time, the children's lived-space was opened once again to its original boundaries within the school property. Five factors were at play in reestablishing their previous lived-space. First, when interacting with the children, I was better able to elicit responses when I knelt down and "got on their level," so to speak. This showed them that I was sensitive to their lived-perspective.

Second, the children reached backward in time for their old security and engaged in what has now come to be known as social referencing. The children looked to the already familiar and trusted teacher for signs as to the meaning of my presence. Having witnessed the teacher show no fear in speaking to me, the children slowly develop a sense that I must not have been a danger. Interestingly, it would not do for the teacher to simply appear fearless, as the children were on alert for pretense. It was only when the teacher repeatedly acknowledged my presence by speaking to me that the children were relaxed somewhat. Undoubtedly, part of the reason for their level of tension and the extents required to relax them was my gender. The children had grown much more accustomed to the comings and goings of females in this classroom, though adult females were construed as more dangerous than children as well. Still, a male was a particularly foreign body to them. The familiar and trusted teacher speaking to me showed the children that the possibility of engaging me in the present was consonant with their previous affective attunement within the classroom

Third, making the children laugh broke down significant boundaries between the children and me. This, perhaps more than anything, transformed their outlook toward me and increased their level of activity and interaction in my presence. I noticed early on in my visits that my personal space seemed to loom large in the children's presence. However, simply by making strange faces and noises that made me appear self-deprecating gave the children the feeling that I was safe. To be sure, I did not have to tell jokes or resort to elaborate gags. In fact, I got the sense that those kinds of behaviors would not have been as efficient in changing the children's lived-space. What they were after was a return to the space of intimacy above all else. Self-deprecating humor was perfectly suited to this aim. The children felt safe enough to return to play in a manner that closely resembled their movement in the class before my arrival.

The fourth element in the bonding process between the children and me was the use of magic (i.e., illusion) on my part. Having established a rapport with the children, I eventually began employing some basic techniques of illusion that my father had demonstrated to me when I was young. For instance, I would pretend to remove the top of my thumb from my hand by masking my knuckle with a forefinger. On other occasions I would stand near a wall with a baseball cap on backward and blow into my finger while pushing my head nearer to the wall. This gave the impression that blowing into my finger raised my cap. These simple acts roused the children into an excited state where they literally yelled out for more. This was quite a transformation considering that I had initially been a person whom the children would not address. By employing magic, I had entered their magical world. The children had come to embrace me within their space of intimacy. By the end of my visits, some children were actually approaching me, grabbing my hand, and requesting that I do magic for them. One child actually raised her arms in a nonverbal request that I pick her up. Their freedom of movement retuned to normal and the call of things was reestablished. Their lived-space was no longer constricted, but it was a slow process occurring over several visits. Thus, the fifth and final element in reestablishing their previous lived-space was time, which required patience on my part.

What I learned through my visits to this classroom was that a child's sense of space is such that he or she seeks to establish (under healthy conditions) a comfortable equilibrium, not unlike that of air or water pressure, within the space that he or she dwells. The child's personal space fills the room, thus, and extends slightly beyond the confines of the property (unless accompanied by the teacher). Beyond the property line (especially the fence), the horizon of lived, felt space expands infinitely to the unknown, unfamiliar, and thus potentially dangerous. Thus, the child does not willingly wander away from the class without the teacher. Walks to the library, for example, entail everyone holding hands in a great chain that provides not only physical safety, but also psychological security. Being without the hand of a trusted adult (or a hand that eventually leads to an adult) leads to an explosion of the horizon and the loss of a security beacon. The child feels lost, vulnerable, and anxious.

A child's space can be upset and disturbed not only by an explosion of the lived spatial horizon, but also by the threat of implosion. My initial presence in the classroom created stilling and freezing. The presence of the unpredictable or unfamiliar is experienced as intrusive to lived-space. As I entered the classroom for the first time, personal, lived-space collapsed to the very epidermis of each child. As safety returned to "normal," space was again returned to the boundaries of the whole room. Thus, what appears to be healthy as regards the lived-experience of space is an outward movement or flow of spatial awareness that can be recoiled effortlessly, as a gentle breeze, for the purposes of reflecting on one's relation to the world of things and others. The unhealthy alternatives appear to be twofold. First, there is the feeling of being pulled or sucked outward, as if without a root or anchor into infinite space. The second unhealthy experience of lived-space is the feeling of being spatially compressed, confined, or constricted to one's skin as a boundary between self and world. The latter condition correlates to a world deplete of inviting things to capture the child's imagination.

I also learned from my observations how intensely interpersonal a child's world is. The above description revealed that the lived-time and lived-space of each child was highly dependent upon a certain kind of social relationship. Specifically, the opening of their lived-time and the clearing of lived-space was founded upon the presence of emotional sensitivity and my ability to express this sensitivity in words and actions.

KEY TERMS AND CONCEPTS

Affective attunement
Clock time
Embodied perspective
Focus on the present
Gestalt
Here-and-now
Immediate future
Immediate past
Invitational nature of things
Lived-space
Lived-time

Objective pole of lived-time
Personal meaning
Phenomenological psychology
Presence
Public time systems
Self-discovery
Self-in-relation to things and others
Subjective pole of lived-time
Temporal rhythm
The secret place
Transcendence

CHAPTER 9

FINDINGS FROM A PHENOMENOLOGICAL STUDY OF PSYCHOLOGICAL MALTREATMENT: THE CHILD'S RELATIONS TO THE MATERNAL FIGURE*

The purpose of this chapter is threefold. The first purpose is to demonstrate another phenomenological style of studying childhood experience, one that is different from the direct observations of children in the previous chapter. Here, childhood experience is accessed indirectly through adult recollections via the use of a formalized phenomenological methodology that will be described later. The second purpose of this chapter is to better understand the child's experience of a highly powerful environmental threat to healthy development: psychological maltreatment. The third purpose of this chapter is to hopefully gain some insight into the nature of childhood maternal relations by looking at what happens when the childrearing process lacks emotional sensitivity. At the very least, this chapter ought to provide some empirical-phenomenological clues as to the nature of good parenting and healthy development by illuminating their counterpoints, telling us what good parenting and healthy development do *not* look like. In other words, one may derive some basic ideas regarding the nature of health-conducive mothering and healthy child development by inverting the research findings, so to speak. This would serve to complement the self-psychological and phenomenological material explicated thus far on the nature of healthy development.

In the inaugural issue of the *Journal of Emotional Abuse*, Hart, Binggeli, and Brassard (1998) outlined the six major categories of psychological maltreatment recognized by psychological researchers. The categories represent the particular kinds of psychological abuse that have been identified thus far and are not meant to imply that the possibility of identifying new forms of psychological maltreatment

---

* This chapter is based on an article entitled, "The Impact of Long-Term Psychological Maltreatment by One's Maternal Figure: A Study of the Victim's Perspective." *Journal of Emotional Abuse*, Volume 4, No. 2, 27–51. (Copyright 2004, The Hawthorn Press).

is precluded. Drawing from the *Psychosocial Evaluation of Suspected Psychological Maltreatment of Children and Adolescents* (American Professional Society on the Abuse of Children 1995), these categories are as follows: (a) spurning or the verbal and nonverbal degrading and rejecting of a child; (b) exploiting/corrupting or encouraging a child to develop behaviors that are self-destructive or socially unacceptable; (c) terrorizing or behavior that threatens or is likely to place the child or child's loved ones in danger; (d) denying emotional responsiveness, ignoring a child's attempts to interact, or interacting without emotion; (e) isolating or preventing a child from socializing; (f) mental health, medical, and educational neglect or refusing or failing to provide needed treatment in these areas (Geffner & Rossman 1998, 2).

Some researchers have suggested that these forms of psychological maltreatment can impede healthy development more than physical and sexual abuse (e.g., Egeland & Erikson, 1987; Ney, Moore, McPhee, & Trought, 1986; Tzeng & Jacobsen, 1988; Vissing, Straus, Gelles, & Harrop, 1991). As Ney (1987) put it, "Professionals suspect verbal abuse may create more intense and longer lasting problems in children than do other types of abuse. Because children tend to identify with their parents, the abuse ... becomes a way in which they then abuse themselves" (371). The extent to which any form of abuse has a detrimental impact on child development, however, always depends on the severity of the maltreatment in question. Thus, rather than pitting one form of abuse against another, the claim that psychological maltreatment is the "core component" of all forms of child abuse has become the prevailing view taken by researchers (e.g., Hart & Brassard, 1987; Navarre, 1987). Whether viewed as a distinct form of abuse or as the essence of all forms of abuse, both perspectives attest to the vital importance of understanding the impact of psychological maltreatment.

The most commonly recognized symptoms of psychological abuse are low self-esteem (e.g., Briere & Runtz 1988, 1990; Egeland, B., & Erikson, M. F. 1987; Engels & Moisan 1994; Gross & Keller 1992; Krugman & Krugman 1984; Leffler 1987; McCord 1983; Moeller, Bachman, & Moeller 1993; Mullen, Martin, Anderson, Romans, & Herbison 1996; Rohner & Rohner 1980; Varia, Abidin, & Dass 1996) and aggression (e.g., Chan 1981; Delozier 1982; Doumas, Margolin, & John 1994; Hickox & Furnell 1988; Loeber & Strouthamer-Loeber 1986; McCord 1982; Ney 1987; Rieder & Cicchetti 1989; Rohner et al., 1980; Varia, et al., 1996; Vissing et al., 1991). However, researchers are observing that it is the victim's interpretation of psychological abuse, its *meaning*, that ultimately determines its developmental impact (e.g., Vissing et al., 1991). To quote Navarre (1987), "The [psychological] assault is not (or not only) upon the physical body but upon the ... individual's perception of the self as valuable ... the world [as] beneficent or neutral rather than innately hostile … the ability to perceive … the desires and needs of others" (49).

Nonetheless, research has tended to remain focused on isolated characteristics of childhood psychological abuse sequelae (e.g., low self-esteem and aggression) to the relative neglect of the victim's interpretive worldview. A noteworthy exception is Ney et al.'s (1986) study, in which the researchers carried out structured interviews and administered questionnaires to children, parents, and staff at a child psychiatric unit to assess victims' perceptions of their physical abuse, verbal abuse, physical neglect, emotional neglect, or sexual abuse. It was found that verbal psychological maltreatment had the most detrimental impact on children by disposing them to more self-directed anger and pessimism about their futures than victims of physical and sexual abuse.

From the perspective of the current investigation, the findings of the Ney (1986) study stand to benefit from further elaboration via a methodology that seeks to provide a description of the individual victim's perspective *holistically*, as a perceptual gestalt. Having utilized questionnaires and interviews structured in advance by the researchers, the Ney study constricted the scope of their available data (i.e., the victim's perspective). To quote Walsh, Perrucci, and Severns (1999), "Survey methods, by their nature, constrain the complexity and variability of the data obtained … [leaving] little opportunity to discover values other than those dictated by the questionnaire" (305). As a result, the Ney (1986) study did not provide a coherent characterization of the victim's worldview. Thus, there remains little empirical data indicating how the specific characteristics of psychological maltreatment arise within the lived experience of abuse.

Phenomenology as a Methodological Option

Phenomenology is a qualitative research method that is used, not only in the social sciences and psychology (W. F. Fischer 1974; C. T. Fischer & Wertz 1979; Giorgi 1985; von Eckartsberg 1986), but also in areas as diverse as student affairs (Manning 1992), physical therapy (Shepard, Jensen, Gall, Schmoll, Hack, & Gwyer 1993), and nursing research (Annells 1996). Phenomenological research can be carried out via the analysis of participants' written protocols. In this regard, phenomenology is similar to the protocol analysis research used in cognitive science where first person descriptions are examined in order to explicate problem-solving strategies (Ericsson & Simon 1980; 1994). The phenomenological approach also resembles field study research in that it utilizes open-ended interviews to collect data (i.e., interviews that require more than "yes" or "no" answers from participants).

Phenomenology as it is employed in this study is a qualitative case-based research method that uses small samples, approximately four to seven participants (Edwards, 1998; C. T. Fischer, personal communication, November 3, 2002). The smallness of the sample allows researchers to explicate in-depth accounts of individual participants' experiences. Phenomenology differs from other qualitative approaches in that its focus is on describing specific phenomena as they are actually experienced rather than building or testing theory (Edwards, 1998). While psychoanalytic authors have also used a qualitative case-based approach to study child abuse, a psychoanalytic case study approach entails maintaining and reasserting its theoretical approach throughout the investigation (e.g., Shengold's 1989 work on the effects of child abuse). The contribution of a phenomenological approach is that holistic accounts of lived meaning can be explicated without the imposition of theory-specific constructs, yielding descriptions that are accessible to professionals of diverse backgrounds. The phenomenological method requires researchers to identify the psychological themes within individual descriptions of a phenomenon, compare the various cases under study, and then holistically articulate the highly relevant structural themes of what is being studied. All in all, the approach bears a striking similarity to the recent corrective proposed by Katzko (2002) for the "disorganization of scientific literature in psychology." In his words, "To get the most out of the data, an effective strategy searches for similarities among diverse situations and similarities in the meanings of the descriptions of those situations" (266).

Phenomenology differs from quantitative research in both its manner of research and its validation procedures. Table 9.1 below briefly contrasts phenomenology with a quantitative research orientation to help clarify their differences in emphasis. The primary purpose of phenomenological research is not to obtain factual data that are as generalizable as possible or descriptive of a norm. Rather, phenomenological research seeks "thick" data that foster an understanding of the meanings inherent in human experiences and actions. Findings are contextualized within the lives of individual participants. Nonetheless, phenomenological research "is not a fuzzy version of real science, but a rather different enterprise—the effort to provide coherent, evocative, useful accounts of our ambiguous, holistic, psychological life" (C. Fischer 1994, 25). The validity of a phenomenological study is achieved through what C. Fischer (1994) has identified as reflexive rigor. By reflexive rigor, Fischer means, "Our turning back on ourselves as our only way to understand human events at a human level.... 'Reflexive' refers to the use of ... self-conscious reflection to perpetually revise our understandings of qualitative data. Doing so rigorously is demanding.... The researcher must ... search, research, and re-search through transcriptions" (25).

Table 9.1
Contrast of Quantitative Research and Phenomenological Research

Quantitative Emphasis	Phenomenological Emphasis
• The researcher as an "independent" observer	• The researcher as a participant observer
• Interprets phenomena under study as part of a singular, "objective" reality	• Interprets phenomena under study as part of a matrix of multiple realities, manifold perspectives
• Tests, experiments, statistically analyzes raw data	• Describes, qualitatively analyzes (explicates significant psychological themes from) raw data
• Strives for identical repetition of research findings	• Strives to articulate the highly relevant constituent meanings of phenomena known only through their varied manifestations
• Focus on obtaining factual data that are highly generalizable (describing norms)	• Focus on obtaining "thick," in-depth data that foster an understanding of the meanings inherent in participants' experiences
• Focus on finding correlations between variables and, ultimately, making statements of causality	• Focus on achieving a holistic characterization of human experience and behavior

The Present Study

The primary objective of this study was to articulate the victim's experience of psychological maltreatment in a holistic manner. It was hoped that a phenomenological methodology could contribute to the existing literature by providing a compelling and coherent description of the victim's perception of psychological maltreatment that was primarily empirical rather than theoretical in nature. It was further hoped that an empirical phenomenology would contribute to the existing literature by making it possible to obtain a cogent description of having been abused derived from the victim's perspective rather than obtaining quantitative data to test hypotheses regarding the significance of psychological maltreatment for the victim. Finally, it was hoped that the isolated facts uncovered by the aforementioned research on psychological abuse would be made more comprehensible when contextualized within the victim's worldview explicated as a perceptual gestalt. In this regard, the rationale for the current study of psychological abuse is expressed in the following quote from Young (1992, 89): "If the above symptomology is, at least some of the time, present in individuals who have been … abused, can we discern an underlying phenomenological coherence which might explain how these psychological difficulties 'go together' and why they might meaningfully be connected?" Thus, the current study hopes to extend the approach utilized by Young in her investigation of childhood sexual abuse to the field of psychological maltreatment in order to broaden the scope of psychological child maltreatment research.

Method

Participants.

Participants for the present investigation were obtained through written advertisements and by word of mouth at two community colleges in New Jersey, one in Paramus and one in Lincroft. These municipalities are suburbs of New York City, primarily composed of blue-collar and white-collar middle and upper-middle-class families. In addition, an advertisement was put in a regional newspaper near Paramus. Eleven young adults volunteered to participate. Three of the volunteers were former students of the author. However, it was decided that they could be considered for participation in the present study because they had ceased being the author's students and were completing their degrees in other disciplines at the time of their participation.

Participants were individually screened by the author to determine their eligibility for participation. Since this study focused on the significance of having been psychologically maltreated in childhood, only individuals whose abuse had begun prior to adolescence (11 years of age) were considered. Also, since the study was on long-term abuse, only participants who were abused for ten or more years were to be accepted. Finally, Vissing et al.'s (1991, 244) conceptual definition of psychological maltreatment was utilized to assess the nature of the participants' abuse. Briefly, this definition characterizes psychological abuse as a verbal or nonverbal "communication intended to cause psychological pain to another person."

Examples of emotional abuse under this definition would include criticisms, threats, derogatory remarks, slamming or smashing things, and stony silence.

To participate in the present study, detailed accounts of psychological abuse that occurred regularly (i.e., daily) were needed. The author's three former students were accepted as participants due to both their detailed memories of the abuse and the author's informal familiarity with them. Two additional people were also accepted due to their appropriateness for the study and the richness of their accounts of psychological abuse. Therefore, five of the eleven volunteers were selected for participation in the present study. No compensation was provided for participation in this study.

Participants were given the pseudonyms Bob, Tia, Jill, Jay, and Sue to protect their anonymity. All of the participants were from middle-class backgrounds and identified their mothers as the source of their victimization. Tia and Jill noted having suffered verbal abuse from their grandmothers as well. Thus, the more general term maternal figure was considered the most precise way to refer to the participants' perpetrators and was chosen over the term mother for this study. With the exception of Sue, all of the participants' parents were separated. Having remained in the custody of their mothers, the participants noted that they were not close to their fathers after their parents' separation. A general characterization of the participants can be found in Table 9.2, which includes categorizations of their abuse related to the six major forms of psychological maltreatment outlined by Hart, et al. (1998). Of the participants, Sue experienced some instances of physical aggression from her maternal figure. This was not viewed as cause for exclusion from the study, however, for two primary reasons.

Table 9.2
Brief Characterization of the Participants

Factor	Bob	Tia	Jill	Jay	Sue
Age	23	21	24	23	18
Ethnicity	Cuban/ Dominican	African American	Italian American	Brazilian American	Irish/ French/ Italian/ German
Gender	Male	Female	Female	Male	Female
Marital Status	Single	Single	Single	Single	Single
Spurning	✓	✓	✓	✓	✓
Exploiting/ Corrupting					
Terrorizing	✓		✓	✓	✓
Denying Emotional Responsiveness	✓	✓	✓	✓	✓
Isolating		✓			
Health Neglect		✓ (Mental Health)			

First, Sue identified herself as a victim of psychological abuse. As she noted in her description, "The stuff that sticks out in my mind more is the way my mom talked to me.... It was just all the mental stuff. She really messed with my self-esteem and who I thought I was when I was growing up." Second, the prevailing conceptualization of psychological abuse as the core component of child abuse eliminates artificial distinctions between psychological abuse and other forms of child abuse. Thus, psychological maltreatment was not viewed as a phenomenon that can only be studied when isolated from other forms of abuse.

Procedure.

The participants were informed that the research involved disclosing their experiences of abuse in written and oral form and each signed a participation consent form. Each participant provided a written response to the following query: "Please describe, in as much detail as possible, what having been psychologically abused by your maternal figure as a child has come to mean in your life. Proceed as if you are trying to get someone who has no idea what it has been like for you to have been maltreated to understand how your abuse has affected you. Include in your description how you became aware of the ways in which your abuse has showed itself in your life and how you have lived with the different aspects of having been abused." All of the participants were told that they had as long as they needed to respond to the research question to their satisfaction.

After dedicating two weeks of perusal to each written response, participants were contacted in order to arrange for face-to-face interviews regarding aspects of their protocols that appeared ambiguous or provided opportunities for further data collection. All participants were interviewed. The interviews were approximately one hour in length. Each interview was tape-recorded and the participants were told that they could terminate the interview at any time. After the interviews, each question and response was transcribed, including any peculiarities in the participant's manner of expression (e.g., tears, laughter). The author transcribed all of the interviews. The written protocols and interview transcriptions were read multiple times in order to get a sense of the psychological meanings integral to the experience of psychological abuse for each participant. When these two steps were completed, the author drafted edited syntheses of the written protocols and interview material as per the methodological requirements of phenomenological research. These syntheses represented cohesive expressions of the participant's experiences with redundancies eliminated. They were organized in terms of the temporal unfolding of the experience as it was recounted by the participants. A portion of an edited synthesis can be found in Table 9.3 for illustrative purposes.

Table 9.3
A Portion of an Edited Synthesis (Bob)

I always felt like … a complex doing whatever, whatever it was. The simplest things, like going to school, I thought I wouldn't do it. I thought I wouldn't go anywhere. You know, I never even finished school. I never wanted to do anything. I wanted to just hang out.

[*What does that mean to you to say that you have a complex?*] I was nervous to be around other people always, especially professors. I thought that they would see me and see right through me. [*What would they see?*] I don't know. Like, what my mother saw. She always used to tell me that I would never accomplish anything.

My mother is a very stubborn and ignorant person.… Her way is the right way.… **Even though it hurts me deeply to admit this, I have to face reality.** Or else I'd have to hold it inside like I have for all of these years. I understand a little more now. [*What was the result of holding that in?*] Holding it in … that person would speak about their parents and it's like, "What does your mother do?" I would change the subject.

The worst part of the whole ordeal is that she doesn't understand the constant pain she gives me.… [*Why is that the worst part?*] Because I want to know about my mother. She don't talk to me, she doesn't say anything.

Note. The material appearing in boldface is from the written protocol. The material appearing in brackets and italics are questions asked by the researcher during the interview. The remainder of the text is comprised of the participants' responses from the interview. All text appears verbatim.

Next, "units" of psychological significance were explicated from each edited synthesis. That is, shifts in meaning were thematically expressed as revelatory of the experience of abuse. A portion of one participant's meaning unit analysis is shown in Table 9.4 below for illustrative purposes. After this process, the themes were brought together for each participant individually in order to arrive at an individual narrative of the significance of long-term psychological maltreatment by one's maternal figure as a child.

Table 9.4
A Portion of One Participant's Meaning Unit Analysis (Bob)

Edited Synthesis Meaning Unit	Theme
[*Does that do anything for you, to understand?*] Yeah, because I'm a more understanding person. Before, when I was young I was always fighting. I don't know if that was the cause of it. I had a bad temper with everybody.	Achieving an increased understanding of his mother has helped Bob to attain a greater understanding of his emotional volatility. This assisted in his becoming less aggressive and developing frustration tolerance.
The worst part of the whole ordeal is that she doesn't understand the constant pain she gives me.... [*Why is that the worst part?*] Because I want to know about my mother. I want to know what goes on inside her head. She don't talk to me, she doesn't say anything. I remember one time, it was two New Years' ago, the first time we ever hugged, and she said she loved me, you know. She actually said it. I guess she was just touched that time.	The most painful aspect of Bob's feeling of maternal rejection is his mother's lack of understanding. An exceptional show of affection on his mother's part stands out as an example of her lack of empathy for Bob. Bob's anguish revolves around the lack of an emotional bond with his maternal figure.

Note. The material appearing in boldface is from the written protocol. The material appearing in brackets and italics are questions asked by the researcher during the interview. The remainder of the text is comprised of the participants' responses from the interview. All text appears verbatim.

The individual narratives were then studied in order to explicate the meanings that were significant to the participants' experiences in general. The general themes were delineated and integrated into a general account of the long-term significance for (these) adults of having been psychologically maltreated as a child. To maintain the holism of the general structure, each meaningful theme was viewed in terms of its unfolding impact on their relations to themselves, their worlds, and others. The purpose of the general structural description was to yield a narrative composed of the psychological themes found to be highly significant to the experience of having been psychologically maltreated by one's maternal figure. The themes that constituted the general structural description appeared in all of the participants' descriptions. This was not a requirement of the research methodology, as highly formative themes are not always evident in each and every participant's description. Such was the case in this study. Thus, two additional themes that were not unanimous to the participants' descriptions will be discussed as supplementary themes. The steps of the entire research method are outlined in the flowchart in Table 9.5.

Table 9.5
Flowchart of the Research Method

Procedure	Brief Description
1. Written Protocols	Obtain written descriptions of victims' experiences, then read, reread, and become familiar with them.
2. Interviews	Interview each participant in person in order to clarify ambiguities and obtain additional data.
3. Edited Syntheses	Synthesize protocols and interviews into cohesive statements of the participant's experience of abuse.
4. Thematically Expressing Units of Meaning	Delineate shifts in meaning and articulate the psychological themes that dominate each "unit" of significance.
5. Individual Narrative Descriptions	Bring the themes together to form individual narratives that answer the question, "What is the essential meaning of each participant's experience of having been psychologically maltreated?"
6. General Structural Description	Synthesize the individual narratives into a general statement of the long-term significance of having been psychologically maltreated. This statement will cohesively express the psychological themes found to be highly formative to the participants' experiences.

For this study, three additional professionals assisted in carrying out credibility checks: Dr. Paul Richer, Dr. Russell Walsh, and Dr. Michael Sipiora. After concealing identifying data, the data analyses were given to these individuals for critique and validation at each step of the research. All three professionals were educators at the time of the study teaching psychology at Duquesne University and were familiar with the methodology used in the analysis. Of the three, only Dr. Richer was not a clinical psychologist. All of the data for Bob, Tia, and Sue was given to all three credibility checkers. These three participants were chosen to be the members of the core analysis due to the fact that they provided the most detailed feedback as well as the largest volume of raw data of the five participants. The author and the credibility checkers always first exchanged comments via mail and then met in person to discuss the validity of the data analyses. Jill and Jay were the additional, adjunct participants. The themes gathered from the core analysis and the insights gained from that process of explication were then used to guide the examination of the remaining participant's descriptions. The researcher fine-tuned the final results of the data analysis during this phase of the investigation. Credibility checkers were not utilized for the fine-tuning process. C. Fisher, cofounder of the phenomenological method in psychological research at Duquesne University, described this process as follows:

> The researcher formally analyzes three or four [descriptions], and comes up with a structure. Then we use the remaining subjects as "adjunct subjects," studying them one by one very carefully for fit with the structure. Often a subject uses a word that's just perfect and which then is used in the structure; other times we see that we overstated something in the structure and modify that. (2002, personal communication, November 3)

Results

What follows is a general structural description of having been psychologically maltreated by one's maternal figure constituted from the individual participants' accounts. Results of the present study are presented in terms of the major themes that existed within this structural description of maternal psychological abuse. Illustrative quotes are included as parenthetical items at points throughout the narrative.

Inadequate maternal nurturing and affection.

The participants felt that they were ultimately unwanted by their maternal figures. They were especially invested in establishing a loving bond with their maternal figures due to the belief that their maternal figures' care was vital to their happiness and well-being. Therefore, participants' perceptions of having been psychologically maltreated arose when they perceived their maternal figures to be opposed to forming such loving bonds with them. (Sue: "My mom was like, 'You know, if I had had the money … you would have been an abortion.'") This unfulfilled desire to get close to their caretakers made the participants vulnerable to experiencing such maternal rejections as abusive.

Participants typically found their maternal figures to be callous, self-involved, or otherwise disinterested in them. (Bob: "I would come home and just like, 'Mom, I did this!' And it's like, 'Yeah, whatever.' My mother didn't care. She was like, 'You want something, go get it yourself.'") The participants felt ignored and disregarded because they were not treated with warmth and caring while they were growing up. For example, their maternal figures were not physically affectionate with them. The participants were not hugged or kissed as children. In addition, the participants grieved over lacking genuine love verbalizations from their maternal figures. (Jay: "She used to tell me she loved me and kissed me. But after a while it got lesser and lesser and I started feeling that.") They saw themselves as having been bribed, given things as a substitute for genuine affection. (Jill: "She'll dish out money, give presents and even heartfelt cards to only tell me I'm a worthless bitch twenty minutes after I open the card.")

The impact of being cast aside.

Feeling cast aside left the participants with a desperate sense of loneliness and isolation growing up. They felt horribly insecure about having no one to turn to in times of crisis. (Tia: "I should have had some support and I don't know how to do these things today. I just felt so alone. To this day I feel lonely. It felt like I wanted to still be a kid, but I had all of these responsibilities.") This insecurity intensified their desire for close, caring relationships with their maternal figures since such relationships promised support and relief from their anxiety. Thus, the more the participants felt deserted by their maternal figures, the more desperately they wished to bond with them. This distressed need to seek care from the people who were their perpetrators, those who made them feel trapped in their abusive relationships. (Jay: "Like, my mom's house, I call it the jail, 'cause that's what it feels like to me. I can't do anything without asking permission, not even get something to eat.") (Jill: "I guess all it comes to is that I feel she is evil toward me but I just can't let go of her … who do I really have?")

Verbal abuse and resultant self-blame.

The participants felt that their maternal figures sometimes intentionally set out to be mean or hurtful to them for "no good reason." They felt that they were made scapegoats for their perpetrators' frustrations. (Jill: "She would call you every name in the book, tell you how worthless you are.") The most salient form of ill will that the participants experienced was verbal aggression. For example, they felt that their maternal figures were viciously and inordinately critical of them. In fact, the participants experienced their maternal figures' opinions that they were not good enough to earn their approval, acceptance, and love to be the most agonizing aspect of their maltreatment. (Sue: "And that hurt more than anything else. I wasn't good enough for her or to her. I wasn't good enough to be her daughter, to go out with her, and have her be proud of me.") Consequently, they found their lives being dominated by frantic attempts to do things that would prove their worth to their perpetrators.

The participants' maternal figures belittled and demeaned them with vulgarity and put-downs. (Tia: "She's always told me I was such a bad little girl or that I was stupid, lazy, ugly, ugly acting, or dumb.") They feared their maternal figures due to the constant threat of being verbally attacked. The participants were often predisposed to isolate themselves from human contact in order to seek sanctuary from these attacks. (Sue: "I don't know, she was weird. Like, sometimes she could be so cool and other times she just scared the shit out of me. So as I got older I would disappear for days … I used to hide under my bed all the time.") At the same time, these attacks motivated them to go and prove their worth to their perpetrators out of a sense of guilt or that they had done something wrong. Thus, their guilt provided further impetus for the participants' despairingly trying to behave in a way that would please their maternal figures. (Jay: "She said music wasn't a career. So I got a job in maintenance. No matter what I did, it wasn't good. I would get a job from eight to five, she would say it wasn't enough hours. What was a 'real' career?")

Resignation and the internalization of abusive messages.

Eventually, however, the participants experienced a sense of resignation, abandoning or not initiating projects because they felt as if they couldn't please their maternal figures. Having acquiesced to their maternal figures' opinions that they were inadequate, they were filled with intense self-doubt in their ability to be good enough to be loved and accepted. Tormented by a sense of disempowerment stemming from their maternal figures' unattainable standards of perfection, the participants felt unable to make good decisions or do things successfully. Thus, they asked themselves rhetorical questions such as, "Why do better since I can't please her?" and "Why should I care if she doesn't?" (Bob: "What am I going to do better for if she is going to scream. I wasn't going to do anything, just hang-out.")

Failing to prove their worth to their maternal figures and thus end their verbal maltreatment left the participants feeling subhuman. (Tia: "I feel like I didn't exist, like, 'Why am I here? My own mother doesn't care for me.'") (Jill: "'Is she right about me?' 'Am I a sicko?' 'Am I really shit?'") This devastating distortion of their self-images predisposed the participants to feeling as if they did not lead lives that bore adequate value. Feeling insignificant to their maternal figures, the participants tearfully concluded that there was little purpose to their being alive. As a result, they lost interest in activities that they loved or found fulfilling and suffered depressed affect. (Tia: "I didn't socialize. I didn't enjoy friendships. I didn't want to cheer anymore. I wouldn't talk to friends I normally talked to.")

Negative comparisons.

As the participants got older they noticed that other children's relationships with their maternal figures were radically different than their own. Namely, they perceived other children to have encouraging and supportive maternal relationships. Consequently, the participants began to see their homes as unstable and dysfunctional in comparison to other children's homes. Their family lives started to appear abnormal to them. They experienced their maternal figures as strange or "weird" because they treated the participants with apathy and animosity rather than the love they saw in other families. They felt that it was incomprehensible for them to be the victims of abuse. The participants experienced a sense of confusion, a torturing inability to understand why they were psychologically maltreated. Moreover, they enviously wondered what life would be like if only they had home lives similar to the ones they witnessed in other families. (Bob: "It didn't make sense. I was wondering what was wrong with my mother. It was strange. My friends would come home, 'Mom, look, this happened!' 'Oh my God. It's nice.' They would help 'em. I would go to my room and play Nintendo.")

Communication deficits.

In an effort to improve their maternal relationships the participants tried to engage their maternal figures in open, honest talk about their abusive relationship despite being afraid of approaching them. However, they found their maternal figures' inability or unwillingness to open up and talk to be due, at least in part, to being in denial about there being anything wrong with their treatment of the participants. (Jill: "I really don't know what to do anymore. I've tried over and over to explain to her that she's got to get a grip and stop doing this to me but that's when she calls me a piece of shit.") Their maternal figures' unwillingness to take responsibility for their actions (i.e., abuse) made the participants feel like they had no interest in giving them the parental guidance necessary for them to grow up and become well-adjusted individuals. For example, when they began to enter adolescence, their maternal figures avoided having substantial discussions with them about how to deal with such potentially difficult issues as relationships, sex, and drugs. (Tia: "The day I started my menstrual cycle I didn't know what it was. I though I was sick. She never even told me about that at all, ever. I didn't know what was going on and my mom just goes, 'Oh ... you're just becoming a woman.' That's it.")

Self-destructive behaviors.

In response to their maternal figures' refusal to care for them, the participants engaged in self-destructive behaviors. The purpose of these self-destructive displays was twofold. First, the participants were expressing their anger at their maternal figures. They felt that perhaps the only way for them to protest their maltreatment was to be spiteful. Thus, the participants were self-destructive because they felt it would irritate and anger their perpetrators. (Jay: "When I stole my first car, she backed-off for a while.") (Bob: "'Fuck her.' You know, 'I'll hang out with these other cool guys and smoke weed.'") Second, the participants' self-destructive behavior was also a cry for help. Their self-destruction was designed to be a glaring exhibition of their sense of inner turmoil, their self-reproach, self-dissatisfaction, anger, and anguish over being psychologically victimized. (Tia: "She didn't come to me and say, 'Why do you want to kill yourself?' I wanted affection. I was asking for help.")

Of the self-destructive behaviors that participants commonly engaged in, drug use was seen as a means of coping with the stress caused by their maltreatment (i.e., a means of self-medicating). In its more innocuous form, this drug use amounted to smoking cigarettes or marijuana to calm their feelings of insecurity. In its more flagrant and dangerous form, the participants' drug use consisted of using of hallucinogens to escape from the depressing character of their worlds of abuse. (Tia: "I'll have to go buy cigarettes, cause I don't like to let people see the real me 'cause I'm afraid that they won't like it.")

Avoidant behaviors.

The participants were also careful not to think or speak about many childhood experiences in order to avoid remembering the terrible nature of their upbringing.

Denying themselves the opportunity to discuss their maltreatment with others, however, made it even more impossible for them to make any kind of sense of their experiences. In particular, they could not understand why the abuse was occurring or how to stop it. This left them with the awful feeling that their maltreatment could simply be due to their own shortcomings. Without communication and commiseration concerning their abuse, therefore, the participants suffered intensified confusion, shame, and guilt. (Tia: "If something goes wrong in my family I feel like it's my fault. I kept all of that bottled up inside. It sometimes made me sick, stressed. I would have stomach cramps, chest pains all of the time and I would constantly be going to the doctor.")

The participants were further predisposed to avoid interpersonal contact with others out of a fear of being victimized. Since they had become accustomed to being victimized and were constantly ready for attacks, they were slow to trust those attempting to communicate with them in a respectful, caring way. The participants were prone to believe that any kindness shown to them was disingenuous. They further thought that anyone who was kind to them would eventually begin to victimize them like their maternal figures did. (Bob: "I figured that my aunt and uncle were going to get tired of me too and start acting like my mother. I thought it was a role at first, like, be all nice to you then treat you like shit.") Consequently, the participants developed strategies for guarding against self-disclosure and interpersonal intimacy. For example, they often pretended to be someone they weren't in order to guard themselves from genuine interpersonal encounters. Unfortunately, however, this social isolation only served to exacerbate their sense of isolation and feelings of being abnormal or uncomfortably different from everyone else. (Bob: "I always wondered why people always had something to say about me. Like, like, I'm isolated. It's true. I am isolated.")

Misplaced aggression and the need for control.

Aside from being defensive and avoidant, the participants also had occasion to express their frustration and anger with themselves and their maternal figures by making people they perceived as vulnerable the scapegoats for their feelings of aggression. They physically or psychologically dominated others in order to attain a feeling of power. These attempts to dominate other people were examples of how the participants attempted to compensate for their frustrated sense of agency or will through the use of control. (Sue: "I didn't feel like I was in control over who I am. But then I met these guys; I could use them as much as I wanted and I could kick them to the curb. It was like a feeling of empowerment. Like I was finally in control.")

Embattled self-awareness and self-definition.

The frustrated sense of agency lingering from their childhood made the participants feel inadequate to the task of figuring out where they were supposed to go and who they were supposed to be when they grew up. They were despairingly indecisive. In preparing for adulthood they found it agonizingly difficult to find a sense of direction or purpose in life. Thus, they were distraught and confused about their place in the world. They lamented over the question "What am I going to do with my life?" (Tia: "I feel like I don't know where I'm going in life. It took me so long to decide on a major. I honestly don't know where to find happiness.")

Discussion of the Research Results

For all of the participants, feelings of shame proved to be the most pervasive and debilitating dimension of their lives. Having maternal relationships that continually predisposed them to question their adequacy as persons (i.e., feeling "not-good-enough"), the participants tended to attribute their maltreatment to defects of their character. They responded to their self-blame with attempts at proving their worth to their maternal figures (i.e., their perpetrators). As the participants' increased their futile efforts to win their maternal figures' affections and end their abuse, their self-worth and sense of value as persons decreased. These results illuminate an important dimension of the relationship between low self-esteem and psychological maltreatment. Though the participants experienced a range of self-depreciating affect (e.g., insecurity, guilt), their low self-esteem was most intimately tied to a specific cycle of shame: a mutually worsening interplay between feelings of inadequacy and resultant self-blame.

Perhaps the most widely held account of aggression in psychological maltreatment sequelae is that victims become aggressive out of hypersensitivity and defensiveness (e.g., McCarthy, 1990; Van der Kolk & Fisler, 1994). Rieder and Cicchetti (1989, 390–391) expressed this view by hypothesizing that psychological abuse could dispose children to be overly attuned to the potentially aggressive components of situations. As a result, victims' social relations may become fraught with fear, tension, and ultimately defensive acting out. However, the data of the current study indicated that shame played a crucial role in the participants' aggression in a way that diverges from the interpretation of defensiveness. The participants agonized over the feelings of self-dissatisfaction and disempowerment that accompanied their verbal victimization. As a result, they were imbued with a certain cognitive rigidity that predisposed them to view people as either perpetrators or victims. Thus, the participants made people they perceived to be vulnerable the scapegoats for their frustration and anger. Becoming aggressive brought with it a pseudo-empowered sense of satisfaction. They derived a feeling of pleasure from finally being on the winning end of an abusive relationship and a sense of regaining control over their lives and interpersonal relations.

Shame was also vital to the development of the participants' pessimism and self-directed anger. As long as their perpetrators were unhappy with them, the participants were unhappy with themselves. Their inability to please their maternal figures made it increasingly difficult for them to perceive their lives as worthwhile. The shame that resulted from their repeated experiences of failure truncated the participants' confidence in their abilities to establish a sense of purpose for themselves throughout adolescence. Thus, the data of this study suggest that the pessimism that Ney et al. (1986) cited as integral to the experience of psychological maltreatment has a ground in the victims' inability to develop a sense of meaning in their lives. Overwhelmed with feelings of rejection, the participants in the current study tearfully concluded that their personal worlds bore little value.

In addition to their depressed affect, the participants responded to their maternal rejection with self-dissatisfaction and anger. The participants experienced the self-directed anger cited in the Ney et al. (1986) study as a function of their self-reproaches. Angry at their maternal figures for maltreating them, the participants' anger was also representative of a sense of inner turmoil and confusion over their abusive maternal relationships. Their self-directed anger, coupled with the anger and frustration they felt with regard to their maternal relations, gave rise to self-destructive spitefulness, cries for help, and subsequent abusive interpersonal relations designed to manage the cycle of shame.

This study found that shame was the dimension of the participants' experiences that brought phenomenological coherence to their perspectives on their maltreatment. Shame themes within the lived context of victims' abuse were threaded through the factual data uncovered by previous studies of psychological maltreatment sequelae. The shame themes that were explicated took a variety of forms, each theme being indicative of the participants' sense that there was something inherently wrong with them. These feelings were found to be the most foundational determinants of low self-esteem, aggression, pessimism about one's future, and self-directed anger.

This investigation suggests that the participants' interpersonal style may be cited as a rich inroad to the further study of psychological maltreatment. The participants in this study sought to cope with their anguish through dependency, isolationism, and aggression. Generally speaking, their development was characterized by attempts to overcome their suffering via these three dysfunctional coping strategies. These results are similar to the findings of Egeland and Erikson on the impact of emotionally unavailable parenting on children. Conceptualizing their findings in terms of attachment theory (Ainsworth, Blehar, Waters, & Wall 1978; Bowlby 1969), Egeland and Erikson (1987, 118) noted:

> Children who had been classified as anxious/avoidant in infancy were observed to be highly dependent on preschool teachers, noncompliant, and poorly skilled in social interaction with peers. Teachers described them as hostile, impulsive, giving up easily, and withdrawn. These behaviors represent the maladaptation we would predict for a child with an attachment figure who is emotionally unresponsive.

Within this account are references to dependent behavior, aggression ("hostility"), and isolationism ("withdrawal"), each of which parallels the findings of the present study. This makes sense considering that the victims' maternal figures in the current investigation were emotionally unavailable in addition to being verbally abusive. The participants' proclivity for dependency, isolationism, and aggression also strongly resembles Karen Horney's (1945) psychoanalytic descriptions of moving toward, away, and against people.

The Research Results Inverted

If psychological maltreatment is the core component of all child abuse, then by inverting the above results one may obtain some valid clues as to the nature of healthy maternal relations and their impact on child development. To be sure, this is no substitute for studying healthy maternal relations or healthy child development directly. Nonetheless, drawing inferences from the current research can serve as a precursor to a more direct study of the phenomena discussed here.

Pedagogical considerations.

If psychologically abusive maternal relations are characterized by hostility and emotional neglect, then good maternal relations would be fundamentally supportive and empathic. Children would need to feel as if their maternal figures genuinely cared for and wanted them. In addition, psychologically supportive maternal figures would be affirming of their children. That is, these maternal figures would convey to their children that they were inherently good, able, and deserving of love.

These sentiments would be conveyed directly through verbalizations and indirectly through affectionate behaviors, such as hugs and kisses. The results of this research indicate that children's maternal relations are very much bound to shared language and the development of a social body (lived-embodiment). The individuals in this study valued and sought verbal communication with their maternal figures. They longed for explicit verbal confirmation that they had a safe, accepting, and affirming place in their homes. They hoped to engage in a caring, mutually nurturing dialogue with their maternal figures; anything less than this was experienced as painful to the participants. The participants also looked to their maternal figures for confirmation of their safety and worth via the manner in which their maternal figures spoke to them. The participant's attended to the manner in which their maternal figures spoke and sought implicit evidence that their speech was laden with positive affection.

Yet another source of implicit communication in the participants' maternal relations was body language. In addition to seeking affectionate words, children "read" affection and sensitivity from behavior. In order to feel cared for, the participants in the current study looked for evidence of their maternal figures' love by reading intentions embedded within their embodied contact (or lack thereof) with their maternal figures. What was of particular importance to the participants was that their maternal figures give welcoming attention to them, hug them, and kiss them. The participants inferred from their maternal figures' not engaging in these behaviors that they were unloved and unwanted as children. In short, the above results suggest that support and empathic care need to be evident in the explicit and implicit aspects of a mother-child dialogue for child development to proceed in a healthy manner.

Developmental inferences.

This affectionate, empathic style of mothering would be conducive to emotional bonding and imbue children with a basic sense of connectedness to others. The feeling of connectedness to the supportive maternal figure would result in children feeling safe and secure in the knowledge that they would have someone to whom they could turn in times of crisis. Moreover, these children would feel good about themselves; they would feel special and valued. Having been treated in an affirming way by their maternal figures, these children would also feel able to make good decisions and feel empowered to handle problems as they got older. In response to their maternal figures' care for them, these children would be self-affirming (e.g., self-acceptance, self-respect, self-esteem). Moreover, they would seek constructive means for coping with peer pressure and other developmental stressors. For example, the children of supportive parents would be inclined to seek and value prosocial contact with others throughout their development. When involved in social relations, these children would allow others the freedom to be themselves.

Finally, the feeling of empowerment from their maternal relationships would give emotionally supported children the sense that they were adequate to the task of finding their place in life as they enter adulthood (i.e., identity formation).

KEY TERMS AND CONCEPTS

Aggression
Avoidant behaviors
Being cast aside
Communication deficits
Credibility checks
Denying emotional responsiveness
Edited syntheses
Embattled self-awareness and self-definition
Emotional sensitivity
Emotional support and sensitivity
Exploiting/corrupting
General structural description
Good parenting
Healthy development
Inadequate maternal nurturing and affection
Internalization of abusive messages
Interpretation of psychological abuse
Interviews
Isolating
Low self-esteem
Misplaced aggression
Narrative descriptions
Need for control
Negative comparisons
Neglect
Pessimism
Phenomenological methodology
Psychological abuse sequelae
Psychological maltreatment
Qualitative research
Resignation
Self-blame
Self-destructive behaviors
Self-directed anger

Spurning
Terrorizing
Units of psychological significance
Validation procedures
Verbal abuse
Victim's worldview
Written protocols

CHAPTER 10

EXISTENTIAL-HUMANISTIC SELF-DEVELOPMENT THEORY (EHSDT)

The purpose of this final chapter is to outline the basic principles of a humanistic self-development theory. This theory will have existential-phenomenological underpinnings. Thus, the theory presented in this chapter will henceforth be referred to as existential-humanistic self-development theory, or EHSDT, for short. Having critically explicated a variety of self-theories and having also presented several related phenomenological descriptions of childhood experience, a unified characterization of EHSDT can now be created. The primary aim of the current theory is to characterize optimal, healthy self-development, not to conceptualize "normal" or pathological self-development. To introduce this theory, a number of fundamental issues need to be addressed. These issues will be posed in the form of questions below.

What Is the Self?

"Self" is a term that is often confused with other concepts in psychological literature. In the interest of clarity, the self ought to be distinguished from these concepts before concentrating on its positive meaning. The self is not the ego of psychoanalytic psychology, the ego of cognitive psychology, or any other rational-functional structure of the mind. The self is neither a faculty of the mind, nor the mind itself, per se. Moreover, the self is not a mechanism inside the brain. Selfhood does not refer to any sort of interior subject or apparatus residing behind the epidermis. There is no assumption of a "little person" inside the body inherent to EHSDT. For the current theory, the self is not actually inside the person the way a jelly bean sits inside a jar, for example. A self is always in-the-world. Selfhood is inclusive of, but not limited to, conscious, reflective understandings of one's world-relatedness. There are senses of self that precede and underlie the conscious self-concept and identity. Finally, the self is not a theoretical concept that is exclusive to a particular philosophical movement or school of psychological thought. The previous pages are but a small demonstration of the wide variety of authors who have had a strong interest in the self.

Self-development is an unfolding process of personality integration. Thus, Koffka (1931), Schachtel (1959), and Stern (1985) each described the origins of self-development in infancy as consisting of an evolving diversity of integrative processes. Particular integrative processes are consolidated with each other to form increasingly large experiential Gestalts, eventually resulting in the formation of a relatively consistent pattern of perceptions, feelings, thoughts, values, and interpersonal relations. In other words, during infancy, the child begins to develop a global sense of self through the amalgamation of manifold integrative processes. Figure 10.1 below illustrates how integrative processes, such as those noted by Koffka, Schachtel, and Stern, evolve to form larger integrations. To make the illustration clearer, particular integrative processes are categorized according to what Murray (2001, 61–92) called the physical, emotional, cognitive, and social-moral-agency domains of self-development. With personal integration beginning so early in development, self-development throughout childhood is not so much a process of becoming increasingly separated out from the mother's existence, but rather a process of forming an increasingly multifaceted style of interacting with the world and other people. Thus, as Stern (1985) noted, an emergent sense of self leads to the addition of a core sense of self, and so on.

I must note, however, that the increasingly multifaceted styles of world-relatedness that arise throughout the course of self-development are not necessarily "better" forms of world-relatedness. EHSDT holds no global negative value judgment against earlier experiences of selfhood, as more multifaceted styles of relating to the world can yield more disjointed, alienating senses of self. This is particularly true of unhealthy self-development. The phenomenology of time (Chapter Eight) may serve to illustrate the general issue being raised here. When a child becomes more adept at symbolic language and abstract, calculative thought, he or she can assimilate our public system of keeping time into his or her repertoire of experience and behavior. This new ability can aid the child in widening his or her personal integration to include responsible action and commitments to projects and other people. At the same time, however, when a child learns clock time, there is a danger that his or her attention will be habitually pulled away from the invigorating, evocative characteristics of the present. The development of clock time can enhance social connectedness (and thus, personal integration as well) or detract one from a vital connection with the lived-present. Thus, what appears to be optimal in terms of self-development is the capacity to add new nuances to one's personal integration without loosing touch with the fresh, vital, holistic perspectives that preceded their arrival. Hence, Schachtel (1959) saw the need for the integration of both autocentric and allocentric perception, while Stern (1985) warned of the dangers inherent to the development of a verbal sense of self (174).

It is not enough to note that an integrative process unfolds throughout self-development. It is just as vital to understand why it takes place. In other words, there must be sufficient motivation for the child to repeatedly engage in the integrative process. Throughout the course of this text, four major motivational tendencies have risen to the fore as the basic motivations intrinsic to self-development. The first of these is the motivation to achieve homeostasis. The purpose of the homeostatic motivational tendency is to reduce tensions and thereby experience a state of calm, stability, or "inner balance." There are three primary goals inherent to the homeostatic motivational tendency. The first is to satisfy biological drives. The second goal is to remove disturbing sensations by recoiling from contact with the world. The third homeostatic goal is to release emotional tension via cathartic self-expression.

The second major motivation inherent to self-development is the motivation to adapt to one's surroundings. The purpose of the adaptational motivational tendency is to manage and regulate one's world-relatedness in a manner that allows one to cope with challenges, fit in with one's surroundings, and attain a sense of security in the world. Accordingly, there are many goals inherent to the adaptive motivational tendency. For instance, the child's adaptational goals might be to adjust to change, to self-manage (e.g., time management), to predict outcomes, to willfully control life circumstances, to follow direction, to take initiative, to harness enthusiasm, to develop technical skills, to calculate, to logically deliberate, to maintain consistency in one's world-relations, or to achieve a constant identity.

Figure 10.1 An Evolving Process of Personal Integration Beginning in Infancy

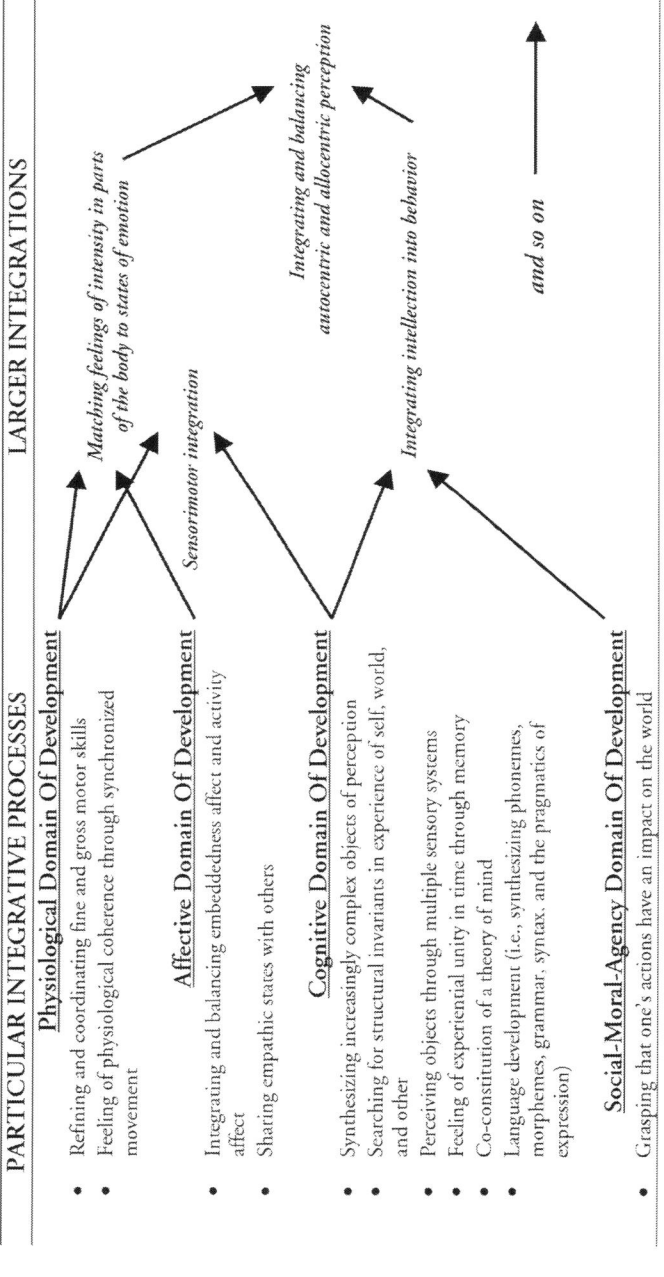

The third major motivational tendency is the motivation toward self-enrichment. The purpose of the self-enriching motivational tendency is to attain and cultivate a personally agreeable quality of life and experience as a being-in-the-world. Self-enrichment denotes the child's striving toward goals that bring enjoyment and "happiness," for lack of a better term. Here, interactions with one's own body, oneself, others, and things are pleasing, not because tensions are removed, but because the contact is itself pleasurable and invigorating.

The fourth and final motivation inherent to self-development is the motivation toward self-transcendence, to borrow Frankl's (1967, 49) apt term. Self-transcendence refers to the inspired, meaningful striving toward things and others in-the-world. Here, the focus of the child's experience is the desire to be in contact with the world out of a care, concern, or dedication that is aimed at things and others in their own right. This is made possible by the development of allocentric perception (Chapter Seven). Self-transcendent goals prevent the child's personality from becoming a system of self-concern, closed in upon itself, so to speak.

The purpose of the self-transcending motivational tendency is to relate to things and others in the most meaningful and profound manner, one that overrides (without necessarily eliminating) concern for one's own enjoyment, happiness, well-being, and so on. Experientially, self-interest is superseded by interest that is directed outward, toward things and others. As is obvious, the chapters in this text tended to focus on the importance of the self-enriching and self-transcending motivational tendencies. This is to be expected, as these are the more uniquely human motivational tendencies. Due to the large number of characteristics that have been noted to represent these two motivational tendencies, examples are provided in Table 10.1 below.

The developing child is always motivated to pursue goals associated with each of his or her basic motivational tendencies throughout development. As Bühler noted, goals act as foci that require the development of integrative processes (Bühler & Allen 1972, 44, 50). Stated differently, integrative processes occur so that the child can effectively pursue the goals toward which he or she is motivated. To cite a simple example, an infant will sharpen and coordinate sensory and motor skills with the aim of establishing contact with the mother. The child will orient his or her body movements and vocalizations in such a way as to facilitate empathic resonance on the part of his or her primary caretaker. This connection provides many benefits, such as a more effective means for communicating hunger and thereby being fed. Consequently, this sort of integrative process leads directly to an enhanced ability to reach a goal consonant with the homeostatic motivational tendency. This is but one example of how a better integrated personality is a more empowered personality, one that is able to pursue the various goals it is motivated toward with more overall efficacy than a less integrated personality.

Ultimately, integrative processes like those noted in Figure 10.1 above occur under the auspices, so to speak, of a global integrative tendency of child development, which involves the pursuit of relatively valued goals through the interpretation, appropriation, and integration of various motivational trends (i.e., homeostatic, adaptational, self-enriching, and self-transcending). In each case, the child's integrative efforts are unique. Referring to the self as the core, center, or nucleus of the personality is meant to call our attention to the distinctive manner in which the child consolidates motivational trends and hierarchically orders his or her goals in life (Bühler 1968d, 340). Every child, even an identical twin, has a particular style of interpreting and organizing his or her world (experientially and behaviorally) throughout development. This is because the child's integrative efforts are the result of the way his or her characteristic imaginative style meets the demands of his or her particular bio-psycho-social, cultural, and historical situation. As Murray (1986) noted, imagination is the unity building power inherent to every human's being-in-the-world. Accordingly, imagination is "the key that unlocks the door to the mysteries of personality integration as we author our own life's mythos, history, and narrative" (2001, 15).

Table 10.1
Self-Enriching and Self-Transcending Motives According to EHSDT

Goals of the Self-Enriching Motivational Tendency	Goals of the Self-Transcending Motivational Tendency
• To accept and affirm one's own uniqueness	• To accept and affirm others as unique individuals different from oneself
• To achieve a sense of competence	
• To attain a feeling of evolution in one's personal development	• To appreciate mystery and develop a capacity for wonder and awe
• To develop a sense of will	• To be oneself with and for others
• To engage in spontaneous self-expression	• To become altruistic, benevolent, and charitable

- To enjoy sustained contact with self, things, and others
- To experience a sense of hope
- To experience a vital feeling of aliveness
- To experience oneself as "fully functioning" (i.e., as actualizing skills, talents, abilities, etc.)
- To experience personal satisfaction in familial and romantic love
- To experience personal satisfaction in friendship
- To feel a sense of belonging
- To feel confident in one's adequacy and value as a person (i.e., self-respect and self-esteem)
- To feel confident in one's skills, perceptions, and evaluations
- To have clarity and understanding with regard to one's feelings, thoughts, wishes, desires, and interests
- To infuse ambitions and personal ideals into one's goal-setting
- To selectively attend to sense perceptions
- To become compassionate, sympathetic, and empathetic
- To become responsible
- To care for or take care of things and others
- To construct an overarching philosophy of life
- To create
- To develop a capacity for fidelity
- To develop a clear sense of values via promises and commitments
- To develop a conscience (i.e., morals, ethics)
- To develop a constructive-productive-creative orientation toward life
- To develop a sense of social values
- To develop an appreciation of the uniqueness of each moment of life
- To learn about things, events, and others in their manifold, multifaceted aspects
- To live in truth with and for others
- To love others
- To respect and appreciate ambiguity
- To uphold a life-affirming nurturance of all living things

    The process of psychological integration is not purely intellectual or calculative, but essentially vital and lived. Throughout the course of self-development, the child actually experiences himself or herself as becoming a more substantive, organized hub of perception and action in his or her direct relations to the world and relationships with others. Though self-development is available to consciousness, it is first and foremost a lived, spontaneous process without having to be a part of reflective awareness from moment to moment. As adults, we have an implicit understanding of selfhood that is sometimes apparent in everyday language. For instance, selfhood is implied when a sad, depressed, or otherwise upset person remarks, "My life is a mess;" or worse, "I'm coming apart." The lived self is similarly implied when someone admonishes to a distraught person, "Pull yourself together!" Given what has been said thus far, a formal definition of the self is as follows: *"The self" is the imaginative, experiential hub of the personality, most intimately associated with (a) the interpretation, appropriation, and integration of motivational trends; (b) the organization and prioritization of personal goals; and (c) the formation of a unique pattern of perceptions, feelings, thought processes, values, and relationships in-the-world-with-others.* In concise, developmental terms, the self is the imaginative-integrative impetus and awareness of the growing person.

What Are the Fundamental Characteristics of Optimal, Healthy Self-Development?

Although self-development denotes a process of personal integration, it is important to bear in mind that the goal of healthy self-development is not the complete and total unification of the personality. Irrespective of an individual's confident feeling of unity or being "at one" with oneself, personality integration is never a completed process, nor is it ever absolutely free of all conflict. Such a perspective would be an anthropological idealism. Human existence is far too complex and ambiguous for any individual to have an absolute understanding of each and every aspect of their development and worldly relations. Self-development is an ongoing process, a perpetual project of becoming. Furthermore, psychological conflict is often an integral part of productive, healthy developmental change. The tendency of the healthy self is to achieve a degree of personality integration that allows for temporary disintegration in the interest of productive reorganization and growth (Bühler 1968c, 18). Moreover, a healthy self has manifold profiles that correspond to different experiential and behavioral contexts. These profiles are not evidence of an unstable, scattered, fragile personality that cannot cope with novelty or difference. On the contrary, optimal self-development is characterized by a tensile strength. The optimal self-structure is one that is not only stable and consistent, but also dynamic and open to possibilities for being-in-the-world-with-others.

In order for the child's personal integration to evolve through productive developmental metamorphoses, the child must maintain a relative openness to experience. When a young child feels secure in the knowledge that he or she has someone to turn to for care, support, and nurturance (broadly conceived), he or she establishes a psycho-emotional "barometric equilibrium" in lived-space that is comfortable and conducive to exploration and pleasurable contact with the world. This equilibrium empowers the child to regulate the amount of new experience that he or she finds tolerable at any given time. In his or her involvement with things and others, the child who is developing a healthy sense of self perceives the world as a horizon of possibilities for inspired, creative action, such as play. Through such actions, the child develops a confident sense of social connectedness while learning about his or her innermost potentials for becoming. Healthy self-development is a process wherein the child is increasingly in touch and in tune with the most personally meaningful aspects of his or her imaginative-integrative efforts while learning and growing through concrete interactions in-the-world-with-others. Optimally, the child would enjoy, accept, and affirm his or her felt experience and characteristic patterns of organizing experiences in response to worldly predicaments—self-acceptance, self-respect, and self-esteem. These three qualities ensure that the developing child's symbolically represented self-concept will remain consonant with his or her genuine lived-experience throughout development.

As is obvious from this description, all four of the basic motivational tendencies outlined above contribute to the child's ability to integrate a unique style of relating to the world. Of the four basic motivational tendencies, it is the self-enriching and self-transcending tendencies that maximize the child's world-openness and ensure that his or her integrative tendency will continually widen and evolve as a being-in-the-world. Thus, these tendencies are the quintessential expressions of healthy self-development and the best gauge of a child's personality integration at any given time of child development. Stated differently, optimal self-development is gauged by the extent to which a child is able to display self-enriching and self-transcending characteristics throughout the lifespan. Without self-enriching and self-transcending motives, the child would fall back on aims that constrict his or her full potential for co-constituting newer, more sophisticated and meaningful forms of organized relating to things and others. Self-development entails something more than attaining homeostatic balance and becoming well-adapted. Homeostasis and adaptation are potent forces in child development that can strengthen the self. When properly nurtured, each of the basic tendencies has the potential to support and be supported by the other basic tendencies, resulting in a more or less unified personality. However, self-development is inclusive of, but not limited to, homeostatic and adaptive tendencies. Self-development also involves productive, invigorating, value-laden action in-the-world-with-others. It involves the inspired desire to experience, to learn, to grow, to love and care, to "create and relate." It is for this reason that secret, hidden places play an important role in self-development. The child's imaginative capabilities are nurtured through the discovery of hidden, secret places. In secret places the child imbues objects with personal meaning, creates scenarios, develops characters, and schematizes fictional predicaments that frame and beckon the construction of aims and goals. The child practices the art of giving the world his or her own personal touch. He or she creatively imbues the world with significance, value, and purpose, free from the constraints of established adult meanings. Consequently, the child becomes more intimately familiar with himself or herself in the process.

Soon after birth, the infant is busy pursuing homeostatic, adaptational, and self-enriching goals, all of which are inextricably interdependent and foundational to growth and maturity. For instance, the child may seek to reduce a need tension or remove an unpleasant sensation by crying, so that a responsive caregiver will bring a nipple to suckle, milk to drink, diapers for changing, and so on. Adaptational goals arise due to the radical shift from intrauterine life to life outside the womb. Once severed from the umbilical cord, biological tensions arise and emotional needs become a reality. As a result, the child will search for evidence that care is consistent, predictable, and reliable. Moreover, he or she will seek physical contact in the form of holding and rocking, for example, in order to derive a sense of security. Again, if the infant cannot achieve these goals, he or she may protest by crying. The child may fuss and perhaps become enraged. The child's protests, if successful, will then yield a feeling of control over the childrearing environment. However, it must be kept in mind that the optimal environment for self-development is one that is so accommodating to the child's needs that the pursuit of homeostatic and adaptational goals do not dominate experience. In advance of the child's arrival, a dedicated, reliable caretaker is sure to have the child's needs "covered," to borrow Winnicott's (1959, 126) term, so that the child will be free to turn toward the world in a relaxed, open manner. In doing so, the child will then seek sustained, pleasurable contact with things and his or her primary caretaker, which are self-enriching goals. The establishment of a relationship that provides a sense of love, of belonging, of hope, of enjoyment and vitality, in turn, creates the most efficient, effective environment for the achievement of homeostatic and adaptational goals. As Schachtel (1959, 50) put it:

> We know, however, that if the mother appears upon the child's crying, but is angry, anxious, tense, or otherwise not capable of giving tender attention to the child and its needs, the crying may continue, feeding difficulties may set in, and even a not hungry child may not feel comforted when it is picked up by an anxious or tense mother.

Thus, in an optimal environment for self-development, the infant would not be full of tension and frustration, would not be riddled with anxiety, and would not be listlessly accommodating. Rather, proactive, sensitive, accommodating caretakers would keep tensions reduced, remove disturbing stimulations, and ward off anxiety to make room for the child's more worldly proclivities. This is the situation most conducive to the integration of a "core" of self-experience, to use Stern's (1985, 46) terminology.

The eventual pursuit of self-transcending goals is made possible by events occurring during the latter half of the first year of life, beginning at approximately the eighth month. As Schachtel (1959) noted, the child begins to perceive in a manner that is essentially allocentric around the eighth month (141). This correlates with Stern's (1985) observation that it is not until the time between the seventh and ninth month that a child will begin to display a sense of "subjective self," characterized by a primitive theory of mind and the sharing of "inner" states (139). The sudden increase in the child's interest in developing a more varied, complex understanding of his or her caretakers' mind represents what is perhaps the first appearance of a primitive self-transcending goal. In essence, the second half of the first year of life tends to involve many cognitive and physiological advances that enhance the child's ability to examine things and others. For example, during this time there are improvements in the infant's vision and his or her ability to grasp and manipulate objects. In addition, it is likely that the child will sit upright, stand, walk, and perhaps utter first words. Thus, as self-development proceeds toward and into early childhood, the healthy child's inclination toward world-relatedness is markedly empowered, increasing his or her potential to pursue self-transcending motives in addition to self-enriching motives.[4]

As the child becomes more physically and mentally adept at exploring the environment, there is an increase in and diversification of more worldly goals. Concretely, play increases, and it becomes blatantly obvious that the child is identifying most strongly with his or her self-enriching and self-transcending motivational tendencies. These developments indicate an expanding imaginative-integrative impetus, one that is widening to span a broader array of creative possibilities in the world with things and others. This is so much the case that early childhood is sometimes referred to as "the play years." Observing a four- and five-

---

4   The reader should not mistake this description of optimal self-development to mean that certain motivational tendencies or goals are the exclusive province of healthy individuals. While optimal development is characterized by a maximization of the child's world-relating potential, unhealthy development consists of varied forms and degrees of *constricted* world-openness. Thus, a person suffering from a severe form of psychopathology might still display traits associated with self-transcendence, for example. In effect, the disparity between optimal development and unhealthy development is not an all-or-nothing issue. Human development and human existence in general are far to complex to be conceptualized in such simplistic terms.

year-old classroom provides striking evidence of the importance of play. On a regular basis, a child will "forget" to eat and delay trips to the bathroom until the last possible minute due to the strong investment in his or her play activities.[5] While adaptive goals continually take on a renewed character throughout development, early childhood should not be mistaken as a time where coping with separation and novel situations (i.e., classrooms) reigns supreme in the child's experience. They are undeniable realities. However, optimal self-development during this time is characterized by the realization that learning is fun, and a confident conviction that the fear of the unknown cannot match the exhilaration of discovery. The healthy developing child maintains a lived, implicit grasp that life is lived in turning toward the world, in invigorating, enjoyable relations to things and others. It is precisely this sort of awareness that appears lacking in certain developmental disorders like autism, for example.

As the child moves toward the age of what Piaget (1963) called "concrete operations" (i.e., between seven and eleven), adults expect him or her to show significant increases in rational thought. However, in the optimal developmental scenario, an adaptational trait like rational thought would not, as is all too often the case, eclipse creative, self-enriching and self-transcending traits. As the child begins to learn how to think in a more logical, calculative manner, he or she ought to be empowered by this new skill to unleash new imaginative potentials for creating an enjoyable, fulfilling, meaningful existence (self-enriching and self-transcending traits). In the optimal scenario, the appearance of rational thought would not eclipse the child's creative power. As Murray (1986, 36–37) put it:

> It is a proper human accomplishment to live both logically and imaginatively, and it may well be that the greatest human achievement of all lies in the experiential realization of genuine poetic living, thus optimizing the strong presence of both kinds of thinking in human existence.

---

5   Certain branches of psychoanalysis would likely interpret a child's delay in going to the toilet as a strategy to derive "anal gratification." However, such an interpretation seems to be more appropriate to the younger child in the designated "anal stage" or to a fixated child. The interpretation offered here deviates from the strictly analytic interpretation as it does not assume that a fixation exists in advance. If a healthy child (no longer in the anal stage) is so attached to play activities that satisfying hunger is of far less importance than the play itself, then is appears reasonable to conclude that not going to the bathroom may be a similar phenomenon. Delaying a trip to the bathroom is a common event, and one that occurs far more often during playtime in particular.

Nor would the appearance of rational thought overshadow the child's inherently holistic, impassioned, social nature. Carol Gilligan's (1982) critique of Lawrence Kohlberg's (1969) theory of moral development comes to mind as an analogue to the current perspective. The formation of highly intellectual moral principles should not diminish the often simpler (though no less profound) morality of care that is its developmental precursor. This is not to falsely romanticize childhood as an especially moral period of life or deny a child's capacity for selfishness and cruelty. Rather, the broader point is that improvements in the child's ability to think logically ought to support and facilitate his or her already developing potential for interpersonal sensitivity and compassion (e.g., empathy development, which is first and foremost a product of imaginative thought rather than reason).

In the optimal developmental scenario, the child's strong tendencies toward world-relatedness will be marked by an increasing value on the importance of achieving self-transcendent goals as he or she moves into and through adolescence. Accordingly, self-transcending motives will become factors in the achievement of the other, relatively less world-oriented goals. For example, competence and self-esteem (i.e., self-enriching traits) might be fostered through the altruistic helping of others (e.g., Yalom 1995, 12–13). As Knowles (1986, 151) noted, the self-transcendent trait of commitment is a prerequisite for the formation of a constant, self-reflective identity (an adaptational trait):

> The identity stage is one in which the young person is centrally concerned with the question of knowing the self. In our view, the question is never adequately answered and can't be, even partially, until the person makes a commitment and lives it out for a number of years.

To cite yet another example, loving another person (a self-transcending goal) might become a prerequisite for attaining fulfilling erotic pleasure and adequate sexual gratification, which are self-enriching and homeostatic goals respectively. Eventually, self-transcending motives might take on such power in the personality that achieving other motivational goals might be of comparatively little significance, as Viktor Frankl's descriptions of life in Nazi concentration camps has shown. In his words:

> The vital requirement [for the health and survival of prisoners] was ... to undergo [a] reversal such that they should no longer ask what they could expect from life, but ... that life was awaiting something from them ... for each of them ... somebody or something was waiting,

whether it was a piece of work to be done or another human being. (1967, 104)

All in all, the conception of a healthy developing self that is central to EHSDT is quite different from the rationalistic, cognitively biased ideal of an increasingly logical consciousness adapting to the challenges of a mechanistic world. A child is not conceived of as a poorly adapted, irrational thinker, but rather as a caring, enjoying, creative, holistically perceiving, and world-relating creature. This aspect of EHSDT was most eloquently expressed in the words of Saint-Exupéry in his book *The Little Prince* (1971):

> Grown-ups love figures. When you tell them that you have made a new friend, they never ask you any questions about essential matters. They never say to you, "What does his voice sound like? What games does he love best? Does he collect butterflies?" Instead, they demand: "How old is he? How many brothers has he? How much does he weigh? How much money does his father make?" Only from these figures do they think that they have learned anything about him. (16–17)

In *The Little Prince,* Saint-Exupéry artfully described the child as needing to "come down" to the "sensible level" of discourse when speaking to adults (5). In the language of EHSDT, Saint-Exupéry described the leveling down of the child's inspired perspective to a more adaptational worldview. When considering matters of great self-transcendent concern, he opined, "No grown-up will ever understand that this is a matter of so much importance" (107). Similarly, EHSDT admonishes that developmental psychologists avoid the temptation to judge childhood from their own rationalistic viewpoint for the child's own good and for the benefit of conscientious pedagogy.

Does Self-Development Occur in Stages?

The stage view of child development is a highly controversial one. EHSDT does not propose that one must be a stage theorist to develop understandings of self-development. Chapters Two and Three illustrated how self-development can be examined without the use of stages. Moreover, phenomenological research regularly explicates significant dimensions of self-development without the use of stages. In the interest of parsimony, EHSDT does not offer another stage theory of self-development.

Nonetheless, as Chapters Four and Five illustrate, EHSDT does not discount the potential of stage theories to contribute to an understanding of self-development. The creation of stage theories is a legitimate way to explore and illuminate self-development. However, phase-like shifts that occur in self-development cannot be viewed as independent of sociocultural and historical forces. Self-development does not occur in stages in the strict sense of biologically predetermined, rigidly segmented periods of growth that begin and end during certain times of childhood for all children at all times. Phase shifts in self-development can only be considered the result of interactions between the child and the people in his or her social world, as self-development is inherently social and worldly from its outset.

The idea that developmental issues arising at certain periods of growth are not exclusive to that period was central to the theories put forth by Charlotte Bühler (Chapter Four), Richard Knowles (Chapter Five), and Daniel Stern (Chapter Six). All of Bühler's basic tendencies were considered present from birth and none were held to become dormant or lose importance as development proceeded. Knowles maintained a somewhat similar position, noting that the issues of each stage are never resolved once and for all, but continually reappear in later development. This same argument was made by Daniel Stern, who did not like to use the term stage because of its traditional meaning of "time-locked" periods of growth. Stern used the term "domains" rather than phases or stages because no developmental issues are lost to adult experience. Nonetheless, he also relied on the concept of predominance as an alternative to the idea of time-locked phases. As he put it:

> There will inevitably be periods when one or two domains hold predominance by default. In fact, each successive organizing subjective perspective requires the preceding one as a precursor. Once formed, the domains remain forever as distinct forms of experiencing social life and self. None are lost to adult experience. Each simply gets more elaborated. (1985, 32)

Based upon the ideas of Bühler, Knowles, and Stern, one may legitimately conceptualize healthy self-development as stage-like, but with four caveats. First, all of the time-specific developmental issues discussed in the previous chapters would be worked on in some manner during all of the major periods of development, with certain issues taking only temporary overall precedence within certain general time frames. That is, though some issues would rise to a predominant status, none would be exclusive to a major period and none would be lost to later experience. Second, the identification of a stage does not necessitate that one issue alone must be predominant. Multiple issues can be viewed as rising to the status of temporary predominance simultaneously. Third, time ranges in stage theories must be viewed as averages, loose approximations, or generalizations and should not be regarded as rigid indicators of the tempo of healthy development. Self-development is first and foremost a highly individualized process, and any assessment of the speed of a child's developmental progress should be guided by an appreciation for the child's unique style of growth. In effect, slower does not necessarily mean poorer. The quality of any developmental achievement ought to be considered in its own right before it is judged based on the speed of its accomplishment. Fourth and finally, the stage-like aspects of a theory of self-development are always the product of their culture and should not be misconstrued as necessarily applying to child development in all cultural settings.

When Does Self-Development Begin?

Self-development begins almost from birth. Infants begin the imaginative-integrative process of distinguishing themselves as a coherent unity from the world around them throughout the first two months. Though early experience is intensely holistic or sensory-motor-affective, children are not born in an autistic state, nor do they live in a symbiotic fashion in early infancy. Still, it is not until the second to the seventh month that children finally establish the firm psychophysical integration that Daniel Stern (1985) called the "core" of self-consolidation (69–70). The primordial form of personal consolidation in infancy is the sense of being an integrated bio-psycho-social unit with a past, present, and future. Later, between the fifteenth to the eighteenth month, children begin the development of a verbal sense of self, which sets the stage for the evolution of the self-concept, which was discussed by Carl Rogers (Chapter Two) and Charlotte Bühler (Chapter Four). Bühler saw the self-concept as developing through childhood into adolescence where individuals begin to become reflectively self-aware. Thus, in adolescence, it becomes possible for the self to burgeon into a "self-responsible identity."

Is Self-Development a Matter of Nature or Nurture?

General position.

Children are born with the potential to behave in healthy, creative, productive ways, and in unhealthy, destructive ways. Nonetheless, EHSDT views child development as basically guided by an inherent inclination to establish interpersonal attachments, integrate one's personality, learn, mature, and grow. There is no guarantee that these healthy tendencies will actualize, however. The reason for this is that the child's innate striving toward health and maturity must be properly nurtured by those in the child's social world. Childhood is very much a time of learning, discovery, wonder, and awe. Learning naturally occurs in the care of adults who support and foster children's desire for experience, knowledge, satisfying interpersonal relationships, and fulfillment in life. In other words, though there is an innate tendency toward healthy self-development, social conditions nonetheless facilitate or impede the child's growth. Thus, self-development is the result of both genetic endowment and environmental forces, such as the demands and opportunities associated with the child's particular cultural and historical milieu, his or her education, and parenting. In Karen Horney's words (1937, 80), "A child can stand a great deal of what is regarded as traumatic—such as sudden weaning, occasional beating, sex experiences—as long as inwardly he feels wanted and loved."

"Nature" and "nurture" alone are not responsible for self-development, however. Since human beings develop enhanced potentials for freewill as they grow, choice comes to be an increasingly significant factor in self-development over time. Thus, in the final analysis, the nature and course of self-development is the result of children's genetic endowment (i.e., so-called "nature"), their child rearing and educational experiences (i.e., so-called "nurture"), and the choices that they make with regard to which motivations, emotions, impulses, thoughts, beliefs, and values will guide their goal-setting in life.

Research-specific position.

Regarding the investigation of particular phenomena related to self-development, EHSDT espouses a phenomenological attitude of neutrality. Phenomenological descriptions do not rest on assumptions regarding nature and nurture in advance of the observation and explication of developmental phenomena. The phenomenological method places its primary emphasis on the accurate description of whatever facet of childhood experience is the focus of study at any given time. The factors that bring the phenomenon under study into existence are illuminated to whatever degree the phenomenological explication allows given the circumstances of each particular investigation.

At the same time, phenomenological psychology is grounded in a nonreductionistic philosophy, which holds that phenomena cannot be completely "explained away" by natural-scientific principles. This is fundamentally consonant with the general position of EHSDT. Phenomenological psychology is meaning-oriented psychology. That is, phenomenological descriptions are descriptions of the meaning of phenomena as lived by the people experiencing them. To make the assertion that a phenomenon is "nothing but" the by-product of genetics or conditioning, for example, eliminates (or at least greatly diminishes) the dimension of meaning from psychological dialogue. Thus, phenomenological psychology and EHSDT both oppose the notion that a phenomenon might be "nothing but" the effect of some mechanistic (or mentalistic) cause.

What Kind of Parenting Is Conducive to Self-Development?

The parent with the highest likelihood of facilitating self-development in a child is a parent who displays a sense of security, self-confidence, self-acceptance, self-esteem, free self-expression, a capacity for genuine intimacy, and a sense of devotion to the childrearing process. Such a parent is best equipped to demonstrate the ten fundamental skills needed to foster self-development throughout childhood. In the interest of brevity and clarity, each of the ten is presented below in the form of a numerical list. Note that these skills are not "stage-specific," but apply rather broadly to parenting throughout the course of child development.

1. *Bringing an Ordered World to the Child.*

    In early infancy, the parent must bring the world to the dependent child in a reliable, predictable fashion. The parent must gratify the child's biological drives and stimulate the child in a responsive, sensitive manner for him or her to feel safe and experience the world as inviting. As the child gets older, especially after infancy, the parent is still responsible for bringing the world to the child, but in a somewhat modified manner. Since self-development involves bringing increasingly sophisticated structure and organization to the personality, the parent needs to set the stage for the imaginative-integrative process by maintaining an ordered, structured world for the child to use as a proper context and model for personal growth. In concrete terms, the parent has an obligation to raise the child in an environment that has guidelines, positive and negative consequences for actions, and rituals that bind the family as a unit in (lived) time and space.

2. *Affectionate Holding and Handling.*

    If the child experiences the parent as basically warm and receptive, the child will be able to manage the feelings of vulnerability and helplessness that come as a result of his or her highly dependent state. The child can thus explore the world without fear and gradually consolidate a sense of self that is in touch with his or her genuine needs, desires, motivations, and impulses. The affectionate holding and handling of the child creates an environment conducive to the development of hope and confidence rather than anxiety. Affectionate holding and handling essentially means that the parent offers a welcoming encouragement to the child's coming-into-being.

3. *Genuine Care and Involvement.*

    The parent needs to display genuine, heartfelt love and care to the child if he or she is to feel secure in the knowledge that he or she is wanted and considered valuable as a person. Genuine care is thus vital to the development of the child's self-acceptance, self-respect, and self-esteem. The parent cannot be perceived by the child as "going through the motions." Self-development is facilitated by a parent who takes an authentic interest in their child's growth and communicates this interest through affectionate words and actions. Involvement means that the parent is interested in being a part of the child's life, not just by intervening to punish and enforce boundaries, but to assist in (a) helping the child develop skills, abilities, and talents that empower and promote self-care, self-reliance, and interpersonal sensitivity; and (b) activating the child's creative expression and passion for life through a nurturing dialogue of shared words and activities.

4. *Constancy and Reliability of Loving Care.*

    The warmth and interest that the parent shows cannot be fleeting or inconsistent. The best conditions for a child's self-development are those in which the child feels that the parent loves him or her no matter what. Even when certain behaviors are frowned upon, the child never loses faith that he or she is adequate and loveable as a person.

5. *Empathic Bonding.*

    The child is best able to benefit from the warmth and care of the parent when the child feels that the parent has the proper "empathic resonance." A parent who has the capability to be empathically attuned to his or her child imbues the child with a feeling of being truly understood and genuinely close to the parent. This psychological closeness implies that the parent is able to identify with the child on a deep emotional level. An affectively attuned, understanding parent can make the child feel accepted and appreciated as a unique individual. Emotional bonding also implies that the parent may allow the child to grow according to his or her individual emotional and psychosocial needs, giving him or her the freedom to pursue courses of action that promise to bring happiness and meaning-in-life. Moreover, the identification process allows the child to use the parent's behavior as a psychological and behavioral model of self-development and later identity. In infancy, empathic resonance is communicated by holding and handling the child in an empathic, affectionate way. As the child gets older, the nature of the empathic relation is more verbal and conceptual, though physical contact is not precluded.

6. *Nurturing Felt and Symbolically Represented Experience.*

    Early experience is conspicuously "sensory-motor-affective" in comparison to adult experience. In other words, the experiential world of childhood is more feeling-oriented and holistic than intellectual (especially in the first year of life). Caring, involved parents must provide the emotional support needed for the child to remain open to felt experience, while simultaneously encouraging increasing openness to the manifold aspects of objects in their own right. Parents need to support and affirm creative, personal, visceral perception as well as the child's inclination to explore and discover the diverse characteristics of things and others. Parents must use support, guidance, and instruction to facilitate an evolving appreciation of both felt, first-person experience and the intricacies of symbolically represented experience (e.g., language, math, visual art, music, and so on), which give rise to a knowledge of alternate viewpoints.

7. *Receptive Mirroring.*

    As the child develops, the optimal parent repeatedly acknowledges and embraces the child's burgeoning creative expression. Receptive mirroring is thus important for facilitating the development of the child's self-acceptance, self-respect, and self-esteem. Repeated reflected affirmations add confidence and strength to the child's personal integration, thus supporting his or her sustained world-openness.

8. *Sensitivity to Changing Needs.*

    A truly empathic parent can gauge his or her demands and expectations against the child's gifts and inclinations. Throughout the course of development, the optimal parent remains sensitive to the child's changing needs and increasingly complex creative impulses. He or she continues to mirror the child in such a way as to convey that he or she is both safe from harm and worthy of attention. At the same time, sensitivity to the child's changing needs also includes knowing when to help the child overcome difficulties and when to allow the child time to overcome hardships on his or her own (e.g., "optimal frustration") (Kohut 1977, 188–189*n*). As the child approaches adolescence, the optimal parent would continue to be sensitive to times when joint problem solving is warranted and when the child requires the privilege of solving problems autonomously.

9. *Tempering the Severity of Discipline without Overgratifying the Child.*

    The development of a loving bond with a child requires that the severity of disciplinary measures ought to be reasonably gauged to the severity of the child's moral infraction. This means that punishment should not be too severe for minor infractions, as a matter of course. At the same time, a child who commits a serious moral transgression cannot be made to feel that there are no substantive consequences for their actions no matter how wrongly they behave. Moreover, a child should not get the impression that he or she is able to extort rewards from the parent at will. Self-development is not facilitated by a parent who has learned that the easiest way to get the child to do what he or she wants is to lace all requests and directives with a bribe. This kind of parenting shows the child that the parent has little self-confidence, thus, poor self-development. This is not a parent that the child can productively identify with for adapting to the civilized, rule-governed social world. The parent must be perceived as having the wherewithal to maintain their role as the adult-in-charge if the child is to be able to look to the parent as a viable model of self-development.

10. *Displaying Prosocial Models of Behavior.*

    Throughout development, the child is gathering information from the primary caretaker in order to integrate an increasingly dynamic personality structure. As the child gets older and the demands of life change, the child repeatedly looks to the parent for guidance and a basic understanding of values. This guidance and understanding is not only communicated through verbal encouragement and advice, but also through role modeling. The child grasps just as much from his or her firsthand observations of the parents behavior as he or she does from communicating with the parent verbally. It is especially important for the parent to display prosocial models of behavior, including love, tolerance, acceptance, peace, commitment, loyalty, dedication, and productive relating.

Are Children Active or Passive Participants in Their Development?

Having examined the self-styled approaches of the previous chapters, it is apparent that developmental self-theory is not a descendent of John Locke's British Empiricism. Each theorist has taken steps to avoid a philosophical-anthropological orientation that reduces the developing child to "nothing but" the by-product of materialistic forces, whether they be genetic or environmental. EHSDT does not consider the child's imaginative-integrative impetus to be "epiphenomenal," as it were.

At the same time, EHSDT does not rest upon a theoretical spiritualism, rationalism, intellectualism, "cognitivism," or any other perspective that views the child as picking himself or herself up by his or her own bootstraps, so to speak. Self-development is always worldly in nature, and thus subject to the influence of genetics, physiology and neurology, biochemistry, conditioning, education, parenting, cultural context (e.g., language, economics, socially constructed meanings), and so on. EHSDT sees the child as a unique individual always at work interpreting and managing varied worldly influences, taking up or rejecting potential motivations for behavior, within the context of these influences. A self is always an influenced-influencer. Selfhood is a perpetual work in progress that is the product of creative discovery. Thus, the issue of whether a child is an active or passive participant in his or her development is not an all-or-nothing issue. EHSDT holds that the healthy child is first and foremost a world-openness with the potential for activity or passivity depending on the child's developmental needs and desires at any given time.

Is Self-Development Continuous or Discontinuous?

Self-development is not discontinuous in the radical sense that developmental issues arise and eventually come to a complete and final resolution or end (as in traditional stage theories). It is discontinuous, however, in that qualitative changes in the way the child experiences the world repeatedly occur throughout development, which modify how the child relates to others as he or she matures.

Self-development is not continuous in the radical sense of development being completely dictated by quantitative increases in abilities occurring in a steady, additive manner (as in behavioral theory). Self-development is only continuous in the more general sense that experience always contains ambiguity and is not theoretically precise or as clear-cut and regimented as biological maturation.

What Kind of Parenting Threatens Self-Development?

There are a multitude of factors that can contribute to unhealthy self-development, including genetic vulnerabilities, poor parenting skills, and a wide array of potential environmental stressors and traumatic experiences. EHSDT does not consider any one force to be universally more detrimental to self-development than all others in all circumstances. For example, when considering the impact of a traumatic experience, one must consider the nature of the trauma, its frequency, its duration, and ultimately its severity. However, the severity of any traumatic experience is itself a function of the manner in which it is perceived and appropriated by the experiencing child embedded within his or her total bio-psycho-social and historical context. Since there is a strong emphasis on the importance of emotionally supportive parenting in EHSDT overall, the focus of the current discussion of unhealthy self-development is emotionally unsupportive parenting. However, this is not meant to imply that poor parenting is the single determining cause of impaired self-development.

That said, the parent who would be the highest risk for hindering the self-development of a child is a parent who is not properly devoted to the task of childrearing or otherwise not adequately attuned to the needs of the child. Due to immaturity or pathology, the parent would be passively or actively resistant to the possibility of the child's psychoemotional emergence from the family unit. It goes without saying that the inadequate, unhealthy parent would not be inclined to display the ten characteristics of optimal parenting noted above. As a result, the child would ultimately come to perceive his or her parental relationship as emotionally unsupportive and significantly related to emotional pain and suffering, even if in a conflicted manner. In one way or another, the child would come to feel that parental expressions of love or care are inadequate, conditional, tenuous at best, or altogether disingenuous.

What Does Unhealthy Self-Development Look Like?

Emotionally unsupportive parenting is a potent force that can increase the likelihood that a child will suffer from unmanageable feelings of frustration and vulnerability (e.g., anxiety, shame, guilt, and so on). These feelings predispose the child to constrict world-openness and curtail his or her transcendent relatedness out of a general need for tension reduction and emotional security. Constricted world-openness indicates that the child cannot freely realize his or her truest feelings, desires, beliefs, values, and so on, in-the-world-with-others throughout development. This prevents the emergence of a strong, flexible personal integration that moves in the direction of authentic goals and ideals. The child cannot adequately integrate his or her personality into a harmonious (i.e., nonconflicting), vital, and fulfilling sense of becoming. In effect, the child's unique imaginative-integrational impetus is impaired. The severity of a child's aberrant self-development is a function of his or her degree of estrangement from his or her unique imaginative-integrative impetus and its creative expansion in-the-world, which differs in character depending on the child's level of maturity. Simply put, estrangement from self and world are but two aspects of the same condition of personal alienation. A rudimentary comparison of healthy and unhealthy self-development is presented in Table 10.2 below.

Table 10.2
Contrasting Characteristics of Healthy and Unhealthy Self-Development

Healthy Self	Unhealthy Self
Secure, confident, hopeful	Insecure, anxious, vulnerable
Relatively open to experience (being-in-the-world-with-others)	Relatively closed off to experience (feeling inordinately needy, isolated, and alienated)
In-touch and in-tune with genuine experience	Intellectualized experience of self and world, relatively alienated from lived experience
Feeling of evolving personal integration	Weak, conflicted, disorganized, or disordered personality
Stable and dynamic character style	Unstable or rigid (i.e., weak or compulsive) character style
Unique style of being-in-the-world-with-others	Stereotyped or symptomological style of being-in-the-world-with-others

Deviations from healthy self-development have been described in various ways in the previous chapters. These descriptions can be used to characterize forms of disrupted self-development along a continuum of severity. Specifically, there are four major varieties of aberrant self-development falling along three general regions or zones of imaginative-integrative impairment. The regions of severity and corresponding forms of aberrant self-development are described below. These descriptions do not trace the evolution of specific forms of psychological suffering. Such a task exceeds the scope of the current text. The current work does not have a clinical focus. To reiterate, the purpose of the current work is first and foremost that of describing optimal, healthy self-development.

Mild imaginative-integrational impairment.

Winnicott (1963c, 102) introduced the idea of the compliant, False Self. The compliant self is a concept that can be used to represent the least severe spectrum of aberrant self-development. Winnicott noted that compliant self-development was characterized by the child adjusting to the needs of the parent early in development. As a result, the child is forced into a functionalistic lifestyle that significantly diminishes spontaneous, creative exploration of the world and disrupts biological functioning (1960, 146). The child's behavior is dominated by acts performed in order to adapt to the desires of the parent. Rogers's (1951, 500–506) account of incongruity is similar to Winnicott's in that the child's self-concept is formed around what will please the parents. The child begins to distort and deny his or her own experiences and identifies with a self-ideal that promises to make him or her appear acceptable to the parent. In effect, a conflict arises between the child's genuine longings and his or her adaptive tendencies. The result is that the child is more or less alienated from spontaneous feelings and motives. Personality integration is thereby weakened. Both Winnicott and Rogers can be said to have characterized a state of compliance with the parent's psychological needs and emotional demands at the expense of genuine, inspired self-development. To be sure, compliant behavior is a common characteristic in hearty, thriving individuals as well. However, when compliance increasingly truncates the child's potential for spontaneous, creative action, his or her genuine self-development is weakened. This is not to imply that such a child is necessarily "mentally ill," but simply that his or her self-development is being stunted. In the language of Knowles's (1986) theory, compliant self-development as described here can be said to consist of an excessive reliance on everyday fallen behavior to the relative neglect of genuine, inspired becoming. All in all, weakened-compliant self-development denotes a primarily functional, adaptive lifestyle marked by deficits and/or difficulties related to the other three motivational tendencies.

Moderate imaginative-integrational impairment.

Kohut's (1977) notion of self-depletion is also similar to Winnicott's ideas pertaining to the compliant self (89). Winnicott (1963c, 102) observed that parents who are more concerned with their own needs than with protecting the child from impinging anxiety increase the risk that the child's self-development will be characterized by compliance rather than spontaneous creativity. Kohut (1977, 89) held that cold, unresponsive parenting results in "self-depletion." The child whose self is depleted lives in a world of unmirrored ambitions. The child does not display the vital, joyful, creative involvement in the world with others that is the hallmark of genuine, fulfilling personality integration. His or her world lacks ideals, which thereby disposes the child to "empty depression." Viktor Frankl's (e.g., 1967) nondevelopmental descriptions of noögenic depression are also indicative of self-depletion in that noögenic neuroses are forms of pathology that result from an embattled sense of meaning-in-life. In other words, depression results from the inability of the self to find its fulfillment in value-laden projects and relationships in-the-world. Whereas Kohut was describing a specific developmental phenomenon relating primarily to a disturbance in self-enriching tendencies, Frankl's noögenic depression has a somewhat different origin. Namely, noögenic depression is the result of a failure of self-transcendence. Nonetheless, despite their etiological differences, both empty depression and noögenic depression result in the same symptomology. That is, both are evidence of a self that is depressed as a result of depleted world-relatedness. The depleted self represents a more advanced and severe disturbance of self-development than compliance as described above. Depressive symptomology represents the formation of psychopathology, which is evidence that the individual's self-structure has been weakened beyond a state of weakened-compliance.

More severe pathological self-development arises when the developing child's estrangement from his or her genuine feelings, desires, and motives is the result of a more pronounced fracturing of the personality when compared to the weakening of self-structure discussed thus far. Fracturing of the self occurs as a result of a more severe striving toward compliance, where desperate needs to adapt to the demands of one's social world result in symptoms associated with psychological disorders, such as those characterized as pathological fallen according to Knowles's (1986) theory. A fractured, pathological self is characterized by a relative deficiency of internal structure and psychological cohesion in comparison to those suffering from weakened personality integration. The developing child increasingly relies on defense mechanisms (e.g., denying and distorting experience) in order to manage intrapsychic and interpersonal conflict. In other words, adaptation has become compromised to the point of dysfunction. The disintegrative process increases the likelihood of the child seeking to derive substitutes for genuine, world-relating fulfillment via isolated aspects of his or her disjointed, disorganized personality (e.g., fixations on psychosexual drives, preoccupations with functionalistic ego qualities, psychological complexes, obsessional ideation, and so on). Karen Horney's (1950, 22) observation that a child with a conflict ridden personality will construct an idealized self-structure as a substitute for healthy personality integration describes fractured self-development at this level of severity. Horney (1950, 18–19) noted that children who suffer from basic anxiety and its resultant "inner conflicts" resort to the strategies of moving toward, moving away, and moving against others in their social relations.

In all three of these strategies, spontaneous, creative involvement with the world and others is bypassed in favor of a compulsive "search for glory" that promises to validate an idealized self-image. The desire to feel confident, secure, and empowered overrides the desire to relate to others in an open, flexible, inspired manner. Thus, Horney believed the search for glory to be the wellspring of neurotic development. Individuals suffering from weakened-depleted self-development and fractured-idealized self-development are further removed from their genuine, healthy imaginative-integrative strivings than those suffering from weakened-compliant self-development. Weakened-depleted and fractured-idealized self-development is characterized by dysfunctional, maladaptive behavior as well as deficits or difficulties related to the other three motivational tendencies.

Severe imaginative-integrational impairment.

The most severe disruptions of self-development occur where world-openness is most constricted and, correlatively, the personality is the least integrated. At this end of the severity continuum, developing individuals suffer from what Knowles (1986) called factical disorders, such as advanced addiction and psychoses, where there is the most fundamental, thoroughgoing disorganization and disintegration of the personality. These individuals are the furthest removed from their imaginative-integrative impetus in that their dysfunction has deteriorated to the point of having a fragmenting, sometimes debilitating effect on their behavior. Here, experience is overwhelmingly characterized by the desperate need for a sense of stability, a sense of security, and homeostatic concerns, such as the need to remove tensions and recoil from disturbing, disrupting sensations. Disrupted self-development as consisting of forms of imaginative-integrative impairment along a continuum of severity is depicted in Figure 10.2 below.

Figure 10.2 Disrupted Self-Development along a Continuum of Severity

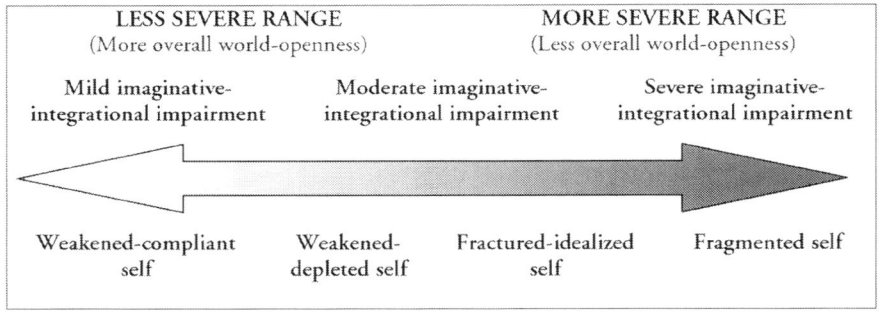

Concluding Remarks

This chapter concludes this text. The fundamental principles of EHSDT have now been sketched out. However, the exact nature of these principles is not set in stone. EHSDT is a dynamic theory, always subject to revision and expansion in the light of more penetrating and expansive theoretical insights and research data. As is evident, phenomenology is the research method of choice for EHSDT. However, EHSDT is not limited to phenomenology as its only option for empirical data. EHSDT welcomes pertinent observations from multiple data sources. Conversely, phenomenologists need not rely on EHSDT for their research, as a matter of course. Nonetheless, phenomenological child psychology may be strengthened by EHSDT as a new avenue for research to add to its knowledge base.

A highly important feature of EHSDT is its appreciative view of childhood. Rather than insisting that children should simply "grow up" and become more like adults, the proponent of EHSDT holds that adults should retain the holistic, creative aspects of childhood experience in their day-to-day living. Childlike qualities in adulthood are not foolish, nor are they exclusive to special "peak experiences." Whereas children can derive benefits from maturing, adults can similarly derive benefits from being more "childlike" without being "childish." Earlier forms of experience are not simply inferior versions of adult experience.

The reader should not mistake the above emphasis on optimal development to mean that EHSDT is a form of "positive psychology," per se. EHSDT does not deny the growth-stimulating potential of conflict, adversity, and suffering in self-development (e.g., "optimal frustration") (Kohut 1977, 188–189*n*). Conflict, adversity, and suffering can sometimes bring out potentials for growth that might not have developed in their absence. This can be seen in its most extreme form when individuals suffering from mental illnesses display outstanding creative potential. In these instances, the alienating effects of emotional stress, strain, and pain provide the individual with a novel perspective on the world. At the same time, strong deficits in adaptive tendencies unleash a potential to propel him or her into moments of intense creativity. What occurs is something similar to when a hydraulic line is uniformly constricted. By applying pressure to the line, its circumference is narrowed and the water flow is thereby propelled further and harder than it would under normal circumstances. Still, the constricted form of existence associated with the fracturing of personal integration loses its extensity (i.e., its potential for a more global creative world expansion) when it gains intensity in this way (Tillich 1952, 69). EHSDT is also different from positive psychology in that quantitative research methods are not considered more valuable than qualitative methodologies when exploring issues relevant to self-development.

For EHSDT to fulfill its potential as a humanistic framework for understanding child development, more work needs to be done on the wider social aspects of self-development throughout childhood. One of the principles of EHSDT is that a child's sociocultural and historical context plays a role in his or her self-development. For example, in contemporary American society, preadolescent and adolescent children, especially females, sometimes suffer from eating disorders (e.g., anorexia, bulimia). This phenomenon did not always exist in our society. Many sociocultural and historical forces have paved the way for this problem. If one were to examine the images of beauty that have dominated art and popular culture since antiquity, one would find that those images have become thinner slowly over time. This is because being large once meant being well fed, healthy, fertile, rich, and powerful. However, those meanings have continually faded from public awareness. Today, being large means very much the opposite. Large people are considered to be overfed and unhealthy. Those who have wealth can afford personal trainers and dieticians to help them maintain a thin, healthy body. These changes in the social meanings of body-type have created a culture that values thinness. Within such a culture, a child's self-image cannot help but be affected by our collective perception of body-image.

The issue of child maltreatment provides another example of how sociocultural and historical forces play a role in child developmental issues. Laws against child abuse and neglect have only come into existence since the 1960s in the United States. Moreover, awareness of psychological maltreatment has lagged far behind other forms of abuse. In early America, children could be beaten quite severely without threat of reprimand or legal intervention. It was socially understood that the likely aim of a beating was to rear the child with proper morals and ethics. Harsh discipline was often considered an effort to train the child in the ways of civility. Differences in child rearing are noticeable in more recent times as well. My students often become uncomfortable when I tell them stories of corporeal punishment that I witnessed at friends' houses in the 1970s. We did not see these acts as child abuse when I was young, except in exceptional circumstances. Today, corporeal punishment is largely frowned upon in comparison to previous eras. The use of corporeal punishment brings with it not only the risk of legal intervention, but also a higher likelihood that a child will look upon his or her parental relationship as abusive. In an era where being beaten was perceived as an attempt to teach valuable life lessons, the child is much less likely to look upon his or her parental relationship in a negative light. In an era where corporeal punishment is often considered child abuse, the child is more likely to develop self-understandings based off the notion that he or she is the victim of some kind of abusive parental relationship.

To be sure, these examples are more complicated than what has been presented here. Nonetheless, they serve to illustrate the fact that self-development is best studied with an understanding of sociocultural and historical context. To this end, a dialogue with the works of Lev Vygotsky (e.g., 1978, 1986) and Urie Brofennbrenner (e.g., 1975, 1979) stand to benefit EHSDT. Vygotsky's work is important because it emphasizes the developmental importance of the way adults use symbols and communicate with children within a culture. His work also emphasizes that what children learn and the speed at which they learn it is a function of the demands of the culture that they are born into. Brofennbrenner's work has just as much potential to benefit EHSDT due to the fact that Brofennbrenner has attempted to develop a schematic to help psychologists grapple with the different kinds of social forces that affect child development. Beyond a dialogue with the works of Vygotsky and Brofennbrenner, EHSDT is most in need of an existential-humanistic account of the historical evolution of childhood with special attention given to how social and cultural forces have affected self-development. No concerted attempt to provide such an account exists to date.

These tasks are too ambitious for the current text and require a volume of their own. However, it ought to be noted that J. H. van den Berg (1961) has done some metabletic research that may be used as a springboard for future work on the wider sociocultural and historical context of self-development. Metabletics is a phenomenological (i.e., descriptive) form of historical psychology. The word *metabletics* means "theory of changes." The fundamental principle of metabletic description is that the very nature of human development can be modified as humans influence and are influenced by changes in their cultural situatedness.

Using his descriptive-historical-psychological method, van den Berg sought to trace the origins of childhood in Western culture. According to van den Berg, childhood is a cultural creation that began with the introduction of the concept of immaturity into Western thought during the Enlightenment. Speaking to the issues of maturity and education, van den Berg (1961, 96–97) noted:

> The child is more infantile than it has ever been, and that is why it is not able to keep up with an educational program geared to the previous generation. Yet educational programs of the last century, and particularly of the last fifty years, have been adapted considerably to the changes in the child. Compared with past programs, modern education is characterized by a definite infantilism, and every change in educational methods will undoubtedly evidence an ever-increasing infantilism. Compare the instruction books of twenty to thirty years ago with those of the present; the older texts are examples of sturdy maturity: the child was supposed to understand those matters, and he did.

Van den Berg goes on to observe that these changes have impacted elementary school through higher education (99).

It has become an increasing challenge for educators to manage the immaturity of their students due to a widening rift between the adult world and the world of childhood. According to Seifert and Hoffnung (2000, 11), offspring were generally expected to carryout the duties that characterized adulthood existence at approximately seven or eight years of age in Western culture prior to the eighteenth century. These young people were entrusted with the basic responsibilities of their social setting, most likely relating to the maintenance of their households or the beginnings of an apprenticeship. This sharply contrasts with the writings of contemporary theorists who warn of the "hurried child," increasingly having their much-needed playtime constricted (e.g., Canning & Lyon 1991; Elkind 1981; Sigel 1987). Over the course of the eighteenth century, the nature of development began to change:

> During the eighteenth century, factory towns began attracting large numbers of workers, who often brought their children with them. "Atrocity stories" became increasingly common: reports of young children in England becoming caught and disabled in factory machinery and of children being abandoned to the streets. Partly because of these

changes, many people became more conscious of childhood and adolescence as unique periods of life, periods that influenced later development. (Seifert and Hoffnung 2000, 11)

Van den Berg (1961) agrees that the earliest evidence of a psychohistorically significant change in the relationship between children and adults can be found in the Enlightenment era. For van den Berg, the more global, thoroughgoing metamorphosis burgeoned in 1762 when Rousseau introduced the Western world to the term *maturation,* marking the first documented appearance of the immature child. The social climate of the Enlightenment provides clues as to why the immature child emerged at this time. A decided weakening of scriptural authority concerning human affairs in favor of modern science characterized this "Age of Reason," as it was termed. While humans were embracing new insights regarding their place in the universe, the natural scientific attitude that dominated Western cultural consciousness fundamentally altered the experience of being-in-time. Westerners came to value the Enlightenment dream of achieving objectivity in their worldviews to such an extent that metaphor, symbol, parable, and myth had begun to be relegated to the status of fiction and fantasy. Natural science was foregoing these foundational elements of storytelling and narration in favor of the search for cause-effect relationships. This new scientific worldview advocated a neutral, detached perspective on the world, admonishing "just the facts." Interpreting events as rich in cultural meaning as valuable for social identity was becoming viewed as subjectivistic and undisciplined.

Despite the great contributions of natural science, an unfortunate consequence of these cultural and historical changes is that the Western experience of history has become progressively more disjointed, so to speak. The past has more than ever become a mass of facts, elusive as regards personal and interpersonal significance (May, 1991). Though continually improving technologies, especially information technology, have given Americans access to more cultural worldviews than ever, a sense of social cohesiveness is increasingly elusive. The feverish pace and increasing diversity of Western society are experienced as overwhelming to children and adults alike; plurality only seems to exacerbate the prevailing condition of sociohistorical disconnectedness. In van den Berg's (1961, 33) words:

> We have no idea how our parents lived. When they tell us ... we are amazed. What our grandparents tell us is even stranger.... Only a story can bring this strangeness to us—if we are inclined to listen. That is why it is so hard for the past to penetrate to us; the past cannot come to us because there are no points of contact, no similarities.

Later, van den Berg continues, "The lengthening and the deepening of maturation thus originates in the multivalent pluralism peculiar to modern maturity" (1961, 42). It is within this wider context that van den Berg sees the gap between children and adults as expanding. For him, the historical alienation that permeates Western culture at large has naturally had an impact on child rearing and evolution through the individual life span:

> Adults' gestures are unsure, since they originate from a domain of maturity whose boundaries are determined by an inability. The mother's hand offering the nipple to the child's mouth is no longer only directed by an age-old code between mother and child—it is also moved by the insecurity which rules all our actions. The child is moved by the insecurity—for besides drinking, it is also tasting maturity—and it is repulsed. (1961, 42)

Gone are the days when parents in their late teens were generally considered quite adequate to the tasks of the adult world (e.g., starting careers and raising families). Westerners have fashioned a world for themselves in which parenting is no longer "second nature," so to speak. This waning of parental efficacy may be evidenced in the plethora of books on parenting and pedagogy available, as well as the proliferation of parenting classes available throughout the United States. It appears that children now have a certain psychosocial foreignness to adults. Children spend months and years in varieties of day care while adults heed the desperate call for scientific and technological advancement in a world teetering on information overload. In the words of Seifert and Hoffnung (2000, 11), "Adults [prior to the eighteenth century] showed more awareness than now of the profound differences among children's formative, childhood experiences."

Integral to the waning of this pedagogical "instinct" is the now pervasive view of children as less competent in comparison to past generations. As Seifert and Hoffnung (2000) noted, the growing concern for children's safety during the eighteenth century assisted in the development of laws to protect their welfare. However, this new attitude of concern had other, more psychohistorical ramifications as well:

> These gains also had a dark side. Viewing children as innocent also contributed to increasing beliefs that children are incompetent, their activities are unimportant, and the people who care for children deserve less respect than other people. This view also contributed to the idea

that children are essentially passive and lacking in opinions and goals worth respecting. (11)

As Mizell (2000) put it, "The messages the students receive from the teachers and administrators with whom they interact is that young [people] are vulnerable, fragile, unable or unwilling to accept meaningful responsibility, likely to erupt in negative behavior any moment, and incapable of serious intellectual work." The Western world has grown accustomed to understanding childhood in terms of inabilities, thereby framing constraints around children's potentials for personality integration by way of intellectual, emotional, and ethical maturity. Thus, the journey into adulthood is longer than ever before and immature children stand in stark opposition to mature adults, much more so than in Rousseau's time. Continuity between the worlds of childhood and adulthood is slowly dissipating. As van den Berg noted, developmental psychologists have begun to explicate a new phase of preadult life toward this end, "post-adolescence" (73).

To be sure, van den Berg's work is not the end of the dialogue that must commence in order to illuminate the wider social context of self-development. It is only a potential beginning. My great hope in writing this book is for humanism to start becoming more readily accessible to students in courses on child development. I am wagering that the most efficient and effective way to accomplish the task of bringing humanism to students of child psychology would be to have EHSDT appear in the theoretical sections of developmental texts alongside the theories of Freud, Erikson, Piaget, Vygotsky, and so on. However, if any one of the critical explications or chapters in this book finds its way into a child psychology course, I will have considered the book a success.

KEY TERMS AND CONCEPTS

Adaptation
Affectionate holding and handling
Basic tendencies of development
Conscious self-concept
Constancy and reliability of loving care
Constricted world-openness
Continuous development
Cultural and historical situatedness
Developmental Stages
Deviations from healthy self-development
Discontinuous development
Drive reduction

Ego
Empathic bonding
Existential-humanistic self-development theory
Felt experience
Freewill
Genuine care and involvement
Homeostatic balance
Identity
Metabletics
Nature
Need satisfaction
Noögenic
Nurture
Optimal self-development
Ordered world
Overgratification
Parenting conducive to self-development
Parenting that threatens self-development
Personal alienation
Personality integration
Phenomenological attitude of neutrality
Productive change
Prosocial models of behavior
Psychoanalytic ego
Receptive mirroring
Self
Self-development
Self-acceptance
Self-enrichment
Self-esteem
Self-respect
Self-transcendence
Senses of self
Sensitivity to changing needs
Spontaneous creative gesture
Symbolically represented experience
Tempering the severity of discipline
Tensile strength
Unhealthy self-development

Unique creative impetus
World-openness

REFERENCES

Adler, A. (1930). Individual psychology. In C. Murchison (Ed.). *Psychologies of 1930*. Worcester, Mass.: Clark University Press.

Adler, A. (1935). The fundamental views of individual psychology. *International Journal of Individual Psychology, 1*, 5–8.

Adler, A. (1939). *Social interest*. NY: Putnam.

Ainsworth, M. D. S., Blehar, M. C., Waters, E., & Wall, S. (1978). *Patterns of attachment: A psychological study of the strange situation*. Hillsdale, NJ: Erlbaum.

Allport, G. (1955). *Becoming*. New Haven: Yale.

American Professional Society on the Abuse of Children. (1995). *Psychosocial evaluation of suspected psychological maltreatment of children and adolescents*. Chicago: Author.

Annells, M. (1996). Hermeneutic phenomenology: Philosophical perspectives and current use in nursing research. *Journal of Advanced Nursing, 23*, 705–713.

Aries, P. (1962). *Centuries of childhood: A social history of family*. NY: Knopf.

Bacal, H. A. (1985). Optimal responsiveness and the therapeutic process. In A Goldberg (Ed.), *Progress in self-psychology, Volume I* (202–227). NY: Guilford.

Bacal, H. A., (1990). Does an object relations theory exist in self-psychology? *Psychoanalytic Inquiry, 10*, 197–220.

Bacal, H. A., & Newman, K. M. (1990). *Theories of object relations: Bridges to self-psychology*. NY: Columbia.

Barritt, L., & Beekman, T. (1983). Human science as a dialogue with children. *Phenomenology & Pedagogy, 1*(1), 36–44. Retrieved May 10, 2005, from http://www.phenomenologyonline.com/articles/beekman.html

Barton, A. (1974). *Three worlds of therapy: Freud, Jung, & Rogers*. Palo Alto, CA: National Press Books.

Benswanger, E. G. (1979). A contribution to the phenomenology of lived-space in early childhood. In A. Giorgi, R. Knowles, & D. Smith (Eds.), *Duquesne Studies in Phenomenological Psychology, Volume III* (111–121). Pittsburgh: Duquesne University Press.

Bertalanffy, L. V. (1950). An outline of general system theory. *British Journal of Philosophical Science, 1,* 134–165.

Boss, M. (1963) Psychoanalysis and daseinsanalysis. NY: DaCapo Press.

Bowlby, J. (1969). *Attachment and loss: Vol. 1. Attachment*. New York: Basic Books.

Briere, J., & Runtz, M. (1988). Multivariate correlates of childhood psychological and physical maltreatment among university women. *Child Abuse & Neglect, 12,* 331–341.

Briere, J., & Runtz, M. (1990). Differential adult symptomology associated with three types of child abuse histories. *Child Abuse & Neglect, 14,* 357–364.

Briod, M. (1986). The young child's sense of time and the clock. *Phenomenology & Pedagogy, 4*(1), 9–19. Retrieved October 25, 2005, from http://www.phenomenologyonline.com/articles/briod.html

Briod, M. (1989). A phenomenological approach to child development. In R. S. Valle & S. Halling (Eds.), *Existential-phenomenological perspectives in psychology: exploring the breadth of human experience* (115–126). NY: Plenum.

Bronfenbrenner, U. (1975). *Influences on Human Development*. Holt, R & W.

Bronfenbrenner, U. (1979). *The Ecology of Human Development: Experiments by Nature and Design*. Cambridge, MA: Harvard University Press.

Bühler, C. M. (1962). Genetic aspects of the self. *Annals of the NY Academy of Science, 96*(3), 730.

Bühler, C. M. (1964). The human course of life in its goal aspects. *Journal of Humanistic Psychology, 4,* 1–17.

Bühler, C. M. (1968a). Early environmental influences on goal setting. In C. Bühler & F. Massarik (Eds.), *The course of human life: a study of goals in the humanistic perspective* (pp.173–188). NY: Springer.

Bühler, C. M. (1968b). The developmental structure of goal setting in group and individual studies. In C. Bühler & F. Massarik (Eds.), *The course of human life: a study of goals in the humanistic perspective* (27–54). NY: Springer.

Bühler, C. M. (1968c). The general structure of the human life cycle. In C. Bühler & F. Massarik (Eds.), *The course of human life: a study of goals in the humanistic perspective* (12–26). NY: Springer.

Bühler, C. M. (1968d). The integrating self. In C. Bühler & F. Massarik (Eds.), *The course of human life: a study of goals in the humanistic perspective* (330–350). NY: Springer.

Bühler, C. M., & Allen, M. (1972). *Introduction to humanistic psychology*. Belmont, CA: Wadsworth.

Bühler, C. M., & Marschack, M. (1968). Basic tendencies of human life. In C. Bühler & F. Massarik (Eds.), *The course of human life: a study of goals in the humanistic perspective* (92–102). NY: Springer.

Burton, R. (2002). *The experience of time in the very young*. Unpublished manuscript. Retrieved September 3, 2005, from http://www.phenomenologyonline.com/articles/burton.html

Canning, P., & Lyon, M. E. (1991). Misconceptions about early child care, education and intervention. *Journal of Child and Youth Care, 5*, 1–10.

Chan, J. (1981). Correlates of parent-child interaction and certain psychological variables among adolescents in Hong Kong. In J. L. M. Binnie-Dawson, G. H. Blowers, & R. Hoosain (Eds.), *Perspectives in Asian psychology* (121–131). Amsterdam: Swets and Zeitlinger.

Chessick, R. D. (1985) *Psychology of the self and the treatment of narcissism*. NJ: Aronson.

Crain W. (2005). *Theories of development: concepts and applications* (5th ed.). NJ: Pearson Prentice Hall.

DeRobertis, E. M. (2004). The impact of long-term psychological maltreatment by one's maternal figure: a study of the victim's perspective. *Journal of Emotional Abuse, 4*(2), 27–51.

Delozier, P. P. (1982). Attachment theory and child abuse. In M. Parkes & J. Stevenson-Hinde (Eds.), *The place of attachment in human behavior* (95–117). NY: Basic Books.

Doumas, D., Margolin, G., & John, R. S. (1994). The intergenerational transmission of aggression across three generations. *Journal of Family Violence, 9*(2), 157–175.

Edwards, D. J. A. (1998). Types of case study work: A conceptual framework for case-based research. *Journal of Humanistic Psychology, 38*(3), 36–70.

Egeland, B., & Erikson, M. F. (1987). Psychologically unavailable caregiving. In M. R. Brassard, R. Germain, & S. N. Hart (Eds.), *Psychological maltreatment of children and youth* (110–120). New York: Pergamon Press.

Elkind, D. (1981). *The hurried child: Growing up too fast too soon*. Reading, MA: Addison-Wesley.

Elkind, H. (1958–1959). On the Origin of the Self. *Psychoanalysis and the Psychoanalytic Review, 45*, 57.

Engles, M. L., & Moisan, D. (1994). The psychological maltreatment inventory: Development of a measure of psychological maltreatment in childhood for use in adult clinical settings. *Psychological Reports, 74*, 595–604.

Ericsson, K. A., & Simon, H. A. (1980). Verbal reports as data. *Psychological Review, 87*(3), 215–251.

Ericsson, K. A., & Simon, H. A. (1994) *Protocol analysis: Verbal reports as data*. Cambridge, MA: MIT Press

Erikson, E. H. (1961). The roots of virtue. In J. Huxley (Ed.), *The humanist frame* (147–165). NY: Harper and Brothers.

Erikson, E. H. (1963). *Childhood and society*. NY: W. W. Norton.

Fantz, R. L. (1965). Visual perception from birth as shown by pattern selectivity. *Annals of the New York Academy of Science, 118*, 793–814.

Fischer, C. T. (1985). *Individualizing psychological assessment*. CA: Brooks/Cole.

Fischer, C. T. (1994). Rigor in qualitative research: Reflexive and presentational. *Methods, 1994 Annual Edition*, 21–27.

Fischer, C. T., & Wertz, F. J. (1979). Empirical phenomenological analyses of being criminalized. In A. Giorgi, R. Knowles, & D. L. Smith (Eds.), *Duquesne studies in phenomenological psychology* (Vol. 3, 135–158). Pittsburgh: Duquesne University Press/Humanities Press.

Fischer, W. F. (1974). On the phenomenological mode of researching "being anxious." *Journal of Phenomenological Psychology, 4*(2), 405–423.

Ford, J. G. (1991). Rogerian self-actualization: a clarification of meaning. *Journal of Humanistic Psychology, 31*(2), 101–111.

Frankl, V. E. (1967). *Psychotherapy and existentialism: selected papers on logotherapy*. NY: Touchstone.

Frankl, V. E. (1969). *The will to meaning: foundations and applications of logotherapy*. NY: Nal.

Frankl, V. E. (1978). *The unheard cry for meaning: psychotherapy and humanism*. NY: Washington Square Press.

Frankl, V. E. (1984). *Man's search for meaning*. NY: Washington Square Press.

Frankl, V. E. (1986). *The doctor and the soul: from psychotherapy to logotherapy*. NY: Vintage Books.

Freud, S. (1960). *The psychopathology of everyday life*. NY: Mentor.

Freud, S. (1962). *Three essays on the theory of sexuality*. USA: Basic Books.

Garrett, L. H. (2006). Childhood reflections of adult male incarcerated child sexual abusers. Unpublished doctoral dissertation, Department of College of Nursing East Tennessee State University. Retrieved April 7, from http://72.14.209.104/search? q=cache:iZ2Zdc-gjG0J:etd-submit.etsu.edu/etd/theses/available/etd-0301106-171002/unrestricted/GarrettL040706f.pdf+lived-pace+in+childhood&hl=en&gl=us&ct=clnk&cd=5

Gavin, E. A. (1990). Charlotte M. Bühler (1893–1974). In A. N. O'Connell & F. F. Russo (Eds.), *Women in psychology: a bio-bibliographic sourcebook* (49–56). NY: Greenwood Press.

Geffner, R., & Rossman, B. B. R. (1998). Emotional abuse: An emerging field of research and intervention. *Journal of Emotional Abuse, 1*(1), 1–6.

Gilligan, C. (1982). *In a different voice: Psychological theory and women's development.* Cambridge, MA: Harvard University Press.

Giorgi, A. (1985). Sketch of a psychological phenomenological method. In A. Giorgi (Ed.), *Phenomenology and psychological research* (8–22). Pittsburgh: Duquesne University Press.

Goldstein, K. (1939). *The organism.* NY: American Book Company.

Gross, A. B., & Keller, H. R. (1992). Long-term consequences of childhood physical and psychological maltreatment. *Aggressive Behavior, 18,* 171–185.

Hall, C. S., & Lindzey, G. (1978). *Theories of personality* (3rd Ed.). NY: John Wiley & Sons.

Hart, S. N., & Brassard, M. R. (1987). A major threat to children's mental health: Psychological maltreatment. *American Psychologist, 42*(2), 160–165.

Hart, S. N., Binggeli, N. J., & Brassard, M. R. (1998). Evidence for the effects of psychological maltreatment. *Journal of Emotional Abuse, 1*(1), 27–58.

Heidegger, M. (1962). *Being and time.* San Francisco: Harper Collins.

Hickox, A., & Furnell, J. R. G. (1988). Psychosocial and background factors in emotional abuse of children. *Child: Care, Health and Development, 15,* 227–240.

Horney, K. (1937). *The neurotic personality of our time.* NY: W. W. Norton.

Horney, K. (1939). *New ways in psychoanalysis.* NY: W. W. Norton.

Horney, K. (1945). *Our inner conflicts: a constructive theory of neurosis.* NY: W. W. Norton.

Horney, K. (1950). *Neurosis and human growth: the struggle toward self-realization.* NY: W. W. Norton.

Kahn, E. (1985). Heinz Kohut and Carl Rogers: A timely comparison. *American Psychologist, 40,* 893–904.

Katzko, M. W. (2002). The rhetoric of psychological research and the problem of unification in psychology. *American Psychologist, 57*(4), 262–270.

Kirova, A. (2001, January 1). Loneliness in immigrant children: Implications for classroom practice. *Childhood Education.* Retrieved March 28 http://www.findarticles.com/p/articles/mi_qa3614/is_200101/ai_n8935302.

Knowles, R. T. (1986). *Human development and human possibility: Erikson in the light of Heidegger.* MD: University Press of America.

Koffka, K (1931). *The growth of the mind.* NY: Harcourt Brace.

Kohlberg, L. (1969). Stage and sequence: The cognitive-developmental approach to socialization. In D. A. Goslin (Ed.), *Handbook of socialization theory and research.* Chicago: Rand McNally.

Kohut, H., & Wolf, E. (1978). The disorders of the self and their treatment: An outline. *International Journal of Psychoanalysis, 59,* 412–425.

Kohut, H. (1977). *The restoration of the self.* Madison, CT: International Universities Press.

Krugman, D., & Krugman, M. K. (1984). Emotional abuse in the classroom. *American Journal of Diseases of Children, 138,* 284–286.

Langeveld, M. J. (1983). The "secret place" in the life of the child. *Phenomenology & Phenomenology, 1*(2), 181–194. Retrieved January 2, 2006, from http://www.phenomenologyonline.com/articles/langeveld2.html

Laplanche, J., & Pontalis, J.-B. (1973). *The language of psychoanalysis.* NY: W. W. Norton.

Leffler, A. S. (1987). Recollection of parental behavior perceived as verbally abusive and its relationship to self-esteem in college students. *Dissertation Abstracts International, 48,* 865-B.

Lefrancois, G. R. (1999). *The lifespan* (6th ed.). Belmont, CA: Wadsworth.

Lefrancois, G. R. (2001). *Of children: an introduction to child and adolescent development* (9th ed.). Belmont, CA: Wadsworth.

Levinas, E. (1969) *Totality and infinity*. Pittsburgh: Duquesne University Press.

Lippitz, W. (1983). The child's understanding of time. *Phenomenology & Pedagogy, 1*(2), 172–180.

Lippitz, W. (2002). Child research and biographical work: Phenomenology and educational perspectives. *Proceedings of the Nineteenth Annual Symposium of the Simon Silverman Phenomenology Center*, Pittsburgh, 3–13.

Loeber, R., & Strouthamer-Loeber, M. (1986). Family factors as correlates and predictors of juvenile conduct problems and delinquency. In M. Tonry & N. Morris (Eds.), *Crime and justice, an annual review of the research, Vol. 7* (29–149). Chicago: University of Chicago Press.

Maiello, S. (1996). Epistemological contribution of the Horney theory to group psychoanalysis. *American Journal of Psychoanalysis, 56*(2), 187–192.

Manning, K. (1992). A rationale for using qualitative research in student affairs. *Journal of College Student Development, 33*, 132–136.

Maslow, A. H. (1954). *Motivation and personality*. NY: Harper and Row.

Maslow, A. H. (1967). Neurosis as a failure of personal growth. *Humanitas, 3*, 153–170.

Maslow, A. H. (1968). *Toward a Psychology of Being* (2nd ed.). Princeton, NJ: Van Nostrand.

May, R. (1991). *The Cry for Myth*. NY: W. W. Norton & Co.

McCarthy, J. B. (1990). Abusive families and character formation. *The American Journal of Psychoanalysis, 50*(2) 181–186.

McCord, J. (1983). A forty-year perspective on effects of child abuse and neglect. *Child Abuse & Neglect, 7*, 265–270.

Mills, J. (1997). The false dasein: From Heidegger to Sartre and psychoanalysis. *Journal of Phenomenological Psychology, 28*(1), 42–65.

Mitchell, S. (1993). *Hope and dread in psychoanalysis.* New York: Basic Books.

Mitchell, S. A., & Black, M. J. (1995). *Freud and beyond: A history of modern psychoanalytic thought.* NY: Basic Books.

Mizell, H. (2000, July). "What works? Who cares?" Paper presented at the 2000 National Symposium on Curriculum, Instruction, and Assessment in the Middle Grades. Abstract retrieved July 22, 2002, from http://www.middleweb.com/HMcares.html

Modell, A. (1985). Object relations theory. In A. Rothstein (Ed.), *Models of the Mind: Their Relationship to Clinical Work* (85–100). New York: International Universities Press.

Moeller, T. P., Bachman, G. A., & Moeller, J. R. (1993). Combined effects of physical, sexual, and emotional abuse during childhood: Long-term health consequences for women. *Child Abuse & Neglect, 17,* 623–640.

Mullen, P. E., Martin, J. L., Anderson, J. C., Romans, S. E., & Herbison, G. P. (1996). The long-term impact of the physical, emotional, and sexual abuse of children: A community study. *Child Abuse & Neglect, 20*(1), 7–21.

Munroe, R. L. (1955). *Schools of psychoanalytic thought.* NY: Appelton-Century-Crofts.

Murray, E. L. (1986). *Imaginative thinking and human existence.* Pittsburgh: Duquesne University Press.

Murray, E. L. (2001). *The quest for personality integration: Reimaginizing our lives.* Pittsburgh: Simon Silverman Phenomenology Center.

Navarre, E. L. (1987). Psychological maltreatment: The core component of child abuse. In M. R. Brassard, R. Germain, & S. N. Hart (Eds.), *Psychological maltreatment of children and youth* (45–56). NY: Pergamon Books.

Ney, P. G. (1987). Does verbal abuse leave deeper scars: A study of children and parents? *Canadian Journal of Psychiatry, 32,* 371–378.

Ney, P. G., Moore, M. S., McPhee, J., & Trought, B. A. (1986). Child abuse: A study of the child's perspective. *Child Abuse & Neglect, 10,* 511–518.

Paris, B. J. (1996a). Introduction to Karen Horney. *The American Journal of Psychoanalysis, 56,* 135–140.

Paris, B. J. (1996b). New ways in psychoanalysis. *The American Journal of Psychoanalysis, 56,* 217–222.

Paris, B. J. (1999). Karen Horney's vision of the self. *American Journal of Psychoanalysis, 59*(2), 157–166.

Paris, B. J. (2002, June 18). Horney and humanistic psychoanalysis. *International Karen Horney Society.* Retrieved January 2, 2005, from http://plaza.ufl.edu/bjparis/horney/fadiman/fadiman.pdf

Piaget, J. (1961). The genetic approach to the psychology of thought. *Journal of Educational Psychology, 52,* 275–281.

Piaget, J. (1963). *The origins of intelligence in children.* New York: Norton.

Ragsdale, S. (n.d.). *Charlotte Malachowski Bühler, PhD (1893–1974).* Retrieved July 2, 2003, from http://www.webster.edu/~woolflm/charlottebuhler.html

Rathus, S. A., & Nevid, J. S. (1999). *Adjustment and growth: the challenges of life.* NY: Harcourt Brace.

Rieder, C., & Cicchetti, D. (1989). Organizational perspective on cognitive control functioning and cognitive-affective balance in maltreated children. *Developmental Psychology, 25*(3), 382–393.

Rogers, C. R. (1951). *Client-centered therapy: Its current practice, implications and theory.* Boston: Houghton Mifflin.

Rogers, C. R. (1959). A theory of therapy, personality, and interpersonal relationships, as developed in the client-centered framework. In S. Koch (Ed.), *Psychology: A study of a science* (Vol. 3) (184–256). NY: McGraw Hill.

Rogers, C. R. (1961). *On becoming a person: A therapist's view of psycho-therapy.* Boston: Houghton Mifflin.

Rogers, C. R. (1980). *A way of being.* Boston: Houghton Mifflin.

Rogers, C. R. (1986). Rogers, Kohut, and Erikson. *Person-Centered Review, 1*, 125–140.

Rohner, R. P., & Rohner, E. C. (1980). Antecedents and consequences of parental rejection: A theory of emotional abuse. *Child Abuse & Neglect, 4*, 189–198.

Saint-Exupéry, A. (1943/1971). *The little prince*. NY: Harcourt Brace Jovanovich.

Schachtel, E. G. (1959). *Metamorphosis: on the development of affect, perception, attention, and memory*. NY: Basic Books.

Schafer, R. (1980). Action and narration in psychoanalysis. *New Literary History, 12*(1), 61–85.

Seifert, K. L., & Hoffnung, R. J. (2000). *Child and adolescent development* (5th ed.). NY: Houghton Mifflin.

Shengold, L. (1989). *Soul murder: The effects of childhood abuse and deprivation*. New Haven, CT: Yale.

Shepard, K. F., Jensen, Gall, G. M., Schmoll, B. J., Hack, L. M., & Gwyer, J. (1993). Alternative approaches to research in physical therapy: Positivism and phenomenology. *Physical Therapy, 73*(2), 88–96.

Sigel, I. E. (1987). Does hothousing rob children of their childhood? *Early Childhood Research Quarterly, 2*, 211–225.

Stern, D. N. (1985). *The interpersonal world of the infant: A view from psychoanalysis and developmental psychology*. NY: Basic Books.

Stolorow, R. D., Brandschaft, B., & Atwood, G. (1983). Intersubjectivity in psychoanalytic treatment, with special reference to archaic states. *Bulletin of the Menninger Clinic, 47*, 117–128.

Stolorow, R. D., Brandschaft, B., & Atwood, G. (1987). *Psychoanalytic treatment: An intersubjective approach*. NJ: Analytic Press.

Tillich, P. (1952). *The courage to be*. New Haven, CT: Yale.

Tobin, S. A. (1990). Self-psychology as a bridge between existential-humanistic psychology and psychoanalysis. *Journal of Humanistic Psychology, 30*(1), 14–63.

Tobin, S. A. (1991). A comparison of psychoanalytic self-psychology and Carl Rogers's person-centered therapy. *Journal of Humanistic Psychology, 31*(1), 9–33.

Tzeng, O. C. S., & Jacobsen, J. J. (1988). *Sourcebook for child abuse and neglect.* Springfield, Illinois: Charles C. Thomas Pub.

van den Berg, J. H. (1972). A different existence: Principles of phenomenological psychology. Pittsburgh: Duquesne University Press.

van den Berg, J. H. (1961). *The changing nature of man.* NY: W. W. Norton.

Van der Kolk, B. A., & Fisler, R. (1994). Childhood abuse and neglect and loss of self-regulation. *Bulletin of the Menninger Clinic, 58*(2), 145–168.

van Kaam (1966). *Existential foundations of psychology.* Pittsburgh: Duquesne University Press.

Varia, R., Abidin, R. R., & Dass, P. (1996). Perceptions of abuse: Effects on adult psychological and social adjustment. *Child Abuse & Neglect, 20*(6), 511–526.

Vissing, Y. M., Straus, M. A., Gelles, R. J., & Harrop, J. W. (1991). Verbal aggression by parents and psychosocial problems of children. *Child Abuse & Neglect, 15*, 223–238.

von Eckartsberg, R. (1986). *Life-world experience: Existential-phenomenological research approaches in psychology.* Washington DC: Center for Advanced Research in Phenomenology & University Press of America.

Vygotsky, L. S. (1978). *Mind and society: The development of higher mental processes.* Cambridge, MA: Harvard University Press.

Vygotsky, L. S. (1986). *Thought and Language.* Cambridge, MA: MIT Press.

Walsh, R., Perrucci, A., & Severns, J. (1999). What's in a good moment: A hermeneutic study of psychotherapy values across levels of psychotherapy training. *Psychotherapy Research, 9*(3), 304–326.

Westkott, M. (1998). Horney, Zen and the real self. *American Journal of Psychoanalysis, 58*(3), 287–302.

Winnicott, D. W. (1958). The capacity to be alone. In D. W. Winnicott & M. M. R. Khan (Eds.), *The maturational processes and the facilitating environment: studies in the theory of emotional development* (29–36). London: The Hogarth press.

Winnicott, D. W. (1959). Classification: Is there a psychoanalytic contribution to psychiatric classification. In D. W. Winnicott & M. M. R. Khan (Eds.), *The maturational processes and the facilitating environment: Studies in the theory of emotional development* (93–108). London: The Hogarth press.

Winnicott, D. W. (1960). Ego distortion in terms of the true and false self. In D. W. Winnicott & M. M. R. Khan (Eds.), *The maturational processes and the facilitating environment: Studies in the theory of emotional development* (140–152). London: The Hogarth Press.

Winnicott, D. W. (1960a). The theory of the parent-infant relationship. In D. W. Winnicott & M. M. R. Khan (Eds.), *The maturational processes and the facilitating environment: Studies in the theory of emotional development* (37–55). London: The Hogarth press.

Winnicott, D. W. (1962a). Ego integration in child development. In D. W. Winnicott & M. M. R. Khan (Eds.), *The maturational processes and the facilitating environment: Studies in the theory of emotional development* (56–63). London: The Hogarth press.

Winnicott, D. W. (1962b). Providing for the child in health and crisis. In D. W. Winnicott & M. M. R. Khan (Eds.), *The maturational processes and the facilitating environment: Studies in the theory of emotional development* (64–72). London: The Hogarth press.

Winnicott, D. W. (1963a). Communicating and not communicating leading to a study of certain opposites. In D. W. Winnicott & M. M. R. Khan (Eds.), *The maturational processes and the facilitating environment: Studies in the theory of emotional development* (179–192). London: The Hogarth press.

Winnicott, D. W. (1963b). From dependence toward independence in the development of the individual. In D. W. Winnicott & M. M. R. Khan (Eds.), *The maturational processes and the facilitating environment: Studies in the theory of emotional development* (83–92). London: The Hogarth press.

Winnicott, D. W. (1963c). Morals and education. In D. W. Winnicott & M. M. R. Khan (Eds.), *The maturational processes and the facilitating environment: Studies in the theory of emotional development* (93–108). London: The Hogarth press.

Winnicott, D. W. (1963d). The development of the capacity for concern. In D. W. Winnicott & M. M. R. Khan (Eds.), *The maturational processes and the facilitating environment: Studies in the theory of emotional development* (73–82). London: The Hogarth press.

Winnicott, D. W. (1965). *The maturational process and the facilitating environment: Studies in the theory of emotional development.* NY: International Universities Press.

Yalom, I. R. (1980). *Existential psychotherapy.* NY: Basic Books.

Yalom, I. R. (1985). *The theory and practice of group psychotherapy* (3rd Ed.). NY: Basic Books.

Yalom, I. R. (1995). *The theory and practice of group psychotherapy* (4th Ed.). NY: Basic Books.

Young, L. (1992). Sexual abuse and the problem of embodiment. *Child Abuse & Neglect, 16,* 89–100.

INDEX

Note: Page entries followed by an "*f*" and "*t*" indicate that the reference is to a figure or table, respectively.

Activity affect, 134–137
Actualizing tendency
    defined by Rogers, 15–17
    meaning of, 15
    and self-actualization, 19
Affective attunement, 153
Allocentric perception, 130–134
Analytic-developmental self-theory, by Stern
    Cartesianism-empirical philosophy and, 123
    existential-humanism, 112–113
    and self, 113–117
    selfhood concept of, 112–113, 122
    summary of, 117–124
Anxiety
    classification, 26
    coping strategies, 26
    defined by Horney, 26–27
    and embeddedness affect, 135–136
Autocentric perception, 130–134

Behavioral theory, 2
    Bühler's concept of, 66–67
    defined by Rogers, 20
Benswanger, E.
    and Gestalt principle, 154

    invitational nature of things and, 154
    "presence" defined by, 155
    "transcendence" defined by, 155
Boredom, 98–99
Bühler, C. M., 64
    and behavioral theory, 66–67
    developmental context and, 67
    and ego psychology, 68–69
    EHSDT, 64–88. *See also* EHSDT, by Bühler
    existential humanism concept of, 64–70
    Frankl's work and, 85–87
    healthy development and, 70
    human life span development, discussed by, 71, 72*f*, 73
    phases of child development, 73–79. *See also* Child development and phases
    self and, 67–68
    self-development stage theory of, 80–82
    self-fulfillment notion and, 85–87
    treatment of intentionality, 85
    and whole person model, 65, 68

Care Structure, 92, 94
Child development and phases
 adolescence/early adulthood, 78–79, 80*t*
 early childhood, 75–76, 77*t*
 infancy, 73, 74*t*
 late childhood/early adolescence, 76–77, 78*t*
Child development theory
 Freud's psychological concept of, 2
 and humanism, 1–4. See also Humanism and child developmental theory
 and Maslow's hierarchy of needs, 1–2
Child maltreatment, 119, 136, 213–214
Childhood maternal relations, 161
 body language and, 182
 developmental inferences of, 182–183
 pedagogical considerations of, 181–182
Clock time, 145–146, 149–150
Congruent self, 17
Continuity of being, 39, 45
Core self, 114–115

Depressive neuroses, 106
Derobertis, E. M.
 and child psychology, interests of, 3–4
 and evolutionary context of human perception, 11
 goals of humanizing child development theory and, 12

and humanism concept, 5–6
introducing humanistic-developmental methodologies, 1
lived-space-time, illustration by, 156–159

Ego, 60
 crisis, 89–91
 defined by Knowles, 97
 defined by Winnicott, 43
 ego development, 97–99, 100*t*. See also Ego development
 psychology, 68–69
 support, 39
 and true self, 43
Ego crisis, 89–91
Ego development
 and analytic strictures, 97–100
 Knowles's views on, 97–99, 100*t*
EHSDT, by Bühler. See also Existential-humanistic self-development theory (EHSDT)
 behavioral theory, 66–67
 child development and phases, 73–79. See also Child development and phases
 critical remarks on, 82–88
 developmental context and, 67
 ego psychology and, 68–69
 global characterization of, 65–70
 healthy development in, 70
 human life span development in, 71, 72*f*, 73
 and integrative tendencies, 84*f*
 whole person model, 65, 68

EHSDT, by Knowles, 108–109. *See also* Existential-humanistic self-development theory (EHSDT)
    Care Structure and, 92, 94–95. *See also* Care Structure
    ego development in, 97–99, 100*t*
    embodied facticity, 95–96
    and Erikson's psychosocial stages, 89–92
    healthy development in, 104, 105*t*, 106–107
    method and technique, defined by, 99
    psychoanalytic theories in, 93*t*
    schematic representation of, 107*f*
    self-development phenomenology and, 100–101, 102*f*, 103–104
Embeddedness affect, 134, 137
    and anxiety, 135–136
    and security, 135
Embodied perspective, 151–152
Emergent self, 113–114
Emotional development, 133–137
Erikson, E.
    ego crisis defined by, 89–91
    ego development and, 97–99
    and Freud, S.'s theory, 89–92
    and Knowles's Care Structure, 92, 94–95. *See also* Care Structure
    psychosocial stages discussed by, 89–92, 93*t*
Existential going-on-being, 39
Existential-humanistic-developmental fundamentals, 8
    active becoming, 11–12
    contextual perception of, 9
    healthy developmental progress, 12
    as historical perspective, 9–11
    holistic perspective of, 9
    imaginative-integrational impairment, 209–211
    individualistic uniqueness, 9
Existential-humanistic self-development theory (EHSDT), 212–218
    by Bühler, 64–88. *See also* EHSDT, by Bühler
    healthy self-development in, 192–198, 200–202, 206, 208*t*
    by Knowles, 89–109. *See also* EHSDT, by Knowles
    and parenting, 202–207
    participation of children in, 205–206
    self, meaning of, 185–187, 189–192
    self-enriching and self-transcending motives, 190*t*–191*t*
    unhealthy self-development in, 207, 208*t*
Existentialism
    meaning of, 7–8
    and phenomenology, 7–8
Existentiality, 94
Existential-phenomenology, 8
    humanism and child developmental theory, 3
Facticity
    embodied phenomenology, 95–96
    Knowles's views on, 94–96

"taking a stand" phenomenon, 95–96
Fallenness, 94
False self-development, 59
    compliance and, 46
    self-pathology and, 46
    spontaneity and, 46
    and true self, 46–47
    Winnicott, D. W.'s concept of, 46–47
Fanatical feelings, 99–100
First force psychology, 2–3
Freud, S.
    and Bühler, C. M.'s theory, 65–66
    and child development theory, psychological concept of, 2
    and Erikson, E.'s psychosexual development theory, 89–92
    need satisfaction notion of, 49
    psychosexual stages, 93*t*

Going-on-being, 39–40

Historical determinism, 8, 11
Holding, defined by Winnicott, 39–41
Homeostatic pleasure principle, 66
Horney, K.
    classifying basic anxiety, 26
    humanistic self-development theory, 14–15, 20–27. *See also* Humanistic self-development theory
    parental behavior examples, given by, 24*t*, 32
    real self, defined by, 20–22, 25–27, 32
    self-realization, 20–27. *See also* Self-realization
Human life span development, basic tendencies of, 71, 72*f*, 73
Humanism and child developmental theory
    and behavioral theory, 2
    and existential-phenomenology, 3
    first force psychology, 2–3
    Freud's psychological concept of, 2
    Maslow's hierarchy of needs, 1–2
    and positivistic natural science, 3
    second force psychology, 2–3
    in student textbooks, 1–2
    third force psychology, 3
Humanism, meaning of, 5–6
Humanistic currents
    in child development study, 4–5
    humanists contributions and, 4
    Knowles's psychoanalytic theory, 4
    selfhood concept, 5
Humanistic self-development theory
    critical remarks on Rogers and Horney's theory, 33–34
    differences in ideas of Rogers and Horney, 31–33
    healthy parental influence in, 28–29
    by Horney, 14–15, 20–27. *See also* Horney, K.
    mutual concept of Rogers and Horney, 27–31
    by Rogers, 14–20. *See also* Rogers, C. R.

self-actualizing child and, 28–29

self-alienation and, 29–31

self-development in, 28

strengths of Rogers and Horney's theory, 33–35

Imaginative-integrational impairment, 212*t*

   mild, 209

   moderate, 209–211

   severe, 211

Impulsive character, 106

Incongruence self, 20

Infancy, 73, 74*t*

   affectivity and, 115

   and coherence, 115

   feeling of history in, 115

   personal integration, 188*f*

   quantum leaps and, 112

   self-agency and, 115

   Schachtel's perception and, 131–132

Infant handling, good-enough

   empathy, Winnicott definition, 41

   identification, Winnicott definition, 41

   mirroring, Winnicott definition, 42

Intentionality, Bühler's treatment of, 85

Knowles, R. T.

   ego development and, 97–99, 100*t*

   EHSDT, 89–109. *See also* EHSDT, by Knowles

   embodied facticity and, 95–96

   and Erikson's psychosocial stages, 89–92

   psychoanalytic theory of, 4

   and reinterpretation of Erikson's theory, 92, 94–95

   self-development phenomenology of, 100–101, 102*f,* 103–104

   summary of, 107–109

Koffka, K.

   behavior and experience, studied by, 127

   learning concept of, 127–128

   organized perceptual forms framed by, 128

   "perceptions" discussed by, 128–130

   and phenomenology as childhood experience, 125–130, 137–142

Kohut, H., 55

   nuclear self and, 50–52. *See also* Nuclear self

   optimal mother, 47–49. *See also* Mothering, in optimal environment

   self-conceptualization and, 53–54

   self-psychologist, 37–38

   unempathic mother and unhealthy self, 52–53

Lived-space, in childhood, 145

   affective attunement in, 153

   Benswanger's approach to, 154–155. *See also* Benswanger, E.

   and embodied perspective, 151–152

   meaning of, 151

   personal meaning in, 154–156

   self-discovery, 154–156

Lived-space-time, an illustration, 156–159
Lived-time, in childhood
    attuned to present, 147–148
    clock time and, 146
    defined, 145
    language development, 149
    meaning of, 146
    moving beyond present, 149
    objective pole of, 146
    public time systems, 149–150
    in space, 150
    subjective pole of, 146
    temporal rhythm, 147

Maslow's hierarchy of needs, 1–2
Mirroring
    meaning of, 42, 57
    receptive, 204
Mothering, good-enough
    and empathy, 41
    facilitating environment, defined by, 39
    going-on-being and, 39–40
    holding concept and, 39–41
    identification and, 41
    mirroring and, 42
    and object-presentation, 42
    omnipotence feeling and, 42
    Winnicott's views on, 39–43
Mothering, not-good-enough
    devotion and, 45
    emotional deprivation and, 45
    environmental failure, 45
    half-heartedly committed, 45
    Winnicott's views on, 45
Mothering, in optimal environment
    being selfobject, 47–48
    empathy and, 49
    and frustration, 49
    Kohut's views on, 47–49
    nascent self and, 48
    need satisfaction and, 49
    and responsive mother, 47
    unified self and, 48

Need satisfaction
    Bühler's concept of, 85
    defined by Kohut., 54–55
    defined by Winnicott, 42, 49
    in newborns, 73, 74t
Nuclear self
    and ambitiousness, 50
    caring manner and, 50
    Kohut's views on, 50–52
    selfhood and, 51–52

Objective pole of lived-time, 146
Object-presentation, 42
Object-relations self-development theory
    comments on Winnicott and Kohut's, 59–61
    critical remarks on Winnicott and Kohut's, 61
    healthy parental influence in, 55–57
    healthy self-development, 57–58
    by Kohut, 37–38, 47–55. *See also* Kohut, H.

mutual concept of Winnicott and Kohut, 55–59
self-actualizing child in, 55
strengths of Winnicott and Kohut's, 61–62
unhealthy self-development, 58–59
by Winnicott, 37–47. *See also* Winnicott, D. W.
Omnipotence, 42
Optimal frustration, 49, 54

Paranoia, 105–106
Phenomenological study considerations, 165–166
    general results, 173–179
    participants in, 166–167, 168*t*, 169
    procedure, 169, 170*t*–171*t*, 172–173
    research results, 179–181
Phenomenology
    and American humanistic psychologies, 7
    and existentialism, 7
    meaning of, 6–8, 163
    and mental illness, 7
    and phenomenologists, 7–8
    and quantitative research, 165*t*
Phenomenology and childhood experience, 125
    allocentric perception and, 130–134
    autocentric perception and, 130–134
    criticism of Koffka and Schachtel's approach to, 137–138
    emotional development in, 134–137
    introduction to, 138–143
    Koffka's approach of, 126–130
    as methodological option, 163–164
    parental influence on child and, 135–136
    psychological maltreatment, 136. *See also* Psychological maltreatment
    research method flowchart, 172*t*
    Schachtel's approach of, 130–137
Psychoanalytic theories, 93*t*
Psychological maltreatment, 136
    categories of, 162
    pedagogical considerations of, 181–182
    phenomological study of, 161
Psychotic compulsion, 106–107

Quantum leaps, 112

Real self, defined by Horney, 20–21
Rogers, C. R.
    "behavior" defined by, 20
    and congruent self development, 17
    explaining actualizing tendency, 15–17
    humanistic-developmental scheme, foundation of, 14–15
    organism, defined by, 15–16
    person, defined by, 15
    self characteristics given by, 18*t*
    self, defined by, 15–16

self-actualizing versus incongruence self, 15–20. *See also* Self-actualizing tendency
self-concept of, 16, 19–20, 31–32
"self-structure" defined by, 17, 19

Schachtel, E. G.
activity affect and, 134–137
allocentric perception of, 130–134
autocentric perception of, 130–134
embeddedness affect and, 134–137
infantile perception of, 131–132
phenomenology, as childhood experience, 125, 130–142

Schizophrenia, 106

Self
Bühler's concept of, 67–68
defined by Knowles, 100, 102*f*
defined by Rogers, 15–16
disorders, 53
false, 46. *See also* False self-development
idealized, 16–17, 20
Kohut's views on, 47–48
meaning of, 16, 185–187, 189–192
nascent, 48
nuclear, 50–52. *See also* Nuclear self
representation of, 72*f*
senses of, 113–117
true, 43–45. *See also* True self
unified, 48

Self-actualizing tendency
Bühler, C. M.'s views on, 83–85
in children, 17–19, 28–29, 55
in early childhood, 75–76
healthy and congruent characteristics, 18*t*
mutual concept of Winnicott and Kohut, 55
and person's development, 16
Rogers, C. R.'s concept of, 15–20
and self-development theory, 16
and self-structure, 17, 19
versus incongruence self, 15–20

Self-agency and, 115

Self-awareness, 78–80
embattled, 179

Self-concept, 60–61
Kohut's views on, 53–54
Rogers's meaning of, 16, 19–20

Self-depletion, 58–59, 209

Self-development
beginning of, 200
existential-analytic theory, by Knowles, 89–109. *See also* EHSDT, by Knowles
existential-humanistic theory, by Bühler, 64–88. *See also* EHSDT, by Bühler
fundamental characteristics of, 192–198
healthy parental influence and, 28–29, 55–56
humanistic theory, by Rogers and Horney, 14–36. *See also* Humanistic self-development theory
nature and nurture of, 28, 200–202
object-relations theory, by Winnicott and Kohut, 37–62. *See also*

Object-relations self-development theory
- optimal mother and, 56–57
- and parenting, 202–207
- and self-actualizing child, 28–29
- stages of, 198–200

Self-discovery, 154–156
Self-enriching and self-transcending motives, 190*t*–191*t*
Self-fragmentation, 58–59
Self-fulfillment
- in adolescence/early adulthood, 80*t*
- Bühler's notion of, 85–87

Selfhood concept, 5, 9
- Horney's, 21
- Knowles's, 100–101
- mutual concept of Rogers and Horney's, 27–31
- nuclear self and, 51
- Stern's, 112–113, 122
- and true self, 43–44

Self-limiting adaptation
- in early childhood, 75, 77*t*, 81
- in late childhood/early adolescence, 78*t*
- meaning of, 71

Self-realization
- children's relations with caretakers, 21–27
- defined by Horney, 20–21, 23*t*
- healthy self-development characteristics, 22
- person characteristics, 23*t*

Self-structure, defined by Rogers, 17, 19

Stern, D.
- analytic-developmental self-theory and, 112–124. *See also* Analytic-developmental self-theory, by Stern
- and Cartesianism-empirical philosophy, 123
- and existential-humanism, 112–113
- and infant-mother relation, 123–124
- longitudinal research and, 118–119
- selfhood concept of, 112–113, 122
- stage divisions and, 120
- using predominance idea, 118

Subjective pole of lived-time, 146
Subjective self, 115–116

Temporal rhythm, 147
Total action-perception process and, 66–67
True self, 59
- Cartesianism element and, 44–45
- ego development and, 43
- and false self-development, 46–47
- in good-enough holding environment, 44
- and isolation, 44
- selfhood and, 43–44
- solitude and, 44
- Winnicott's views on, 43–45

Unempathic mother, 52–53
Unhealthy self, 53
Unhealthy self-development, 58–59

Verbal self, emergence of, 116–117

Whole person model, 65, 68

Winnicott, D. W.
- Cartesianism elemental work of, 44–45
- child development, views for, 38–39
- ego, defined by, 43
- false self-development, 46–47. See also False self-development
- "good-enough" mother, views for, 39–43. See also Mothering, good-enough
- "not-good-enough" mother, views for, 45. See also Mothering, not-good-enough
- object-relations theorist, 37
- true self, defined by, 43–45. See also True self

Printed in Great Britain
by Amazon